Flights from Realism

Themes and Strategies in Postmodernist British and American Fiction

Marguerite Alexander

Tutor in English Literature,
Extra-Mural Department, University of London

Edward Arnold
A division of Hodder & Stoughton
LONDON NEW YORK MELBOURNE AUCKLAND

For James

© 1990 Marguerite Alexander

First published in Great Britain 1990

Distributed in the USA by Routledge, Chapman and Hall, Inc.
29 West 35th Street, New York, NY 10001

British Library Cataloguing in Publication Data

Alexander, Marguerite
    Flights from realism: themes and strategies in postmodernist
British and American fiction.
    1. Fiction in English 1900 – Critical studies
    I. Title
    823.91209

    ISBN 0–7131–6564–2

Library of Congress Cataloging-in-Publication Data

Alexander, Marguerite.
    Flights from realism: themes and strategies in postmodernist
British and American Fiction / Marguerite Alexander.
      p. cm.
    Includes bibliographical references.
    ISBN 0–7131–6564–2
    1. English fiction–20th century–History and criticism.
    2. American fiction–20th century–History and criticism.
    3. Postmodernism (Literature)   I. Title.
PR888.P69A44   1990
823′.9109–dc20   90–203
                                                       CIP

Typeset by Colset Private Ltd, Singapore.
Printed and bound in Great Britain for Edward Arnold, the
educational, academic and medical publishing division of Hodder
and Stoughton Limited, Mill Road, Dunton Green, Sevenoaks, Kent
TN13 2YA by Richard Clay Ltd, Bungay, Suffolk.

Contents

Note of Editions Used

Paul Auster, *The New York Trilogy*, Faber & Faber, 1987 (Los Angeles: Sun & Moon Press, 1985 and 1986)
  City of Glass
  Ghosts
  The Locked Room
Samuel Beckett, *Murphy*, Pan, 1973 (G. Routledge & Co., 1938)
  Molloy (1955, Olympia Press)
  Malone Dies (1956, John Calder)
  Trilogy including *The Unnamable* (1959, John Calder) Pan, 1979
Saul Bellow, *Herzog*, Penguin, 1965 (Weidenfeld & Nicolson, 1964)
E.L. Doctorow, *Ragtime*, Pan, 1976 (1974)
Lawrence Durrell, *The Alexandria Quartet*, Faber paperback, 1961, 1963
  Justine (Faber & Faber, 1957)
  Balthazar (1958)
  Mountolive (1958)
  Clea (1960)
William Faulkner, *The Sound and the Fury*, Penguin, 1964 (Jonathan Cape and Harrison Smith, New York, 1929)
John Fowles, *The French Lieutenant's Woman*, Triad/Panther, 1977 (Jonathan Cape, 1969)
  The Magus, Triad/Panther, 1977 (Jonathan Cape, 1966, revised version 1977)
William Golding, *Pincher Martin*, Faber & Faber, 1956
Joseph Heller, *Catch-22*, Corgi, 1964 (1961)
James Joyce, *A Portrait of the Artist as a Young Man*, Triad/Panther, 1977 (B.W. Huebsch, New York, 1916)
  Ulysses, Bodley Head, 1960 (Paris, 1922)
Rosamund Lehmann, *The Echoing Grove*, Penguin 1958 (Collins, 1953)
Doris Lessing, *The Golden Notebook*, Panther, 1973 (Michael Joseph, 1962)
Malcolm Lowry, *Under the Volcano*, Penguin, 1962 (Jonathan Cape, 1947)
David Lodge, *Small World*, Penguin, 1985 (Martin Secker & Warburg, 1984)
Iris Murdoch, *The Sea, The Sea*, Chatto & Windus, 1978
Vladimir Nabokov, *Pale Fire*, Corgi, 1964 (Weidenfeld & Nicolson, 1962)
  Lolita, Corgi, 1961 (Weidenfeld & Nicolson, 1959) (Olympia Press, 1955)
Flann O'Brien, *At Swim-Two-Birds*, Penguin, 1969 (Longman Green, 1939)
Thomas Pynchon, *The Crying of Lot 49*, Pan, 1979 (Jonathan Cape, 1967) (Lippincott, 1965)
  Gravity's Rainbow, Picador, 1975 (Viking 1973)

Salman Rushdie, *Midnight's Children*, Pan, 1982 (Jonathan Cape, 1981)
　The Satanic Verses, Viking Penguin, 1988
D.M. Thomas, *The White Hotel*, Penguin, 1981 (Victor Gollancz, 1981)
Muriel Spark, *Not to Disturb*, Penguin, 1974 (Macmillan, 1971)
Kurt Vonnegut, *Breakfast of Champions*, Granada, 1974 (Jonathan Cape, 1973)
　Slaughterhouse 5, Triad Grafton, 1979 (1969)

From Modernism to Postmodernism

1

The Word and the World

The term 'postmodernist', increasingly used to describe certain kinds of late-twentieth-century fiction, sounds like a joke. For many readers of fiction – the 'common readers' to whom the nineteenth-century novelists addressed their work – the very word carries a suspicion of trickery, for how can anything already acknowledged as existing, postdate the modern, if we take 'modern' to mean contemporary?

This common-sense response, which postmodernist novelists see as their business to violate and confound, nonetheless identifies a number of the essential features of this kind of writing. Whatever differences there are separating the novels that may be defined in this way, they have in common an element of playfulness, or even trickery, that is only rarely found in novels before this period. In some this may take the form of withholding information or cheating the reader of an expected resolution. John Fowles in *The French Lieutenant's Woman* offers alternative endings to his story, while Thomas Pynchon takes the increasingly mystifying narrative of *The Crying of Lot 49* to the brink of a revelation which is then denied. Sometimes where there is closure, as in William Golding's *Pincher Martin*, it carries with it the demand that the whole novel be re-read in the light of it. Where the supernatural is used – as it is, for example, in Salman Rushdie's *Midnight's Children* – it is not naturalized at a later point in the narrative. This marks a radical break with earlier uses of the supernatural in fiction – in, for example, the Gothic novel. Ann Radcliffe's *The Mysteries of Udolpho*, published in 1794, titillates the reader throughout with apparent manifestations of the supernatural which are all ultimately shown to be of human agency.

In other words, the postmodernist novelist has re-drafted the contract between writer and reader along lines which many readers of more conventional fiction find unfavourable to themselves. A recurring theme of late-twentieth-century fiction is treachery – enacted between individuals, obscurely at work within society and, more generally, the treacherous nature of appearance. And for baffled readers that treachery is not always held within the frame of the novel, but something of which they are themselves victims.

So there is a new distance between writer and reader which a term like postmodernist – albeit one more often employed by critics than by writers themselves – does nothing to bridge. The assault on common sense implicit in the term itself is entirely appropriate and symptomatic of divisions deeper than the tension that has always existed between the practice of serious novelists and the expectations of the general reading public. The great English and American novelists of the nineteenth century shared with their readers certain assumptions – about the ultimate value of society, whatever specific criticisms of it might be made; about the place of the individual within that society; about the existence, if not of God (though open expressions of disbelief were rare, even for an avowed free-thinker like George Eliot) then of a body of universal truths which included an agreed concept of human nature – but that concord can no longer be said to exist, at least as far as postmodernist novelists are concerned. My intention in this introductory chapter is to explore some of those changes in twentieth-century thought and experience which lie behind the changes in fictional practice.

In one of his authorly intrusions into the narrative of *The French Lieutenant's Woman*, John Fowles comments on the godlike omniscience that he has so far assumed in relation to his characters, which he admits as being at variance with the practice of his own times: 'But I live in the age of Alain Robbe-Grillet and Roland Barthes; if this is a novel, it cannot be a novel in the modern sense of the word' (p 85). This statement is interesting as an example both of that shattering of fictional illusion and of the self-consciousness about the act of writing that are among the requirements of postmodernist fiction. Equally illuminating is the suggestion that these two representative figures have definitively altered the course of the twentieth-century novel. Alain Robbe-Grillet, who since the early 1950s has been a leading practitioner and apologist of the *nouveau roman*, is the less surprising, since novelists have always acknowledged indebtedness to earlier writers on whose innovations their own work might depend, though the choice of a French writer is significant. More intriguing is the citing of Barthes (1915–80), philosopher and literary theorist whose work encompassed both structuralist and post-structuralist approaches, in the context of fictional practice. Fowles's tribute to Barthes may be said to mark a new development, in that creative writers have traditionally been wary of acknowledging the influence of critics on their work.

There has always been more resistance to theory in England, at all levels of national life, including the universities, than in the rest of Europe and in America. When in *Middlemarch* George Eliot describes her heroine's mind as 'theoretic',[1] the reader rightly takes this as a signal that dangers lie ahead for Dorothea: in acquiring wisdom, she will abandon theory. And writers like Fowles who admit the reliance of practice on theory have often found that their work, at any rate initially, is more enthusiastically received abroad. While there are many serious and respected contemporary English novelists whose work is free of the writerly anxieties that characterize postmodernist writing, most of the greatest advances in English fiction in this century have been made by users of English who were not themselves English – Joyce, Conrad and Henry James, for example. As we shall see, and seek reasons for in the course of this book, America has produced more extreme forms of postmodernist writing than Britain (Ireland is a separate matter). That said, however, since the last war many British writers have, like Fowles, become more sensitive to the theoretical issues involved in the writing of fiction; and one of the intentions of this book is to examine some of the conditions and historical circumstances that have helped bring about that change.

Fowles mentions Barthes as an agent of radical change. A detailed critique of his work lies outside the scope of this book, but it should be said that part of Barthes's significance as a figurehead – not just for a novelist like Fowles, but for critical theorists – lies as much as anything in the range of his writing: anthropology and psychoanalysis, besides linguistic philosophy and literary theory, and always with an awareness of the ideological colouring in areas of inquiry once thought to be 'neutral' or 'objective'. He is in fact an example of a new kind of polymath to have emerged in the decades since the war. A number of the writers whose work I shall consider – Beckett, Iris Murdoch, David Lodge, Saul Bellow, Nabokov – have held university appointments, so that Joyce's claim that his work would provide employment for professors has gathered new meaning with the emergence of the academic novelist, who often feels obliged to define his or her approach to fiction in the light of Joyce's achievements. It cannot be accidental that the growth in the study of modern literature in universities has paralleled an increasingly theorized and self-conscious attitude to fiction by novelists themselves.

To claim actual indebtedness, except in specific cases, is perilous, but throughout the modern and postmodern periods there has been a remarkable degree of concordance, however casual and by whatever means reached, between novelists and theoreticians on the status and function of language. Ferdinand de Saussure (1857–1915), who taught in Paris and Geneva, is the ultimate point of reference for structuralist linguistics. His most important contribution was the concept of language as an arbitrary system of signs which acquire meaning, not as they mediate reality, but in relation to each other, in terms of the system as a whole. This has bearing on the central theory of the Russian Formalists who were active during the Revolutionary period, that the function of poetry is, through language, to 'de-familiarize' the everyday world in order to return the world in a form where it might be 'seen' rather than merely recognized. Using these terms of reference, a distinction can be made between 'realist' fiction, on the one hand, and modern and postmodern on the other, by saying that whereas the former creates worlds that the reader recognizes, using language as a mediating agent, the latter defamiliarizes the world in language that draws attention to itself.

Structuralism allows us to interpret diverse forms of human activity (advertising, social organization, myth) in terms of a code: only when the code is decoded can the individual referent be understood. In other words, individual referents do not in themselves mediate reality. Apart from its application in literary theory, anthropology and sociology, structuralism has been a useful tool in Marxist dialectic (the self-contained, self-referential nature of the structuralist sign system has clear links with Marxist materialism, which rejects the idea of a reality beyond or outside the immediate historical, cultural and economic context), and has had a bearing on the development of psychoanalytical theory, which suggests that all statements, narratives and dreams carry meaning, though they do not necessarily relate to external reality directly.

I should make it clear that I am not suggesting that linguistic theory should be given priority over other twentieth-century initiatives in examining, codifying and understanding human beings; but that outside the natural sciences a new concern for language has characterized most such endeavours. A sensitivity to language is no longer confined to writers whose raw material it is. The writers that I shall be discussing, who have rejected naïve realism, often, as it happens, show more than a passing acquaintance with those other forms of twentienth-century discourse – psychoanalytical, political, philosophical – where language is felt profoundly to matter.

Although my concern is with the postmodern period (which I shall shortly attempt to define), some account must be given of modernism but with the acknowledgement that the area has already been well mapped out by others.[2] As I have already suggested, a foregrounding of language is among the principal characteristics. The poets Eliot and Yeats, and Joyce and Virginia Woolf among the novelists, worked on the principle that language elicits a direct response from the reader, independently of meaning. Moreover, their work, at its most characteristic, is self-referential, generating meaning only as the parts relate to the whole, rather than through an implied reference to the 'everyday' world: from that point of view, *Ulysses* is the paradigmatic modernist text. The aesthetic of modernism demanded that the text be seen as an impersonal artefact, comparable to other art forms, so that William Faulkner, a late modernist whose work I shall be considering, saw his own novel *The Sound and the Fury* as 'a vase'.[3] This in turn meant that the position of the author – by convention, the mediator of meaning within the novel – demanded to be re-defined. In the course of a discussion on aesthetics in *A Portrait of the Artist as a Young Man*, Joyce's hero, Stephen, defines the ideal work as one where the artist is 'invisible, refined out of existence, indifferent'.[4]

One solution to the problems posed by this requirement was for the writer to conceal himself or herself behind the 'voices' of the characters, as Faulkner does in *The Sound and the Fury* and *As I lay Dying*, Virginia Woolf in *The Waves* and, in poetic form, Eliot in 'The Waste Land'. In *Ulysses* Joyce uses the interior monologue and in the 'third-person' episodes such a wide diversity of style that it is impossible to identify the author with any one of them.

These changes were accompanied by a new approach to character. One clear way in which the author's authority is asserted in fiction of the classical realist period (late eighteenth and nineteenth centuries) is in the knowing tone adopted towards characters – something that John Fowles parodies and exposes in *The French Lieutenant's Woman*. The author knows all, and in the course of the novel, tells all. The effect of this in the work, for example, of Jane Austen and Dickens is that peripheral characters are fixed and complete, though there may be mysteries to uncover before a full understanding of them is reached, while development is reserved for the central characters. That development however – usually taking the form of the gaining of wisdom through experience – is, once achieved, complete and irreversible. And while there are exceptions to this pattern – most notably Laurence Sterne's *Tristram Shandy*, to which I shall be returning – it became the model by which later, non-realist novelists might define the terms of their own reaction.

Where the nineteenth-century English novel and the twentieth-century realist novels that have succeeded it fed and continue to feed off the aspirations of their readers, modern and postmodernist fiction has more often found inspiration and justification for change in the broader intellectual climate. On the issue of characterization, the writings of Freud suggested that the inner life of the individual was a good deal more turbulent, and expressed itself in action more deviously, than fictional technique had yet taken account of. D.H. Lawrence was almost certainly directly influenced by Freudian ideas, Joyce and Virginia Woolf more indirectly by a climate of interest in psychoanalytical theory. A challenge of a different kind is implicit in Marxist theory, which sees the concept of the individual on which the nineteenth-century idea of character largely depended, as historically determined by bourgeois capitalism, without the universal validity that it appeared to claim for itself. As we shall see, some post-modernist fiction makes accommodation with Marxist theory, while it is by and large (though with notable exceptions) more openly political than modernist fiction. The politics of modernism, while discernible (and as we shall see, often to the right of the political spectrum), frequently tend to be concealed by a concentration on the inner life, which required ways of presenting character to be more fluid, more alert to moral ambiguity.

Of the modernist novelists, I see Joyce as the most significant influence on the subsequent development of non-realist fiction and for that reason I shall in the following chapter examine his work in more detail. There is a point to be made here, however, which helps to elucidate some of the differences between modernist and later non-realist fiction. Modernist writing in English reached its peak in the early 1920s, with the publication of *Ulysses*, 'The Waste Land', Pound's 'Hugh Selwyn Mauberley', Virginia Woolf's *To the Lighthouse*, Lawrence's *Women in Love* and a number of important Yeats poems. And it has to be said that, with the exception of Joyce, who described himself with some justification as 'apolitical' and of Virginia Woolf (whose work for a variety of reasons stands just outside the mainstream) these writers were all touched by an ideological climate that later hardened into fascism.

'Fascist' is an easy label to use and a hard one to justify, especially when speaking of a time when attitudes (particularly racist) which are completely unacceptable now held wide currency. Of these writers Yeats only briefly associated himself with the fascist party in Ireland, Pound more disastrously in Mussolini's Italy. Nonetheless, a casual anti-Semitism marks their work, as it does that of the more popular writers of the period (incidentally making Joyce's choice of a Jew as the hero of *Ulysses* the more remarkable). They lamented, from a variety of positions, the undermining of authority. At the same time their distaste for the increased mechanization and urbanization of their own times and its effect on the quality of the individual life and personal relationships, as well as on the broader culture and social values – indeed, the whole of Western civilization – encouraged widespread use of myth in modernist writing. Whether the source of that myth was the classical period (Pound), or the Renaissance (Eliot), or an Ireland of aristocratic heroes and peasants (Yeats), or Nietzsche's concept of the superman and celebration of power (Lawrence), what was being suggested was some earlier golden age, innocent of the industrial revolution, which showed up the time that they were living through for the tragically shabby thing that it was. By comparison, it has to be said for Joyce's use of Homeric myth in

Ulysses that the ironies generated by the comparison work as much in favour as at the expense of his own time.

Critical theorists recently[5] have argued against the separation of ideological colouring from aesthetic value encouraged by the liberal humanist tradition; and the politics of modernism, now more of an embarrassment for admirers of individual modernist writers, has become the object of critical inquiry. Less committedly political in approach is Frank Kermode's valuable collection of essays *The Sense of an Ending*, which looks at the links between the myths in modernist writing and fascist mythology, in particular the common sense of apocalypse. Kermode, in discussing this point, argues for the usefulness of fictions in helping us to understand reality, but with this caution: 'Fictions, notably the fiction of apocalypse, turn easily into myths; people will live by that which was designed only to know by.'[6]

It could be argued that in the period since the last war an awareness by writers of the common ground shared by myth and fiction, and of the accompanying dangers of confusing one with the other, underpins some of the initiatives of postmodernist writing. Fascism powerfully exemplifies the way a fiction (of racial supremacy and purity) can, in acquiring the status of myth, become something that people live by. Postmodernist fiction not only displays extreme caution in the use of myth but a new puritanism about the nature of the fictional process. I shall return to this point later.

The break with modernism, however, was made not by non-realist writers in the period since the last war, but by a return to realist writing in the 1930s. In England, the response to the pressure of events – the Depression at home, the rise of fascism in Europe – by a generation of writers which included Auden and Spender among the poets and Isherwood and Orwell among the novelists was an attempted separation, only partly successful, from the aestheticism of modernism, in favour of political commitment and social realism. The debate concerning the formal qualities of a work of literature and political commitment has gathered momentum since the 1930s, and writers may now feel authorized by the theorists to combine formal experimentation with a radical political position. In *Writing Degree Zero* (1953), for example, Barthes attacks the use of the preterite tense, one of the conventions of realist fiction:

> The narrative past is therefore a part of a security system for Belles-Lettres. Being the image of an order, it is one of those numerous formal pacts made between the writer and society for the justification of the former and the serenity of the latter.[7]

Barthes's argument – that formal subversiveness is the only effective way of communicating a subversive meaning – is, as we shall see, highly relevant to late-twentieth-century non-realist fiction. Orwell and other writers of the 1930s, however, were in accord with the prevailing Marxist aesthetic of the time: that formal experimentation and political commitment were at odds with each other.

Political considerations, however, are only one factor in determining an aesthetic position. In his essay 'Modernism, Antimodernism and Postmodernism' David Lodge sees the successive phases in the twentieth century when one kind of writing is in a position of dominance over its antithesis in terms of a pendulum which, having swung as far as is possible at the time in one direction, will move in the opposite direction.[8] American writers of the 1920s and 1930s like Scott Fitzgerald and Ernest Hemingway, who were exposed to European innovations and innocent of political intent, made some kind of accommodation between modernist and realist writing. They used modernist techniques to express an inwardness – a romantic belief in the value of feeling – in a realized social context and with a realist attention to narrative. They share with near-contemporary English writers like Evelyn Waugh and Graham Greene a sense of the rootlessness of modern society and the resulting social and personal disintegration.

Alienation, personal despair and disintegration are recurring themes in postmodernist writing (Samuel Beckett's novels and plays being paradigmatic texts from this point of view), and in novels like Malcolm Lowry's *Under the Volcano* and William Golding's *Pincher Martin* which I shall consider as bridges between the modernist and postmodernist positions. There is, moreover, some overlap between the careers of these writers and those of Greene, Waugh, Fitzgerald and Hemingway. This suggests the important point that 'postmodernist' is not to be identified with a particular historical moment. The most obvious quality separating the work of Beckett, Lowry and Golding (in this instance) from that of more or less contemporary writers exploring much the same themes is that in the case of the former the stylistic and formal qualities of their work reinforce the bleakness of the content. Form and content, in other words, as in the work of Joyce, exist in a particular relation to each other, forcing the reader to a degree to 'experience' what in realist fiction is 'told', and therefore at a different kind of remove. Beckett, Lowry and Golding (in *Pincher Martin*) offer none of the consolation that form can give to otherwise disturbing material; and their austerity in this matter illustrates another of the ways in which certain twentieth-century writers have broken the traditional pact between writer and reader. The world that Evelyn Waugh, for example, writes about is cruel and heartless, his vision of human nature pessimistic in the sense that his 'decent' characters are always at the mercy of the predators.

Yet Waugh nonetheless belongs to that tradition in the English novel which sees the novelist's function as principally to entertain – through humour and a sense of the variousness of life and character, and through the movement and final resolution of the plot.

It would be wrong to suggest that postmodernist writing is necessarily austere, or that it excludes the possibility of narrative satisfaction or an interest in character, though the latter are often the subject of redefinition. Playfulness, as we have noticed, is one of the distinguishing characteristics of a postmodernist text, though it is often of a rather grim order and at the reader's expense. If alienation is one of the principal themes of postmodernism, then it is also fair to say that as a mode of writing it has been very successful at alienating the general reading public. One of my intentions is to suggest reasons why writers might feel compelled to violate readerly expectation in this way, and to look at the different kinds of pleasures that the novels that I shall discuss have to offer.

The phenomenon itself is not a new one. In the 1760s, within twenty years or so of the appearance of Richardson's and Fielding's novels, *Tristram Shandy*, the first English anti-novel, was published. Its author, Laurence Sterne, anticipated many of the developments of the late-twentieth-century novel by writing a kind of pastiche on the whole narrative process – interrupting his story so often that the digressions carry more cumulative weight than the plot; violating not only time sequence but the reader's common-sense expectation of how much narrative time specific episodes should take; sidestepping a satisfactory conclusion; and creating a tension between the rational workings of the hero/narrator's mind and the rational requirements of a linear narrative. Sterne inspired no immediate imitators, and until our own century *Tristram Shandy* was regarded as a literary curiosity, likely to attract only the more eccentric reader.

When *Tristram Shandy* appeared, Richardson and Fielding were struggling for control over the direction that the English novel would take. It belongs to a time, therefore, when there was some degree of self-consciousness in the writing of prose fiction, when the whole enterprise was in the process of definition. At the time, *Tristram Shandy* was read as a one-off satire, its self-reflexiveness turning back on itself to form a blind alley, while elsewhere the ground rules of realist fiction, about to dominate the scene for a century and a half, were being laid.

Postmodernist fiction, so many characteristics of which are found in *Tristram Shandy*, emerged at a time when the certainties that underpinned realist fiction had in their turn been undermined. Joyce (himself an admirer of *Tristram Shandy*) had worked at creating a form which would accommodate those thought processes and odds and ends of lived experience to which traditional realist fiction had given low priority. Events since his time – in particular the Second World War – have given a new impetus to further developments in the novel. A truism which had some currency in English criticism until recently was that the Second World War had failed to produce anything like the same body of material – in poetry and prose – as the First. This is a point to which I shall return, and discuss in some detail, in a later chapter on 'War'. Meanwhile it may be said that there is some surface truth in the truism, if we restrict writing about war to the experience of combat and if we admit it to be truer of English than of American writing. There were, as we shall see, special reasons for the enormous body of writing that emerged from the trenches of the First World War, and for the emphatic realism – even of the poetry – that characterized that writing, at a time when the modernist writers, away from the battlefields, were engaged in their experiments with form.

There is moreover the fact that, since the response of writers to the First World War was mostly, thought not entirely, in poetry, it was published much closer to the event. With one or two exceptions, it was not until the late 1950s and 60s that novels about the Second World War, realist and non-realist, began to appear, in Britain and America, dealing both with military experience (as in novels by Evelyn Waugh, Anthony Powell, Kurt Vonnegut and Joseph Heller) and civilian (Olivia Manning's, Rosamund Lehmann's and, though it resists categories, Thomas Pynchon's *Gravity's Rainbow*). It must be said, however, that the impact of the Second World War on the course of fiction is not registered principally in those realist novels which use the war as a backdrop for an exploration of personal and social relations, however outstanding such novels as Evelyn Waugh's *The Sword of Honour* Trilogy or Olivia Manning's sequence of novels may be in themselves. More to the present purpose is a novel like *Gravity's Rainbow*, which is an attempt to find a form that accommodates aspects of the war which defeat a linear narrative mode.

British and American novelists have tended to avoid direct representation of the more appalling outrages of the war, in particular the concentration camps; and when such representations are attempted – as in Thomas Keneally's *Schindler's Ark*, published in 1982 and D.M. Thomas's *The White Hotel*, in 1981, questions are always raised of sensationalism or exploitation, suggesting a deep unease that such a subject should be appropriated by fiction at all. It will nonetheless be noticed that the outrages of the war are a reference point in a number of the novels that I shall be discussing; while in a general way postmodernist fiction, whatever specific subject might be foregrounded within a particular novel, may be seen as a response to the events of the war and to the continued threat posed by nuclear weapons. The fact of the 'unbelievable' happening, in recent and remembered history, has placed a strain on that distinction between the credible and the incredible on which the eighteenth- and nineteenth-century bourgeois realist novel depended. One of the terms of this 'contract' which implicitly existed between reader and writer was that the reader would only collude in a fiction that at least on some level held a mirror up to the everyday world, so that the fiction was to a degree neutralized by the everyday world that it reflected. And that everyday world, with its belief in reason and progress, had banished the supernatural except in the practices of organized religion. (When in *Bleak House* Dickens has a character die of spontaneous combustion, he draws his reader's attention, in an Introduction, to a newspaper account of just such a bizarre event.)

The late twentieth century, on the other hand, has seen a revival of the fantastic on a scale unprecedented since the Middle Ages, a time when so few natural explanations for the expected were available. Among the writers that I shall be discussing, Salman Rushdie, Thomas Pynchon, John Fowles and Iris Murdoch make use of fantasy in their writing, although it would be misleading to describe them primarily as fantasists. Although I shall not be considering their work, it is worth mentioning that South American novelists (Gabriel Garcia Marquez, Mario Vargas Llosa, Isabel Allende) routinely employ the new conventions of magical realism, suggesting that there is a link between the culture and conditions of particular societies and the extent to which the novelist feels that he or she can present a stable view of reality.

While in the late-twentieth-century British and American non-realist novel fictions have become wilder, more extravagant, less constrained by the commonplace and common sense, there is running parallel to this – often in the work of the same novelists – a new scrupulousness, some would say over-scrupulousness, about the use of fiction at all. This manifests itself in a variety of 'metafictional' techniques – interruptions into the narrative flow by the writer to remind the reader that this is indeed fiction; an insistence on the unreliability of the narrative voice. These techniques will be considered in due course as individual novels are discussed in later chapters. I suggested earlier that this, for many readers quite unnecessary caution (caution in the sense both of a warning to readers and a nervous anxiety on the part of writers) might be seen as a manifestation of a new puritanism. One of the most notorious acts of the Puritan ascendancy in England (1640–60) was the closing of the theatres. There were a number of reasons for this, including the belief that the theatre encouraged political dissent, but political expediency was reinforced by religious ideology. Fiction, it was felt, was bad for the soul, in blurring the distinction between what was true and what was false. It was an acknowledgement both of the power and of the inherent dangers in fictional representations of reality. The Puritan edict created tensions even among those who identified themselves with the cause and paradoxically contributed to the emergence of the English novel. Daniel Defoe (1660–1731) was an active Dissenter in his youth and *Robinson Crusoe*, published when he was nearly sixty, has been seen by commentators, including Marx, as the archetypal Puritan novel, combining the Puritan faith in Providence with the Protestant work ethic.[9] Yet to gain acceptance for his book he perpetrated a fraud, presenting it to the public as a true account, like Alexander Selkirk's account of shipwreck and survival.[10] *Robinson Crusoe* gained acceptance, and helped create a taste for other fictions, by its convincing evocation of a life being lived and time passing, thus launching the English novel on its realist course.

It seems to me that similar tensions lie behind the contradictions in postmodernist writing. One may assume that Defoe justified his 'fraud' because *Robinson Crusoe* satisfied other criteria of truth, by being a morally instructive account of the workings of Providence and of the individual's response to them. Moral instruction and entertainment were the two imperatives of the classical realist novel, both abandoned by the modernists in favour of an aesthetic foregrounding which had an oblique bearing on moral issues only in as far as the reader's perceptions of external reality were altered by the aesthetic experience. A good deal of postmodernist writing marks a return to moral enquiry – almost certainly in response to recent history – but in a world where moral issues are perceived to be more complex and the writer is more reticent about authorizing a particular moral position.

This has been accompanied by a new anxiety about language – both more powerful as a self-generating system of meaning than was once felt, and more inadequate as a direct means of communicating the inner self. In 1973 the experimental British novelist B.S. Johnson committed suicide. In her book *Metafiction*, Patricia Waugh draws a parallel between Johnson and the fictional Hugo, a character in Iris Murdoch's first novel, *Under the Net*:

> Both believe in the supremacy of the self and the incapacity of language to express that self. Like Hugo, Johnson also failed, tragically and inevitably, to get out from under a 'net' which increasingly closed in on him until his suicide. His work and life reveal the tragic potential in the assumption by a self-conscious writer of an extreme 'falsity' position.[11]

Johnson, like Iris Murdoch's character Hugo, was influenced by French existentialism, a philosophy which, although in the process of formulation in the early decades of this century, was effectually moulded by the experience of the French during the Occupation. The existential emphasis on personal freedom, and the choices available to the individual in pursuit of an 'authentic' existence in a world that is fundamentally irrational, acquired a particular meaning for those who lived through the German Occupation; while the novel – a genre in which considerations of personal freedom have always assumed particular importance – was inevitably touched by existentialism. These three elements – the experience of Occupation, its effect on philosophical inquiry and the kind of novel that existentialism helped to form – come together in the work of Jean-Paul Sartre, philosopher, novelist and, during the war, active in the Resistance: a career which demonstrates one of my central propositions, that experimental fiction since the war has been fed both by theory and by the pressures of certain kinds of experience for which existing fictional models have seemed inadequate. The existentialist novel is not to be confused with the postmodernist novel, but there is some interplay. Of the novelists that I shall be discussing, there are traces of existential philosophy in the work of Beckett, who settled in France before the war and, like Sartre, was active in the Resistance; and John Fowles and Iris Murdoch too both entertain existentialist ideas.

Of more bearing on American postmodernist writing is post-structuralist theory, which is derived from the work of the psychoanalyst, Jacques Lacan (1901–   ) and of the philosopher Jacques Derrida (1930–   ). Post-structuralism, as it has been appropriated by literary theorists, argues for the destabilizing of meaning in any text, usually by exploiting possibilities within the text which undermine the overt meaning and of which the writer was perhaps not conscious. As a way of reading, post-structuralist techniques can be applied to any text, usually with the effect of overturning what appear to be the author's intentions (though modern critical theory would argue that, whatever those intentions were, they are irrecoverable). Whatever specific influences there may or may not be on individual works of fiction, it is nonetheless the case that the postmodernist novelist, by virtue of a shared philosophical position, renders the post-structuralist reading redundant: the text which refuses to stabilize its own meaning cannot be further destabilized.

Post-structuralist theory has had its effect on all the human sciences, questioning priorities which were thought to be unchallengeable – the priority of sanity over madness, of culture over nature, of work over play – and to suggest that they might be inverted. It helped to fuel the revolutionary student movements of the late 1960s in

France and in America; encouraged a revival of Marxist dialectic in the universities; and helped provide a theoretical basis for the feminist and homosexual rights movements.

These developments have all presented a challenge to mainstream culture and have in common with some postmodernist writing a conscious subversiveness. The techniques of postmodernism are subversive of established literary practices and these are often combined with 'outrageous' subject matter. The 'hero' of *Under the Volcano* is a drunk whose insight and sensitivity are intimately connected with his drunkenness; the presences that people Beckett's work are tramps and social outcasts; *Lolita* is a morally ambiguous celebration of the love of a middle-aged man for a pubescent girl. In other words, kinds of experiences and ways of living which are marginalized in the classical realist novel, placed on the periphery as socially and morally undesirable, are now being allowed a central position, whatever moral judgements may obliquely emerge.

Lowry, Beckett and Nabokov have all in their turn provoked moral outrage. When the American actor Bert Lahr played Estragon in a production of *Waiting for Godot* in Florida – the play's American premiere – he received hate mail, of which the following, quoted in Deirdre Bair's biography *Samuel Beckett* – may serve as an example of the response of Middle America:

> How can a man, who has charmed the youth of America as the lion in *The Wizard of Oz*, appear in a play which is communistic, atheistic and existential?[12]

The subversiveness, however, can take a less flamboyant form. There has been a revival of interest among non-realist writers in historical writing, but usually, as in Doctorow's *Ragtime*, in ways that challenge received versions of history. Thomas Pynchon in *The Crying of Lot 49* and *Gravity's Rainbow* suggests a mystification in the corporate process that is so sinister and pervasive as to amount to a general conspiracy. Joseph Heller's account in *Catch 22* of the Mediterranean campaign in World War II also suggests mystification, perpetrated by the authorities controlling the war and compounded by muddle. *Catch 22* was measurably subversive in effect: published in the early 1960s, it soon became a cult book among the young and helped fuel the protests against the Vietnam War.

In *Catch 22*, *Gravity's Rainbow* and *The Crying of Lot 49* mystification is incorporated into the narrative process, so that the reader is subjected to the conditions which apply within the world of the novel. This in part is what makes such fictions 'difficult', and for some readers unsatisfactory, since any experience when 'told' (rather than being, as is the case in these novels, reproduced on some experiential level for the reader) is already in the process of being tidied up. So considerations of form in postmodernist fiction can never be separated from those of theme or subject matter. This has encouraged in the work of those critics who are beginning to evaluate kinds of late-twentieth-century non-realist writing, like Patricia Waugh in *Metafiction* (1984), and Brian McHale in *Postmodernist Fiction* (1987), a tendency to give priority to the new conventions and techniques, over a detailed examination of individual novels. Valuable though their work is, it seems to me to place too little emphasis on the pleasure of the text. Most readers still think of novels in terms of what they are 'about'; and it is as appropriate to take account of this in postmodernist as in realist fiction, since many of the best postmodernist novels seem to be written under the pressure of experience, either personal or of the particular historic moment, bearing in mind always the theoretical positions that underpin these novels. Apart from any other consideration, this approach is one way of countering one of the most common ways of dismissing non-realist novelists, that they write as they do because it is 'fashionable'.

For these reasons I have in the following chapters divided the material according to subject matter or, in the case of Chapter 2, on Irish writing, in terms of particular cultural and historical conditions. Because I wanted some basis of comparison within individual chapters, I have included some novels (like William Faulkner's *The Sound and the Fury*, published in 1931) which might more appropriately be described as late modernist. This, along with other late modernist novels like Malcolm Lowry's *Under the Volcano*, should help suggest how Joyce's form of modernist writing (a considerable influence on a number of the writers that I shall be discussing) developed into postmodernism. For this reason, I often use the term 'non-realist' in preference to 'postmodernist'. A point that I shall return to shortly is that rigid distinctions between 'postmodernist' and 'modernist', or even in some cases (like the novels of Iris Murdoch), between 'realist' and 'postmodernist' are not always possible, and the attempt to make hard and fast rules can be sterile. Among areas of experience that have encouraged non-realist responses I have omitted 'women's' writing, not because I wish to distance myself from the feminist position, but because it seems to me that many recent novels by women about specifically female areas of experience (by writers like Margaret Drabble, Anita Brookner, Mary Gordon, Marilyn French, for example) have had the effect of revitalizing realist writing. That there are non-realist approaches to the subject (by, for example, Angela Carter) is beyond question, but I feel that a detailed comparison between the two would be more fruitful than anything that could be attempted here. I have included Doris Lessing's

The Golden Notebook and Rosamund Lehmann's *The Echoing Grove* – both of which lend themselves to a feminist approach – but in other contexts.

In his essay, 'Authors and Writers' Roland Barthes makes a distinction between authors for whom writing is an intransitive activity, and writers for whom it is transitive, and argues a higher value for the first than the second.

> – the author is a man who radically absorbs the world's *why* in a *how to write*. And the miracle, so to speak, is that this narcissistic activity has always provoked an interrogation of the world: by enclosing himself in the *how to write*, the author ultimately discovers the open question par excellence: why the world? What is the meaning of things? In short, it is precisely when the author's work becomes its own end that it regains a mediating character: the author conceives of literature as an end, the world restores it to him as a means: and it is in this perpetual inconclusiveness that the author rediscovers the world, an alien world moreover, since literature represents it as a question – never, finally, as an answer.[13]

Barthes's categories are not restricted in application to particular literary movements or historical periods. They have nonetheless clear bearing on the present subject. The 'narcissistic' 'how to write', the 'perpetual inconclusiveness' and the questioning are all features of postmodernist writing which, for all its self-reflexiveness, does take on a mediating character towards the world. To use for a time Barthes's terms of reference, authors, as opposed to writers, have always existed. The question that I have touched on, and as yet sketched in only partial answers to, is why the 'intransitive activity' of authors should now, in the late twentieth century, be such a wide-spread phenomenon. This can only be partly answered by first posing another question. Is the experience of living in the late twentieth century radically different from the experience of other human beings at other points in history?

I have already stressed the importance of the Second World War – and in particular, the evidence that it offered of man's inhumanity to man – as being perceived to mark a radical division in experience. There are other issues, however, and to touch on some I shall quote from an episode in Doris Lessing's *The Golden Notebook*, where the heroine, Anna, is describing her feelings of doom to her psychoanalyst:

> I don't want to be told when I wake up, terrified by a dream of total annihilation, because of the H-bomb exploding, that people felt that way about the cross-bow. It isn't true. There is something new in the

world. And I don't want to hear, when I've had an encounter with some mogul in the film industry, who wields the kind of power over men's minds that no emperor ever did . . . that Lesbia felt like that after an encounter with her wine-merchant. (p. 459)

The feelings of despair and impending annihilation which characterize so much late-twentieth-century writing alienate many readers, who feel that it is possible to lead perfectly satisfactory lives with the world as it is. The 'world' of the novel often seems not to correspond to the 'real world' – something that non-realist novelists implicitly acknowledge with the counter-claim that we create a world from our own perceptions of the 'real world'. There is a challenge of a different kind in *The Sense of an Ending* from Frank Kermode,[14] who might be said to voice some of the criticism that Anna in *The Golden Notebook* anticipates to her conviction that the world is indeed, different. He considers, in a general way, the expression of apocalyptic thinking in fiction and notes the recurrence of ideas of apocalypse in Western thought in particular, which he argues has its roots in the Old and New Testaments. Apocalyptic fears, it seems, have a way of coinciding with momentous dates – the ends of centuries or of millennia – which could certainly be argued as having a bearing on the late-twentieth-century spate of apocalyptic writing. He states that a collective sense of being specially doomed or marked out is not unique to the twentieth century but a feature of a number of periods of recorded history. We may feel, as Anna does in *The Golden Notebook*, that the technological capacity for global destruction creates an absolute division between our own period of crisis and any that has preceded us, but is there any real difference between having the technological means of annihilation (which we may expect now to be expressed in environmental[15] rather than military terms) and living in fear of an annihilation which may come from an unspecified supernatural agent? Technology has created new fears, but has at the same time set limits for most of us on what may be feared from the natural workings of the universe.

Kermode does not use the term 'postmodern' in *The Sense of an Ending*, which was published in 1966, but he has little time for what he calls 'schismatic modernism', by which I take him to mean the mutated expression of modernist techniques and attitudes by later generations of writers. If one takes the attitudes struck by postmodernist writers to be fundamentally without substance, then it is a short step to seeing their fiction as decadent. There is an interesting parallel here with English drama in the few decades that the theatres remained open after Shakespeare and his immediate contemporaries. Jacobean drama, like postmodernist fiction, is often morally ambiguous, deals with relative values rather than absolutes, and often when the meaning is stabilized before the final curtain it is in terms of such conventional piety as to suggest parody. The suspicion it creates is that the linguistic virtuosity – another feature that it shares with postmodernist fiction – and often spectacular theatrical effects disguise a fundamental hollowness, are in fact empty gestures. The questions this raises are whether an earlier generation of dramatists, who were privileged by their historical position to establish the English secular theatre, had left the Jacobean and Caroline dramatists with a public stage but nothing much to say; or whether there was indeed a hollowness or decadence in early-seventeenth-century English society which the theatre of the time makes manifest. It is not always easy to distinguish.

Similarly, postmodernist fiction can be seen as a gesture, a decadent tailpiece to a couple of generations of writers (which would include Henry James and Conrad, as well as Joyce and Lawrence) whose innovations, rather than pointing the way forward, had blocked the road. The criticism that the Marxist critic, Terry Eagleton, makes of postmodernist art might be felt by its detractors to apply just as well to postmodernist fiction:

> Postmodernism takes something from both modernism and the avant-garde, and in a sense plays one off against the other. From modernism proper, postmodernism inherits the fragmentary or schizoid self, but eradicates all critical distance from it, countering this with a poker-faced representation of 'bizarre' experiences which resembles certain avant-garde gestures.[16]

Postmodernist fiction validates itself through the merits of individual texts, which is the approach that I intend to take. But a defence can also be made on historical grounds, which leads me back to a consideration of whether that qualitative difference in experience, expressed in novels like *The Golden Notebook*, is not a convenient fiction by novelists themselves. Frank Kermode who, as we have established, sees no more substance to twentieth-century apocalyptic thinking than to that of earlier apocalyptic periods, does concede that the technological advances of the twentieth century, with the increase in social mobility that has accompanied them, have changed people's lives.[17] The proliferation of machinery has created the paradox of more freedom of choice with a sense of no longer being in control. Moreover, in considering the prevailing pessimism of so much late-twentieth-century writing, it might be worth stating the obvious: that with the rapid advance in communications technology, it is no longer possible to live in ignorance of the fact that at any moment, some-where in the world, appalling things are taking place. Incidents of man's inhumanity to man or natural disasters are no longer, as they might be in more isolated communities, sporadic but intrude into our consciousness with depressing frequency.

Philip Roth, in 'Writing American Fiction', gives an account of a particularly squalid news item before assessing the possible effect of such reported events on the writing of fiction:

> And what is the moral of the story? Simply this: that the American writer in the middle of the twentieth century has his hands full in trying to understand, describe and then make *credible* much of American reality. It stupefies, it sickens, it infuriates, and finally it is even a kind of embarrassment to one's own meagre imagination. The actuality is continually outdoing our talents, and the culture tosses up figures almost daily that are the envy of any novelist.[18]

On the qualitative difference, if such there is, between our own and earlier times, there is one further point to be touched on at this stage where the philosophy underpinning many of the novels is in collision with common sense. This is the question of how far the individual has control over his or her destiny. Such freedom is the cornerstone of the classical realist novel; and in an age and society such as our own, which has invented notions like 'consumer choice', it is possible for individuals whose lives have been lived peacefully, untouched by disaster, to see no reason for such a concept to be questioned or displaced. Yet the twentieth-century novel has been particularly resistant to the idea that our destinies, as individuals, lie in our own hands. At its most extreme, that resistance can be seen in the work of Beckett and is present in the work of a number of the other novelists that I shall be discussing. But it is by no means confined to non-realist fiction. The emergence of the anti-hero who is completely at the mercy of events, in novels of the early decades of the century like Evelyn Waugh's *Decline and Fall* (1928), is also a rejection of the autonomous self.

Personal freedom has, throughout the century, been the subject of philosophical inquiry; and even those philosophies such as existentialism which have given it a paramount position stress the irrational nature of the world in which such freedom may be exercised, which in turn limits its effectiveness. In other words, it is important for the individual to behave 'authentically', whatever effect such actions may have. It seems to me that at least as important as the direct influence on a novelist of any particular philosophy is something that I have not yet touched on – that is, the steady undermining of religious belief throughout the century. Free will is a central tenet of Christian belief, encouraging in the believer the conviction that, on the ultimate issue of personal salvation, he or she has absolute choice, however circumstances may limit personal control of destiny in the world of appearances. The importance of such conviction, however illusory it may seem to the non-believer, can scarcely be overestimated. If it is allowed that Frank Kermode's medieval peasants experienced the same kind of fear over the possibility of annihilation as we may experience, even though the technological means were not available to them, then it must also be allowed that the sense of being in control of their eternal fate may have gone some way towards mitigating despair.

It can also be argued, and sometimes is, that examples of the wide-spread destruction of human life, comparable to the actions of Nazi Germany and Stalinist Russia, have occurred throughout recorded history without provoking anguished scholarly debate about the 'real' nature of 'human nature'. But perhaps it is not just the fact of such horrors but their moment in history, when supportive systems of belief, like Christianity, were already in the process of being under-mined. There is a sense in which contemporary novelists who are sensitive to such issues are groping in the dark, often, as in a post-Apocalyptic world, returning to first principles and feeling towards re-definitions. To that response to events may be added the assault on traditional models of human nature which has come from feminist and civil rights theorists, on the grounds that such models are instru-ments of oppression. As yet, the new models are still to appear. Within this broader context, the term 'postmodernist' begins to acquire a particular suggestiveness, as of a state of limbo, of waiting, a moment of poise between worlds.

In the Preface to his book, *Postmodernist Fiction*, Brian McHale provides a neat and useful definition, hinging on the difference between 'modernist' and 'postmodernist':

> That idea is simply stated: postmodernist fiction differs from modernist fiction just as a poetics dominated by ontological issues differs from one dominated by epistemological issues.[19]

In other words, postmodernist texts pose questions about the nature of reality, modernist texts about how we can know a reality whose existence is not ultimately in doubt. He admits *Postmodernist Fiction* to be 'a one-idea book', and must be given credit for exploring that idea with great thoroughness, drawing on novels from Europe and North, South and Central America.

I have chosen, however, to map out the terrain differently and to concentrate on fiction written in English. McHale's definition results in the exclusion of all but a handful of British novelists. Among the issues that interest me is the way that a number of British novelists, working in a climate which has been largely hostile both to theory and to postmodernist techniques, have attempted to make some terms with postmodernism; and why in British fiction there is still such a strong pull towards realism. In a number of the following chapters, the comparison that is set up between British and American novels exploring similar themes generates, I hope, some useful discussion of these issues.

The foregrounding of ontological questions can lead to a concentration on the nature of reality which is curiously lacking in context. While all the novels that I have chosen raise such questions, they also indicate the pressures experienced by novelists in exploring certain material (historical or romantic, for example) in the late twentieth century, so that the ontological issue may not finally be the central one. To take the example of a writer who falls both within my spectrum and McHale's: Nabokov. A late novel, *Ada*, favoured by McHale, is finally about ontological uncertainty, whereas *Lolita*, a novel that I shall be discussing, raises that question peripherally, in a narrative which profoundly defamiliarizes the reader's concept of 'love'. Apart from the fact that I find *Lolita* a more interesting novel than *Ada*, I also think it likely that it shakes the reader's certainties more profoundly. It plays with the reader, it violates expectations.

In the following chapters, in the interests of some kind of historical structure, I shall begin with a brief discussion of Joyce's work, because he of all the novelists of the high modernist period seems to me to have been the greatest influence on the subsequent course of non-realist fiction; and I shall use the somewhat arbitrary date of 1960 to divide the material. I shall organize the texts in a way that draws attention to the subject matter – Desire, Breakdown, War, Society, for example – in order to identify the particular areas of late-twentieth-century experience which have given momentum to non-realist writing.

2

'In the beginning was the pun'

James Joyce: *Portrait of the Artist as a Young Man, Ulysses*
Samuel Beckett: *Murphy*
Flann O'Brien: *At Swim-Two-Birds*

> The language in which we are speaking is his before it is mine. How different are the words 'home', 'Christ', 'ale', 'master', on his lips and on mine! I cannot speak or write these words without unrest of spirit! His language, so familiar and so foreign, will always be for me an acquired speech. I have not made or accepted its words. My voice holds them at bay. My soul frets in the shadow of his language. (p. 172)

This reflection by the young Stephen Dedalus in Joyce's *A Portrait of the Artist as a Young Man*, arising from a discussion on semantics with an English priest, offers an insight into the extreme linguistic self-consciousness and virtuosity that are features of Irish writing. We are now, in the light both of the emphasis placed on language by twentieth-century philosophy, and of the attention currently given on university syllabuses to cultural sub-groups, more prepared than Englishmen of the colonial period to see Stephen's, and Joyce's 'unrest of spirit' as 'real' and not the product of a deliberately cultivated sensibility. There was a sense in which Joyce had no 'native' language. As a Dublin Catholic whose first language was English, not Gaelic, he had no linguistic roots in the Irish folk-lore tradition which he draws on only to satirize in the 'Cyclops' section of *Ulysses*. Significantly, the impetus behind the revival of that tradition in Joyce's own lifetime came from Douglas Hyde, Lady Gregory, Yeats and Synge, all members of the Anglo-Irish Protestant Ascendancy. On the other hand English, his first language, was also the language of the imperial oppressor, from whose cultural values he wished to distance himself.

If, as is now more widely accepted, a language system does not simply mediate the individual versions of reality of its users, but to a degree imposes a structure within which the individual must negotiate, then that nexus of imposition and negotiation is more exposed when the language is that of an imperial power. It cannot therefore be regarded as coincidence that some of the most virtuoso and self-conscious writers in English have been Irish, nor that Irish prose writers have never had the same attachment to realism as their English counterparts. The same may be said of an Indian writer like Salman

Rushdie and of a number of Caribbean writers. I am confining my discussion of this point to Irish writing, however, while acknowledging that it applies more widely, because historically Irish writers made a significant contribution in establishing a tradition of non-realist writing in English, when realism was otherwise in the ascendancy; while the work of Joyce and Beckett in particular are important landmarks in modernist and postmodernist writing.

The tradition of subversiveness and linguistic virtuosity in Irish writing is not, for reasons that I shall be examining, confined to Catholic writers, and may be said to begin with Jonathan Swift (1667–1745), whose influence is apparent in the work of the three writers who form the main subject of this chapter. *Gulliver's Travels* can lay claim to being the first work of science fiction in English; its fantasy is never finally naturalized and, written in an age which placed a high value on reason, it outraged common sense. The distinctively Irish character of his position, however, is more apparent in those works on specifically Irish themes. Like a number of Anglo-Irish Protestants, his loyalties were divided. A High Churchman and a Tory, his allegiance was to England; but as Dean of St Patrick's in Dublin, he witnessed the effects of English policy on the Irish population. His most savage attack on that policy, 'A Modest Proposal', published in 1729, in which he suggests that the children of the Irish poor should be bred as delicacies for the tables of the rich, is a masterpiece of sustained ironic inversion in which the English version of reality, that the Irish are sub-human, is exposed and taken to its logical conclusion. That inversion has been a feature of Irish writing ever since, even when its purpose has not been as overtly satirical as Swift's, and of the work of writers like Joyce and Beckett, who evade political definition.

Dissent and subversiveness remain active in Anglo-Irish writing between Swift and Joyce, the first major Catholic writer, most notably in the work of Laurence Sterne and Oscar Wilde, both important historical markers in any account of modernism and postmodernism. I have already given a brief account of *Tristram Shandy* as the first anti-novel, self-consciously exposing fictional devices to draw attention to the absurdities of narrative fiction.[1] Both *Tristram Shandy* and Sterne himself were touched by notoriety, and that was to be the fate of Oscar Wilde too, for his homosexuality, and for what was seen as the decadent aestheticism of at least two of his works, *The Picture of Dorian Gray* and *Salome*. He achieved greatest success, however, with his plays, which like 'A Modest Proposal', subvert from within.

The cunning of a play like *The Importance of Being Earnest* is that it appears to accommodate itself so comfortably to the prejudices and expectations of West End audiences. The plot is a conventionally unimaginative farce which is lifted by the brilliance of the language. What makes it, within my present terms of reference, peculiarly Irish, is that the language is used with the kind of absolute control over effect which comes from distance, from being able to see it as raw material rather than a colourless mediator of meaning. The chief characteristic of Wilde's language is, again, ironic inversion; like Swift's use of the same device, it can be read as satiric in intent. When Lady Bracknell says of a widowed friend that 'Her hair has turned quite gold with grief', the gap between the conventional expectation and the likely reality of mourning in high society is exposed; and by this means, most of the shibboleths of late Victorian society – marriage, class, money – become targets.

Wilde's subversiveness, however, is larger than specific social satire, and forms links with a number of the modernist and post-modernist writers who followed him. Realistic presentation is rejected, in characterization, in situation, in dialogue, and the action is never governed by moral consideration. Instead, the audience is presented with an imagined world which acquires validity, not as a convincing representation of the 'real' world but from the brilliance with which it is imagined. It is an alternative world, and offers dandyism as an alternative strategy for living. There are elements of dandyism in the work of Joyce, Flann O'Brien and early Beckett, but one of Wilde's most important contributions, to modernism, to the Irish tradition, and to postmodernism as Irish writers helped to shape it, was the priority he gave to the self-invented world – the micro-cosmic world of the mind – over the natural world.

This particular inversion is a characteristic that Wilde shares with Joyce; and just as with Wilde it is partly to be traced to his rejection of conventional English morality, so with Joyce it can in part be seen as a rejection of English cultural imperialism, as the passage that I quoted earlier from *A Portrait of the Artist* indicates. But that is not the whole story as far as Joyce is concerned. In *A Portrait* Stephen is encouraged by a Jesuit priest to enter the priesthood, and he is briefly enticed by the prospect of power – the power to administer the sacraments, particularly Communion. In the end he decides to pursue a career as a writer, both because he has no taste for the discipline of the religious life, and because writing offers him sacramental power of a different kind. He sees himself as

'a priest of eternal imagination, transmuting the daily bread of experience into the radiant body of everliving life.' (p. 200)

It is a commonplace of Joyce criticism that Joyce – who was, as

Stephen describes himself in *Ulysses*, 'a horrible example of free thought'[2] used the elaborate symbolic structure of the Catholic Church to create his own aesthetic. What is interesting, for our present purposes, in the parallel Joyce draws between the function of the priest and the function of the writer is not just the transforming power thereby given to the imagination: this was a cornerstone of the romantic movement, after all, and hardly new to Joyce. But here and elsewhere in his work Joyce shows himself particularly drawn to the doctrine of Transubstantiation – a doctrine central to Catholicism and outrageous to common sense in its claim that something (bread and wine) can be what it appears and then actually become something else (body and blood), after the performance of a rite and while retaining initial appearances. In wanting to 'transmute the daily bread of experience', Stephen wants to show the everyday world more fully for what it is, behind the accidents of appearance. It seems to me that if we drain Stephen's perceptions of the accidents of his own religious inheritance (while not in any way denying that that is where they are rooted), then they provide the basis for a theoretical justification for fictional worlds which are finally just themselves, but which enable us to see the everyday world more fully.

Salman Rushdie, the now notoriously lapsed Muslim and an inventive creator of fictional worlds which deny the everyday world of appearances, recently described himself as having 'a hole'[3] where religion used to be. This corresponds to Stephen's lack of pride in his own loss of religious faith. It is certainly tempting to see at any rate some kinds of non-realist writing in the twentieth century as meeting needs once met by religion; while often the most pained objections to specific non-realist texts – Rushdie's *The Satanic Verses*, Beckett's work, Nabokov's *Lolita* – have come from religious believers.

A Portrait of the Artist includes detailed discussion on aesthetics, and in particular Stephen's (and one supposes, Joyce's) well-known distinction between static and kinetic art:

> The tragic emotion, in fact, is a face looking two ways, towards terror and towards pity, both of which are phases of it. You see I use the word 'arrest'. I mean that the tragic emotion is static. Or rather the dramatic emotion is. The feelings excited by improper art are kinetic, desire or loathing. Desire urges us to possess, to go to something; loathing urges us to abandon, to go from something. These are kinetic emotions. The arts which excite them, pornographic or didactic, are therefore improper arts. The aesthetic emotion (I use the general term) is therefore static. The mind is arrested and raised above desire and loathing.
> (p. 186)

Stephen's dismissal of 'kinetic' art, as defined here, is in line with the requirement of 'impersonality' made by other modernist writers like Eliot. In part this stance by the modernist movement (which on this issue would include Wilde, Woolf, Conrad, Pound and Henry James, as well as Eliot and Joyce) can be seen as a reaction to the calculated manipulation of emotion by their Victorian predecessors. In *Ulysses*, Stephen sends Buck Mulligan a telegram which is a quotation from Meredith's *The Ordeal of Richard Feverel*: '*The sentimentalist is he who would enjoy without incurring the immense debtorship for a thing done.*'[4] A feature of much modernist and postmodernist writing is a deliberate avoidance of the emotional set-piece which is such a feature of the Victorian novel; often accompanied by teasing the reader into the expectation of something which is then withheld. The climactic meeting of Marlow and Kurtz in *Heart of Darkness*, Mrs Ramsay's death in *To the Lighthouse* are, in narrative terms, asides, with no emotional gratification in them for the reader. In *Ulysses* Bloom's reunion with Molly and his meeting with Stephen, his spiritual son, are momentous in terms of the novel's overall structure, but presented with a calculated banality.

The evasiveness of the modernist writers marked their distance from their predecessors. In postmodernism it is part of the general climate of distrust of the power wielded by fiction, a distrust that has been reinforced by the interest shown in academic circles since the last war in decoding other constructs, in politics, society and the general culture, whose power lies in the mysteriousness of their processes. On this point, it is worth noticing that Joyce's rejection of sentimentality (which can also be decoded and thereby exposed) extends to its expression in Irish nationalism, which he felt did the issue a disservice. The 'Cyclops' section in *Ulysses* is an extended satire on Irish nationalist sentiment, which takes the form of emotionally powered fictions, told by an assortment of bar-room characters who forcibly reject Bloom's reasonable interventions.

The crux of Joyce's thinking, however, is that the aesthetic satisfaction to be gained from a novel (as from any other work of art) is derived not from specific and localized emotional effects, but from a contemplation of the work as a whole. This is a more difficult idea to grasp in relation to a work of fiction which takes the reader through a linear process from the first page to the last, than in relation to a painting or other finished artefact which can be viewed in its entirety in space. Yet this is one of Joyce's most significant contributions to the later development of non-realist fiction in English.

It has become commonplace to talk about the 'world' of *Ulysses*, by which we mean something rather different than when using a phrase like 'Dickens's world'. In the latter, we mean that whatever elements of the 'real' world Dickens has used (in his descriptions of London, for example) have been touched in such a way by the idiosyncracies of his imagination that they become in his novels, no longer quite themselves, but 'his'. The work of a number of major writers demonstrates that kind of transformation. Some of that process is at work in Joyce, and we may speak of 'Joyce's Dublin', as of 'Dickens's London'.

The 'world' of *Ulysses*, however, refers rather to Joyce's attempt to create a world, or re-create the world, in his great novel. Such an enterprise would be unthinkable in a representational or mimetic work with a narrative development of plot. What Joyce has done is create a microcosm – less than twenty-four hours in the life and consciousness of Bloom, and to a lesser degree of Stephen and of Dublin itself – which allows him endlessly to extend the possible frames of reference. *Ulysses* encompasses the colour spectrum, the parts of the body, the principal branches of human knowledge. 'Oxen of the Sun' is a sustained historical survey, in the form of parody, of English prose styles; while elsewhere in the novel there are parodies or popular magazine fiction, newspaper headlines, nationalist rhetoric and theological discourse. Academic careers have been built by assembling lists of the writers, from the classical period to Joyce's own day, whose work is either paralleled, parodied or discussed within the novel; here it is enough to emphasize Joyce's inclusiveness.

The day in Dublin dramatizes the imperial relationship of the English to the Irish in the transactions between Haines, Stephen and Buck Mulligan; and the confrontation between the Judaic and Christian cultures in Bloom's dealings with everybody else. The beginning and end of the human life cycle – Paddy Dignam's funeral and Mrs Purefoy's confinement – are included in the events of the day; and while throughout much of the novel the female principle is given less weight than the male, the balance is to a degree redressed towards the end in Bloom's sexual transformation in the 'Circe' section and in Molly's closing soliloquy. So a novel which, by the conventions of linearly developed narrative fiction, may appear chaotic and random, reveals itself to the initiated as a model of painstaking organization.

Among the novels that I shall be discussing, Lowry's *Under the Volcano*, Bellow's *Herzog*, Pynchon's *Gravity's Rainbow* and both the Rushdie novels, *Midnight's Children* and *The Satanic Verses*, may be said to have exploited further the possibility made available by Joyce through the example of *Ulysses*, of the encyclopaedic novel. It is a kind of novel which through an extensive range of reference, through parody, and through setting no limits on the life of the individual mind, can take on the world.

The frame of reference for which *Ulysses* is most noted, of course, is the Homeric one, through sustained parallels of character and episode between *Ulysses* and the *Odyssey*. The use of myth is, as has been noticed, a feature of modernism which is viewed with more suspicion by postmodernist writers. There are features of Joyce's use of myth, however, which may be said to have left the door open, in particular the multiple ironies which resist final closure in favour of a heroic golden age at the expense of the present. Bloom emerges well from the comparison with Odysseus, as husband, father, citizen. And while there is an inevitable degree of comic absurdity in the comparison between Bloom's daily round and Odysseus's epic journey, Bloom's day acquires significance thereby. *Ulysses* is a work of celebration, closing on a note of affirmation with Molly's repeated 'Yes'; and it is here more than anywhere that Joyce's imitators and admirers, who do not find much cause for celebration, part company with him. Very few of the novels that I shall be discussing (Bellow's *Herzog* is perhaps the most notable exception) seem to find affirmation possible.

It remains to say something of Joyce's methods of rendering the inner life of the individual. A term like 'stream-of-consciousness', once used to describe the way the constant flux of immediate experience and the remembered associations that it generates are registered by the individual mind, already sounds antiquated; nor can it be claimed that Joyce pioneered the technique. Some of Dorothy Richardson's sequence of novels (together entitled *Pilgrimage*, completed in 1935) and Proust's *À la Recherche du Temps Perdu* pre-date *Ulysses*; while Virginia Woolf's major work is immediately contemporary. Moreover, with the widespread shift to a flat, often journalistic mode of writing in the 1930s, with the inner life of the individual giving precedence to events in the world, it looked for a time as though the innovations of the modernist writers in rendering the minutiae of experience had been rejected.

That the pendulum began to swing back towards the end of the 1930s will become clear through the discussion of individual novels; apart from the fact that many realist novelists since the modernist period have incorporated modified forms of interior monologue into their work. So it is worth trying to identify those features of modernist innovation which later non-realist writers picked up and developed further. Joyce and other novelists of the modernist period broke existing barriers, not only in the way that the individual's perceptions might be presented, but also in the kinds of human material that might by these means emerge to the surface of the novel. I shall quote from an essay that Beckett wrote on Proust which, in this particular passage, applies just as well to Joyce's writing and to the novels that Beckett would later write himself. Beckett writes that what Proust is concerned with is the

non-logical statement of phenomena in the order and exactitude of
their perception, before they have been distorted into intelligibility in
order to be forced into a chain of cause and effect. . . . And we are
reminded of Schopenhauer's definition of the artistic procedure as 'the
contemplation of the world independently of the principle of reason.'[5]

If material is allowed into the novel before it has been 'distorted into
intelligibility', then kinds of experiences may be admitted which part
of the mind routinely edits out when shaping a narrative. This raises
an interesting point of difference between Joyce and Beckett on the one
hand, and, if we confine ourselves to English writers of the modernist
period, Virginia Woolf on the other. Bloom's day includes the registering of physical sensations – taste, warmth and so on – , concerns
about his bowels, masturbatory fantasies and, in the 'Circle' episode,
a disturbing masochistic fantasy. Virginia Woolf was engaged in a
similar enterprise in her novels, but because her 'characters' are self-
aware in a way that Bloom is not, her novels are more refined – in the
sense both of more 'genteel', and of the material being more distilled.
Her 'characters' encounter a variety of fears – of madness, death,
feelings of inadequacy and failure – but they do not really confront
the workings of their own bodies or those impulses over which they
have little control. And more writers since, including Beckett, have
exploited the freedom of expression that Joyce helped to win than
have attempted to refine further in the direction of Virginia Woolf.

We think of Joyce as moving the novel forwards in terms of what it
is possible to write about. There is a sense also, however, in which he
moved it back – back from the world of getting, striving, achieving,
choosing, of the realist novel, to a sense of existence. Beckett, Lowry,
Golding, Faulkner, Bellow and others have found this to be highly
productive ground to explore; and one of the ways in which fiction
has developed in the late modernist and postmodernist periods has
been through exploring the margins of existence – the particular
experiences of the drunk, the dying, the social outcast, the mentally
disturbed and disabled.

All of these inhabit their own separate worlds which, in late-
twentieth-century non-realist writing, have been allowed as much
validity as any other. In some cases (William Faulkner's rendering of
the mentally disabled Benjy's inner world in *The Sound and the Fury*,
for example) this requires from the writer the imaginative penetration
of this closed world, and this may be said to mark an advance on
Joyce. Although *Ulysses*, in terms of narrative voice and authorial
intrusion, fulfils Joyce's requirement that the writer be 'refined' out
of existence, it is none the less a coded celebration of his own life.
The date of the action, 16 June, 1904, marks the beginning of Joyce's

relationship with Nora, later his wife; Stephen, who reflects Joyce's writerly concerns, is the age that Joyce himself was on Bloomsday; Bloom, who reflects Joyce's family concerns, is the age of Joyce at the time of composition. Other characters are based on known originals. The world of *Ulysses* is in a special sense (though not in a strictly representational one) Joyce's world. He penetrates other worlds only through the interior monologues given to female characters; but since his rendering of Gerty draws heavily, by way of parody, on women's magazines, and of Molly on some kind of concept of 'universal' womanhood, they can hardly be said to be 'closed' worlds.

Ulysses is affirmative, celebratory, and rests on the belief that an intense particularity will yield up the universal. Bloom, who decoded points us back to Joyce, is also a representative figure, a hero reconstructed in early-twentieth-century terms. *Ulysses* embodies Joyce's conviction that the writer need only look to himself to find the world; and in that, it is one of the last, great, unquestioning expressions of humanism. In later, non-realist writing 'the world' fragments into separate 'worlds' which de-stabilize the reader's sense of his or her own world as 'universal'; while such expressions of humanism as they contain are often anguished and modified. Joyce's 'trick' was to expose previously marginalized areas of experience and incorporate them into the 'universal': the nighttown sequence, 'Circe', exposes Bloom's masochism and transsexual fantasies before returning him to the diurnal round. As we shall see, however, his work proved a most valuable point of departure for later writers.

Ulysses was published in 1922, a year which marked the peak of the modernist achievement in English. In the 1930s in Britain a new generation of writers emerged (Orwell, Isherwood, Greene) whose return to realism was an expression of growing social and political concern; while others, for whom there was no going back, were consigned to a kind of wilderness for years before their work was recognized. Among the latter were Joyce's fellow countrymen, Samuel Beckett and Flann O'Brien. Beckett, who was born in 1906 in Dublin, had by the 1930s settled in Paris, where he became Joyce's friend, disciple and, for a time, as Joyce's eyesight failed, assistant. The association, while clearly fruitful, was probably also partly responsible for Beckett's delay in finding his own voice, his most remarkable trilogy of novels, which I shall discuss in a later chapter, belonging to the period immediately after the war.

For his first novel, *Murphy*, he had difficulty finding a publisher; and when it was published, in 1938, it was largely misunderstood, the *Times Literary Supplement*, for example, reviewing it as part of a group headed 'political and social novels'.[6] For this the novel's form, which is in some ways a retrenchment on modernist principles, is partly responsible. However, apart from being an extraordinarily polished and linguistically brilliant piece of writing, it helps us to sketch in some of the links between modernism and postmodernism; and demonstrates the continuing influence of Irish modes of writing on non-realist fiction. *Murphy*, like many early works, is highly revealing. All of Beckett's work may be said to express philosophical positions which, while in some ways peculiar to himself, form links with other strands in postmodernist writing. In his later fiction and drama, those positions are largely implicit, expressed obliquely by 'characters' lacking in self-awareness. In *Murphy*, on the other hand – a transitional work both in the development of non-realist fiction and of Beckett's assurance in handling his material – much of the discourse is openly philosophical, expressed in dialogue; through the self-awareness of the central character, Murphy, and by an omnipresent authorial voice.

The use of that authorial voice is one of the features that distinguishes *Murphy* from Joyce's theory and practice. However, it is not so much omniscient in the manner of classical realist fiction as arch and knowing: liberal with puns, playful with characters and reader alike, it is more a parody than a comfortable acceptance of the role of the author in classical realist fiction, and in that sense points more towards postmodernism than to Joyce.

The other apparent retreat from modernism in *Murphy* is its heavy reliance on narrative. The plot is a farce, resembling the eighteenth-century picaresque novel both in the increasingly complicated movements of a group of largely undifferentiated characters (described by the author as 'puppets',[7] with the single exception of Murphy himself), and in the marginal social position of all the characters, including Murphy. However, where in the conventional picaresque novel there is some normalizing standard by which the activities of characters may be judged, *Murphy* subverts all social norms.

Subversiveness is arguably *Murphy*'s most insistent characteristic, a link both with later postmodernist fiction and with the methods used by Irish writers since the eighteenth century to distance themselves from 'realities' imposed from elsewhere. The central character, Murphy, is an Irishman living in London who, against his better judgement, has fallen in love with a prostitute, Celia. The affront to his judgement, however, comes not from Celia's profession, which even her grandfather, Mr Kelly, considers an honourable calling, but from the fact that love violates his stated ideal. This is, to be free of all those desires which tie him to the material world. His recreation is to strap himself naked into a chair in order to appease the body and liberate the mind: 'And life in his mind gave him pleasure, such pleasure that pleasure was not the word' (p. 6). His love for Celia interrupts that life of the mind, not only by introducing an object of desire, but because of Celia's insistence that Murphy find a job, a condition that Murphy finds deeply distasteful.

Already the twin goals of the classical realist novel – an object of love and work as a sphere of achievement – have been undermined. When Murphy does find work, as a nurse in a mental hospital, the Magdalen Mental Mercyseat, he finds it surprisingly congenial, largely because of his admiration for the patients:

> the impression he received was of that self-immersed indifference to the contingencies of the contingent world which he had chosen for himself as the only felicity and achieved so seldom. (p. 96)

In this, too, Murphy's system of values subverts received wisdom, 'the complacent scientific conceptualism that made contact with outer reality the index of mental well-being' (p. 101).

Murphy had warned Celia that an inevitable consequence of his finding work would be his loss of desire for her, and this proves to be the case as she is replaced at the Magdalen Mental Mercyseat by another object of affection. This is Mr Endon, one of the patients, 'a schizophrenic of the most amiable variety' (p. 105) whose inability to respond to Murphy's friendship is a further reminder to Murphy of his own deplorable attachment to the world outside his own mind:

> Mr Endon would have been less than Mr Endon if he had known what it was to have a friend; and Murphy more than Murphy if he had not hoped against his better judgement that his feeling for Mr Endon was in some small degree reciprocated. (p. 135)

After playing a game of chess with Mr Endon in which Murphy notably fails to attract the attention of his opponent, who moves his pieces only to return them to their original positions, Murphy retreats dispirited to his room where he meets his death. He is strapped to his chair when his room fills with gas released when the lavatory is worked on the floor below, the result of an arrangement of his own devising to heat his room. What the novel leaves unclear is whether, at the time, he wills his own death; the possibility of dying in this way was of course an implicit risk.

Murphy's story can be read in two ways. Conventional wisdom might see it as a cautionary tale of a man, himself sane, who is driven by his admiration for the insane, by his own failure to give priority, as society does, to sanity over madness, to an act of self-destruction. On the other hand, the world in *Murphy* – as judged by Murphy himself and the authorial voice – is absurd, but those who are puppets remain oblivious to this fundamental condition of existence:

Not the least remarkable of Murphy's innumerable classifications of experience was that into jokes that had once been good jokes and jokes that had never been good jokes. What but an imperfect sense of humour could have made such a mess of chaos. In the beginning was the pun. And so on. (p. 41)

Murphy is a tragic figure in being able to see the absurdity of existence without being able to retreat from a consciousness of it into insanity.

The collection of bizarre characters and events against which Murphy's story is played out reinforces the sense of absurdity in the novel. Murphy is the object of a quest by a group of his fellow countrymen and women who look to him to resolve a vicious circle. He is beloved by a Miss Counihan who thus links him in a chain of unrequited love. He is sought by Miss Counihan and by Neary because, if Murphy turns her down, then she is resolved to accept Neary . . . and so on. But because Neary becomes less enthusiastic about Miss Counihan as the prospect of winning her draws closer, he comes to see Murphy as an end in himself rather than as a means to an end; and when Miss Counihan is attainable, he transfers his affections to Celia. So desire in *Murphy* is thwarted as much by fulfilment as by denial. This is so, too, of Celia's desire that Murphy find work: seen by her as the solution to their problems, the means to an ideal state, work becomes for Murphy an end in itself.

There is considerable play in *Murphy* with ends and means, which amounts to a discourse on the nature of existence. Characters endlessly invent 'ends' or goals for themselves, so that the process of living becomes part of the 'means'; and this is part of a wider failure to acknowledge that life has no 'end', in the sense of point or meaning. This is implicit throughout the novel in the foregrounding of language, which distances it from external reality. Partly this is a matter of insistent ironic inversion, in the manner of Swift or Oscar Wilde, of which a number of examples have already been quoted. More radical, however, is the way that the linguistic virtuosity which characterizes the novel is ironically undercut by an explicit sense of the pointlessness of language itself. At the end of an argument with Murphy, Celia

felt, as she felt so often with Murphy, spattered with words that went dead as soon as they sounded: each word obliterated, before it had time to make sense, by the word that came next; so that in the end she did not know what had been said. It was like difficult music heard for the first time. (p. 27)

The idea that language is a self-contained system – an end as well as a means – is, as has already been remarked, central to twentieth-century philosophical discourse on language, but few creative writers of the twentieth century have dramatized that concept for us in quite the way the Beckett has, building it into a vision of life which is precariously poised between comic and tragic absurdity.

Beckett's later novels make great play with his characters' disorientation in time and space. Landscape is minimally indicated, but left vague as to geographical location, to suggest the isolation of its human inhabitants. The London of *Murphy* is by contrast precisely rendered, its seedy world of cheap lodging houses not dissimilar to realist writing of the period (Orwell's, for example), with the difference that social and political commentary has no place in Beckett's work. The passing of time is indicated with unusual precision through the movement of the stars; and Murphy at one point has his horoscope cast. This helps provide the novel with a structure which is comparable to the Homeric parallels in *Ulysses*, though it is nothing like as highly developed, and has the effect of undermining significance rather than conferring it. The movement of the stars, cyclical and preordained, provides further ironic commentary on the quest for means to ends among the characters – a human need which, in fiction, is satisfied by linearly developed plots. This is the last time that Beckett uses such a narrative development, and he does so in order to expose the nature of the need it satisfies and within his own philosophical system, its futility. Murphy's last, posthumously revealed wish, that his remains be cremated and flushed away in the lavatory of the Abbey Theatre bar in Dublin, which in itself is an expression of futility, is in turn thwarted: after a series of accidents, his remains are scattered about the floor of a London pub during a drunken brawl.

The unnamed narrator of Flann O'Brien's first novel, *At Swim-Two-Birds* (1939) bears a close family resemblance to Beckett's Murphy and to the Stephen of *A Portrait of the Artist as a Young Man*. He has no taste for honest toil, spending the greater part of his time in bed, or for cleanliness (like Stephen, he has lice). A student at University College, Dublin, he has a taste for theoretical discussion on the nature of fiction, and takes an ironical view of lower-middle-class Dublin mores as enshrined in the home of his uncle, where he lodges. The conclusion must be that, whatever else they were doing, the Irish novelists of the first half of the century were explicitly distancing themselves from the Anglo-Saxon Protestant virtues – the Protestant Beckett as much as the Catholic Joyce and O'Brien: virtues which are central to the English realist tradition of the nineteenth century. In their place what is valued in the Irish novel is the life of the mind. O'Brien's narrator speaks of 'the privacy of my mind' (p. 9) and 'the kingdom of my mind' (p. 13). As in *Murphy*, where it is an expression

of Cartesian dualism, the mind is a place enjoying a discrete and autonomous existence.

The fruit of that mental activity in *At Swim-Two-Birds* is the
narrator's labours in fiction, about which he has strong views:

> One beginning and one ending for a book was a thing I did not agree
> with. (p. 9)

So three alternative beginnings are supplied, all calculated to strain
the credibility of readers whose ideas of what a novel should be have
been formed by realist fiction. (*At Swim-Two-Birds* explicitly plays
with such a reader, rather than assuming a reading public already
capable of accepting its own terms of reference; a stance justified by
its virtual neglect by the public until the late 1950s, when it was
'discovered'.) The first 'beginning' concerns a Pooka, or devil, from
the Irish folk tradition; the second, Mr John Furriskey, who is born
into the world with a memory, but no experience, at the age of
twenty-five; the third, Finn McCool, a legendary Irish hero. These
narratives, which are interspersed with more commonplace events in
the life of the narrator, come in time to overlap; while the reader's
orientation within the text is further de-stablized by the presence of a
novelist, Desmond Trellis, within the frame of the novel, who is responsible for the Furriskey plot and who bears more than a passing
resemblance to the narrator himself.

Other conventions of realist fiction than the requirement of a beginning, a middle and an end (and only one of each) are parodied in *At
Swim-Two-Birds*, in particular those related to characterization. The
realist novelist aims to convey a sense of human difference, though in
popular genre fiction the technique is often reduced to unacknowledged cliché. So, a servant girl in the Trellis narrative is described by
the narrator's literary confidant, Brinsley, as bearing, like the red
swan in the fanlight above the door. 'the ineluctable badge of mass-
production' (p. 32). Trellis himself is is introduced twice in the
novel – once in the narrative style usually associated with the narrator, and later in a parody of eighteenth-century prose. He has dis-
cernibly the same characteristics in both, but emerges from the first as
lazy, tyrannical and unsavoury, and from the second with some
dignity and honour. This calls into doubt the very possibility of
objectivity in a third-person narrative by demonstrating the inability
of language to mediate pure meaning. The birth of Furriskey at the
age of twenty-five, already possessing attributes of physical decay
(filled teeth and nicotine-stained fingers) and of attainment ('having
an unusually firm grasp of the Latin idiom and a knowledge of
Physics' (p. 40)) exposes the devices used by novelists to create an illusion of reality in their characters.

In order to preserve that illusion, the world of the novel is, in realist fiction, framed and contained, and consistent in all its parts. In *At Swim-Two-Birds*, as the novel proceeds, the separate narrative threads acquire their own dynamic and break through the frames. So, Trellis fathers a child, Orlick, on one of his own characters. Orlick has inherited his father's literary skills and these are in demand by a group of Trellis's characters (Furriskey, Lamont and Shanahan) who are seeking revenge on their creator for the roles he has forced them to play: in particular, for being cast as rogues when they aspire to a life of lower-middle-class propriety. When in the Orlick narrative Trellis is finally brought to trial, after undergoing a series of physical ordeals inflicted by his vengeful characters, he is accused of inflicting 'considerable mental anguish' (p. 197) on his characters by virtue of the morally opprobrious behaviour into which they are forced.

The revenge element in the Orlick narrative calls into question the purity of motive in those who write fiction; while Trellis, the representative of 'the writer class' within the novel, is a far from admirable figure. Nor is the reading of fiction regarded as any more worthy an activity than the writing of it. The narrator, in a reported conversation with Brinsley, refers to fiction as a kind of drug, furtively administered in private:

> The play was consumed in wholesome fashion by large masses in places of public resort; the novel was self-administered in private. The novel, in the hands of an unscrupulous writer, could be despotic. In reply to an inquiry, it was explained that a satisfactory novel should be a self-evident sham to which the reader could regulate at will the degree of his credulity. (p. 25)

There is certainly no question of the reader being duped by Flann O'Brien's novel. With its frequent interruptions, medley of styles, and miscellaneous jokes at the expense of a variety of genres, from the western romance to the Irish folk-tale, it lays bare the whole fictional process and eliminates the possibility of that kind of readerly 'involvement' on which the use of fiction as a drug depends. In avoiding these pitfalls, however, it raises other questions about fiction, which obliquely recalls Beckett's discourse in *Murphy* on means and ends. When a novel is as self-reflexive as this, so that its subject may be said to be fiction itself, its very purity raises the question of whether fiction serves any end beyond itself.

To an extent, this question is answered by the exuberance and vitality of the narrative itself, so that throughout the novel pleasure is foregrounded as the purpose of fiction, even as a puritanical aloofness is maintained from those fictional practices which allow it to be used as a drug. Beyond that, it is worth at this point recalling Barthes's justification of self-reflexive fiction from the passage in 'Authors and Writers' that I quoted in Chapter 1: that 'it is precisely when the author's work becomes its own end that it regains a mediating character: the author conceives of literature as an end, the world restores it to him as a means.'[8] The 'world' that At Swim-Two-Birds mediates is lower-middle-class Dublin society, which is an object of satire throughout. This is true, not just of the narrative which forms a kind of realist core around which the other narrative threads are spun – the account of the narrator's stay in his uncle's house for the academic year ending in his final examinations – but of those other more bizarre fictions.

The 'Finn McCool' story which, like the 'Cyclops' section of Ulysses confines itself to the hyperbolic excesses of the Irish folk-tradition, emerges from its context as a reflection on the gap between a heroic tradition which is kept very much alive, and the realities of early-twentieth-century Irish life. The other fiction with its roots in folk-lore concerns the conflict between a Pooka, or devil, and a Good Fairy for the soul of Orlick at his nativity. The joke on which this narrative turns is the extreme propriety of the Pooka. He is at the end quick to seize his advantage over the Good Fairy when he beats her at a game of poker and she is without the means to settle her debts, but by then there are no fears as to how he will use his influence over the infant. He is the very model of a Dublin family man – affectionate towards his wife, reviling bad language and drunkenness when he encounters them, anxious to observe the niceties due to a house where a birth is expected: in every respect the essence of decency. What we see here are the values of Catholic Ireland colouring a much wilder, amoral tradition with which it has had to make common cause.

The aspirations to blameless gentility of the characters 'caught' in the Trellis plot have already been mentioned. One of the finest sustained comic episodes in the novel is the account of a tea-time conversation between Furriskey, Shanahan and Lamont which meanders round the topics of music and illness. There is no development of ideas, no communication, no linear 'plot' to the conversation, but a series of assertions as each tries to cap the others:

> 'Ah, but the boil's the boy, said Furriskey with a slap of his knee, the boil's the boy that will bend your back.
> I'll tell you what's hard, too, said Shanahan, a bad knee. They say a bad knee is worse than no knee at all. A bad knee and an early grave.'
> (p. 158)

This passage works as social satire by reproducing in a highly stylized form a number of the characteristics of everyday conversation and exposing it as ritualistic and finally inconsequential. Where the conversation does not communicate ideas or information, however, it does communicate pleasure and a sense of being in the moment – both among the characters in the novel to the reader. And this has as much of a place in non-realist fiction as the existential anguish encountered elsewhere.

All works of fiction are ultimately about themselves in the sense that, no matter how mimetic the novel, the novelist recreates the world in the act of writing. In realist fiction, however, that self-reflexiveness is concealed in order to draw attention to the novelist's representation of the 'real' world. Flann O'Brien has, in the manner of non-realist fiction, reversed that priority, but he still has much to say about 'the world'. Moreover, the fact that all the fictions in the novel tend, no matter how fantastic they are initially, to stabilize around the same social norm, which is identifiably that of the unnamed narrator, makes its own point about the act of writing fiction – that the imagination, however fantastic, is still rooted in the known world.

3

'A dingy way to die'*

William Faulkner: *The Sound and the Fury*
Malcolm Lowry: *Under the Volcano*
William Golding: *Pincher Martin*
Samuel Beckett: *Molloy, Malone Dies,*
   The Unnamable

Twenty-five years or so span the publication of the novels that I shall
be discussing in this chapter, so I make no claims for them as a group
marking a definable historical shift or, like *Murphy* and *At Swim-
Two-Birds*, a particular historical moment. Unlike the writers of the
last chapter (Beckett, of course, figures in both), the writers here do
not share a common cultural background – Faulkner was born in
Mississippi, Lowry and Golding in England, Beckett in Ireland – and
since Beckett chose to write his Trilogy originally in French, they
cannot properly be described as, in this instance, sharing a language.
Moreover, while the Beckett Trilogy is undeniably a postmodernist
work, the others might more properly be described as late modernist
in that there is some final stabilizing of meaning, though there is a discernible difference from fiction of the high modernist period in the
degree to which readers are teased and de-stablized along the way.

Nonetheless, they have in common a certain quality of experience
which the reader is obliged, by the terms of the novels, to share. Using
a variety of techniques, including the interior monologue or soliloquy, they all create claustrophobic and unsettling worlds from the
minds of the 'characters', into which the reader is drawn, and then
forced to share the uncertainties and contradictions of those worlds.
In the previous chapter I discussed what was one of the principal
achievements of the modernist period – the discovery of ways to
explore the workings of the individual mind and catch the flux of
experience. But with the exception of the shell-shocked Septimus
Warren Smith in Virginia Woolf's *Mrs Dalloway*, the minds that are
explored fall within the boundaries of what is commonly regarded as
'normal'.

In these novels, Faulkner, Lowry, Golding and Beckett all show
themselves to be heirs to the modernist tradition in their exploration

---

* Malcolm Lowry, *Under the Volcano*

of the 'worlds' created by individual minds. All but Golding, whose work, here and elsewhere, has links with moral fable, have made explicit their indebtedness to Joyce, but they have all pushed their exploration of individual consciousness to limits seemingly unimagined by Joyce. Part of Joyce's achievement, as was noticed in the previous chapter, was to take previously marginalized areas of experience and incorporate them into the 'universal'. Faulkner's congenital idiot, Benjy and Lowry's alcoholic Consul are in a sense the least of it, as Golding casts doubts on the value of the individual consciousness altogether and Beckett arguably takes that consciousness beyond the limit of what we ordinarily understand to be human. Together they suggest the kind of fragmentation of experience – the loss of a sense of shared humanity – that is registered in so much twentieth-century non-realist writing, particularly since the last war.

William Faulker (1897–1962) is foremost among that group of American writers (which includes Thomas Wolfe and John Crowe Ransom) to emerge from the American South in the years between the two world wars.[1] They shared a common subject, which is both intensely regional and rooted in their own history, yet appropriate in a larger sense for the times in which they lived: that is, the defeat of what was by then seen as the corrupt ideal of the Old South (a compound of chivalry, close family ties and privilege based on land and skin colour), and the South's failure to find something to replace it. Faulkner and other southern writers of his generation write as though still in the aftermath of the Civil War – in that sense reflecting a society that had stagnated since – but with a perspective that was only achieved after the First World War.

The Sound and the Fury tells the story of four children, Benjy, Jason, Quentin and Caddy, who are effectively orphaned with the death of their grandmother because of the self-absorption and emotional sterility of their parents. A term like 'story' – used by Faulkner himself, as we shall see, of *The Sound and the Fury* – would seem to mark a distance between this novel and the aesthetic of the modernist movement. But Faulkner's entire career as a writer demonstrates the need to reclaim the art of story-telling – one of the traditional prerogatives of the novelist – in the light of modernist principles, focusing on memory and on individuals' experience of events. Faulkner's own account of the genesis of *The Sound and the Fury* – that it began as a short story with Benjy as narrator – is instructive:

> And that's how that book grew. That is, I wrote that same story four times. . . . That was not a deliberate *tour de force* at all, the book just grew that way . . . I was still trying to tell one story which moved me very much and each time I failed.[2]

There is an apparent contradiction here of his own description of his novel elsewhere as a 'vase'[3], which suggests a highly wrought artefact, only obliquely expressing the artist's emotional commitment to his material, in the manner of modernist writing. The focus on a story which is never finally told, however, brings Faulkner closer to the infinite regressiveness of postmodernist writing, which has allowed writers to reclaim the role of story-teller while abandoning the author's traditional authority over the final version of events.

The *tour de force* of *The Sound and the Fury* is the contribution of Benjy, the idiot brother who has no language and no sense of time and who makes connections, not through reason, but through the associations generated by remembered sensations. Faulkner was an admirer of Conrad's novels, and his rendering of the relationship between Benjy and his sister Caddy owes something to Winnie and Stevie in *The Secret Agent*, but Conrad did not really attempt to enter the world of Stevie's mind. Faulkner's imaginative penetration of Benjy's mind carries conviction and engages the reader in Benjy's suffering and bewilderment. Lacking a sense of linear time, Benjy at the age of thirty-three has no concept of the finality of the past, nor therefore of the impossibility of his sister Caddy's returning to inhabit the world of their shared childhood. His need for her is continually revived by the calls of 'caddie' from the golf course.

From the following accounts, by Quentin and Jason, the reader is able to piece together something of a linear narrative, though with the emphasis still on the selectiveness of the individual memory. In these we learn of a series of disgraces, misfortunes and financial reverses in the Compton family: of Caddy's sexual adventures, of the collapse of the marriage which was to have brought her independence and her brother Jason a job, and of the subsequent return of her daughter Quentin, now seventeen, to the family home; of brother Quentin's idealization of Caddy, with his accompanying anxiety that his feelings for her are potentially incestuous, and of his suicide at the time of Caddy's marriage.

The point is, however, that while Jason's and Quentin's 'stories' illuminate the linear sequence of events in ways that Benjy's cannot, in other respects their memories have no more validity than his: theirs are not privileged versions. This is partly because, while not genetically flawed, they have been damaged by events and family history, and this colours their perceptions. Moreover, although they can distinguish the sequence of events as Benjy cannot, they are as emotionally locked in the past as he is and as incapable of moving on from the loss of Caddy to the family. Quentin's account is dated 'June Second, 1910', the day of his death and eighteen years before the narrative 'present' of Benjy's and Jason's, but the living brothers have advanced from that event no more than the dead. Jason, who thinks he has, is locked as much in his hatred of Caddy as Benjy is in his love for her.

There are other features than the refusal to allow the accounts of those of 'sound' mind to carry more weight than Benjy's which link *The Sound and the Fury* to certain kinds of postmodernist writing as well as back to Joyce. There is the relentless teasing of the reader as key information is withheld or offered in such a way as to delay understanding (although it is closer to modernist than to postmodernist writing in the completion of the jigsaw by the end). Then there is the way that language, particularly names, signifies more by association than by a direct correspondence between word and object. This is particularly apparent in Benjy's confusion of 'caddie' with 'Caddy', but apparent also when, after a disgrace involving his mother's brother, Maury, Benjy's name is changed from 'Maury' to 'Benjy'. Names recur in the Compson family (Jason and Quentin as well as Maury), reinforcing the sense of cyclical rather than linear development in a way that is particularly appropriate for a family locked not just in its own immediate past but in the vanished glories of the Old South.

A feature of twentieth-century non-realist writing which will be noticed again is that time, instead of being an invisible and inert medium in which events take place, is foregrounded and problematized – a development which is comparable to changing concepts of language. In *The Sound and the Fury* the linear progression of time is shown to be at least in part a construct and immaterial in relation to the 'world' inside the mind, most notably for Benjy but for other characters too. On the other hand, time does move and a failure to acknowledge that traps the individual in an enclosed and private world. Quentin, in an attempt to arrest time at a point before Caddy's marriage, gives considerable attention on the day that culminates in his suicide to breaking his grandfather's watch, bequeathed to him and therefore a link with the family's past as well as a way of measuring time.

The Sound and the Fury is, like *Ulysses*, a coded book, not only in the kinds of demands that it makes on readers, but in the way that it encloses much of Faulkner's own family history and personal reference. Like Joyce and Conrad, both writers whom he admired, he chose to present his material obliquely, but one can make distinctions between the three in their preference for the oblique manner. Joyce's aesthetic, the carefully argued priority that he gives to impersonal and 'static' art over 'kinetic', is reinforced by a fear of lapsing into sentimentalilty,[4] and one senses a similar anxiety behind Conrad's indirect approach to his material. Some of his novels (*The Secret Agent, Heart of Darkness*) suggest a taste for melodrama combined with a kind of failure of nerve, a need to avoid the direct representation of emotion. Faulkner, by contrast, appears to have chosen obliqueness because of its emotional effect, because it helped him reclaim for the novel the power to move. I quote from his biographer, David Minter, who is part quoting, part paraphrasing *Faulkner at Nagano* (by Robert A. Jeliffe):

> by the time he came to the fourth telling, he wanted a more public voice. In addition, he thought indirection more 'passionate'. It was, he said, more moving to present 'the shadow of the branch, and let the mind create the tree'.[5]

The fourth telling of *The Sound and the Fury* is a third-person narrative which finally stabilizes the meaning. The immediate effect is one of shock as characters are described for the first time from without, the picture of Benjy particularly claiming an emotional respose from the reader:

> a big man who appeared to have been shaped of some substance whose particles would not or did not cohere to one another or to the frame which supported it. His skin was dead-looking and hairless; dropsical too, he moved with a shambling gait like a trained bear. His hair was pale and fine. It had been brushed smoothly down over his brow like that of children in daguerro-types. His eyes were clear, of the pale sweet blue of cornflowers, his thick mouth hung open, drooling a little. (p. 244)

Ulysses and other great modernist works avoid the climactic moment and the sense throughout of something still pending, in favour of a seamless and finished perfection where the parts are subordinate to the whole. One of the features of late modernist fiction, however – and this is as true of *Pincher Martin* as of *The Sound and the Fury*, besides Durrell's *Alexandria Quartet* and Rosamund Lehmann's *The Echoing Grove*, which I shall discuss in the next chapter – is that the indirection of modernist writing, the withdrawal of the narrative voice that knows and is prepared to tell all, are used to create a sense of deferral with the prospect of final satisfaction. In the purest forms of postmodernist writing, that deferral becomes infinite.

Once the picture clarifies, the events of *The Sound and the Fury* – Quentin's suicide, Caddy's alienation from her family, and particularly from her daughter, Benjy's castration (on the mistaken grounds that he is a sexual threat to young neighbouring girls) and Jason's tyrannical control over the family after their father's death – are shocking, and at the moment of the novel's conclusion no prospect is offered of anything better. The young Quentin makes her escape but, it seems, only to repeat the cycle of her mother's life, while hanging over the oblivious Benjy is the threat of the asylum. Nonetheless, it seems that some sense of redemption is intended, somewhat in the manner of Shakespearean tragedy. The title is a quotation from *Macbeth*, but *The Sound and the Fury* is closer in spirit to the other tragedies, particularly *King Lear*, in expressing a sense of human goodness, albeit that it is thwarted and powerless. The love between Benjy, Caddy and Quentin, the care given to Benjy by the black servants, are matched by Faulkner's own emotional commitment to his material. The other novels under discussion in this chapter, dealing with similarly extreme and marginal human experience but written upwards of ten years later, during and in the aftermath of World War II, illustrate the subsequent undermining of a humanism which, in Faulkner's work, is still precariously held.

Under the Volcano, published in 1947, is the only really significant work of fiction to have been written by Malcolm Lowry (1909–57). It was nonetheless enough to make a cult figure of its author, and to become itself a cult book in the 1960s when postmodernist modes of writing were gathering momentum. One obvious reason for that late flowering of interest in a writer whose own attempts to interest publishers in his work had not always met with success was that the value he gives in his novel to the insights and sensibility of his central character, Geoffrey Firmin, who for the greater part of the novel is apparently stupefied by drink, found an answering response in the drug culture of that 1960s.

Just as relevant, however, is that, like *The Sound and the Fury*, *Under the Volcano* is a heavily-coded work, though with an important difference. The code in *The Sound and the Fury* can finally be broken and is confined to the novel itself, whatever of Faulkner is enclosed within. The Russian Formalists made a distinction in the analysis of narrative between 'fabula' and 'sjužet': 'fabula' is the order of events referred to by the narrative, 'sjužet' the order of events presented in the narrative discourse. So the act of decoding *The Sound and the Fury* is in recovering the 'fabula' from the 'sjužet'. The coding of *Under the Volcano*, by contrast, is of a more arcane order, generating multiple meanings which both recede further and further within the novel and fan out beyond it.

Lowry's acknowledged model for his novel was *Ulysses*. His concerns are, like Joyce's, intensely autobiographical, with the authorly 'self' split, as in *Ulysses*, between an older and a younger man: Geoffrey Firmin, the dismissed consul of Quauhnahuac, a provincial Mexican town, who is given the author's alcoholism, paranoia and distinct modes of perception – attributes which, while intermittently viewed with irony, are also presented as in some sense heroic; and his younger brother Hugh, who is given Lowry's early experiences as a merchant seaman and at Cambridge, together with his anti-fascist political position. Firmin's estranged wife Yvonne completes the trio, while the affair she had with Hugh in the past, which may or may not be on the point of reviving on the day to which the novel's action is confined, contributes a theme of treachery and betrayal.

Under the Volcano, which is on one level a domestic drama, is made to signify far beyond itself by a careful placing in time and space and by a wide range of literary reference. One of the more remarkable features of the novel is its evocation of a landscape both beautiful and sinister, dominated by two volcanoes, which is given a global centrality and such variety of geographical feature as enables it to suggest both more distant and mythic locations:

> How continually, how startlingly, the landscape changed! Now the fields were full of stones: there was a row of dead trees. An abandoned plough, silhouetted against the sky, raised its arms to heaven in mute supplication; another planet, . . . a strange planet where, if you looked a little farther, beyond the Tres Marias, you would find every sort of landscape at once, the Cotswolds, Windermere, New Hampshire, the meadows of Eure-et-Loire, even the grey dunes of Cheshire, even the Sahara, a planet upon which, in the twinkling of a eye, you could change climates, and, if you cared to think so, in the crossing of a highway, three civilizations; but beautiful, there was no denying its beauty, fatal or cleansing as it happened to be, the beauty of the Earthly Paradise itself. (p. 15)

The image of the Garden of Eden recurs, but spoiled, in the tangled undergrowth of the Consul's garden where emergency supplies of alcohol are hidden.

The novel is set on 2 November, the Mexican Day of the Dead, a day of carnival, religious ritual and random acts of violence, which gives apocalyptic significance to the individual deaths, before the sixteen-hour time sequence borrowed from *Ulysses* is completed, of Yvonne, trampled by a horse, and the Consul, at the hands of a fascist agent. The year is 1938, just after the Munich agreement. The Spanish Civil War, in which Hugh has been involved, is a frequent point of reference, as is the casual and widespread anti-Semitism of pre-war Europe; while there is evidence on all sides of the political turbulence of Mexico itself, with fascist and para-military groups working against the socialist government. There are spies and suspicion of spies everywhere, extending the theme of treachery from the domestic to the political sphere, which is further reinforced by reference to Mexico's troubled history. In the political arguments

between Hugh and Firmin which punctuate the novel, Hugh's ideal-
ism (that of an 'indoor Marxman') and Firmin's liberal humanism are
shown to be equally ineffective.

Throughout the novel it is not just Firmin who stands at the edge of
the ravine which he is thrown down by his murderer at the end, in the
company of a dead dog, but the world of which Quauhnahuac is the
symbolic centre. So the Consul's last words – 'this is a dingy way to
die' (p. 374) – take on a resonance beyond his own death.

Under the Volcano, as well as signifying its own historic moment so
comprehensively, aspires in its range of literary reference to the
encyclopaedic, to be a book of books.[7] The debt to *Ulysses* is clear,
in the parallel assumptions of the inclusiveness of the individual
consciousness which can yield up the whole of a man's life in a day,
and of the capacity of any text to 'contain' such other texts as have
bearing on it. Dante is quoted, but in a larger sense presides over the
novel by virtue of the latter's evocation of the underworld of the mind,
the burden of which may prove to be intolerable. There are numerous
casual references to Elizabethan and Jacobean drama and poetry,
most persistently to *Doctor Faustus*, the most apocalyptic text of that
period. The title evokes Hardy's *Under the Greenwood Tree*, the
most purely pastoral of his novels; like the references to the Garden of
Eden, it places *Under the Volcano* in a world of lost innocence, while
the evocation of T.S. Eliot's 'The Waste Land' in the Consul's spoiled
garden helps to locate that world in recent literary history.

Under the Volcano's intertextuality is very much in the modernist
mode, but there are other features of the novel which enable us to see
it as an important bridge between modernist and postmodernist
writing, particularly its persistent dualism. Central to this is the treatment of the Consul's drunkenness. Modernist writers still claimed
some kind of universality of perception, but readers' expectations of
this tend, more often than not, to be flouted in postmodernist writing,
which places a new value on 'deviant' forms of perception. While
Under the Volcano does not shirk from presenting the damage
inflicted on Firmin's life by drink – as for example the way that every
decision (in particular of what to do about Yvonne's offer of reconciliation) is endlessly deferred beyond the next drink or two – there is
nonetheless a sense that this is the price he pays for a heightened
perception that Yvonne cannot share.

> 'And, by the way, do you see that old woman from Tarasco sitting in
> the corner, you didn't before, but do you now?' his eyes asked her,
> gazing round him with the bemused unfocused brightness of a lover's,
> his love asked her, 'how, unless you drink as I do, can you hope to
> understand the beauty of an old woman from Tarasco who plays domi-
> noes at seven o'clock in the morning?' (p. 55)

The Consul's assertion that, 'a woman could not know the perils, the complications, yes, the importance of a drunkard's life!' (p. 89) is to a degree ironized within the narrative, but not to a point where we can dismiss his claim to importance altogether: there is a measure of collusion, even as the absurdity of such a position is acknowledged. There is throughout the novel – most especially in the representation of Firmin's paranoia – , in Ronald Binn's words, 'an underlying complicity between the narrative and the Consul'.[8] Although Firmin is not presented exclusively in his own terms but projected also through the perceptions of others – not just Yvonne and Hugh, but his friend Dr Vigil (an oblique reference to Dante) and Jacques Laruelle, a former lover of Yvonne – , whatever judgements they form of his drunkenness are not 'privileged' by their sobriety; while enough is shown of their past lives and former relations with the Consul to render them less than objective witnesses.

I have already mentioned the frequent references in *Under the Volcano* to English texts of the sixteenth and seventeenth centuries. Although it is not given any particular prominence by Lowry, it seems to me that the work of that period which is most persistently suggested is *Hamlet*, in that it is impossible always to distinguish between the world of the hero's mind and the material world that he inhabits. Like Hamlet, the Consul is paranoid, often appearing to over-interpret what is going on around him. On the other hand, he has been a victim of treachery in the past, and the narrative leaves it open whether the various disappearances of Yvonne and Hugh, which arouse his suspicions, are innocent or not. The Mexico of *Under the Volcano* is, like Elsinore, full of spies, but who is a spy and who is not, and who is spying on whom? Then, it is made clear that not everybody witnesses an event in the same way. In the course of a bus journey, the bus stops and there is a dying man, the victim of violence, beside the road. When the journey resumes, the Consul notices that a fellow passenger is clutching a handful of bloodstained coins, taken from the dying man, but not everybody notices the coins, or the blood. Like Hamlet, he inhabits a mysterious and treacherous world where appearances are deceptive – a world to which paranoia may be the only appropriate response for the sensitive man.

The distinction between the world of the mind and the physical world is even harder to make in *Pincher Martin* in that the only character, other than those who enter the novel by way of,his memory of them, is the survivor from a ship torpedoed in the Atlantic during World War Two; and he alone inhabits the physical world enclosed by the novel.

Since *Pincher Martin*, his third novel, published in 1956, William Golding (1911–   ) has published a further nine, in a widely-ranging and still active career; until the last three, a sequence of novels, always breaking new ground in terms of form and theme, though usually, with one or two exceptions, choosing 'large' subjects and extreme situations. *Pincher Martin* should not, therefore, be taken as representative of his work as a whole. He is a difficult writer to classify, resisting labels like 'realist', 'late modernist' or 'postmodernist'. Moreover, he emerges from his work as a novelist in a recognizably Christian tradition – a claim that could be made for only a few of the novelists whose work will be discussed in later chapters. *Pincher Martin* serves, therefore, to illustrate a point that I made in the opening chapter – that while it would be impossible altogether to dismiss the claim often made by their critics that non-realist or 'experimental' novelists are merely jumping on a fashionable bandwagon, it can be argued that such writing is at its most successful when the form has clearly been determined by the pressure of the subject-matter.

Because *Pincher Martin* is about the capacity of the individual mind to create its own world – and then to use that world as an instrument of self-deception, to deny external reality – the mind of the protagonist, Martin, is central to a remarkable degree, drawing the reader into that world to share in the deception. The novel opens with the struggling body in the water after the torpedo attack, a cry for 'Help', a half articulated appeal to 'Mother' ('Moth . . .'), before the face contracts into a snarl. This takes us about a page and a half into the novel; and thereafter, while the third-person narrative voice persists, it is Martin's own consciousness that is in control, concentrating on and sifting the images that arise in his mind, assessing his physical state, willing his own survival:

> I won't die.
> I can't die.
> Not me —
> Precious. (p. 14)

He colonizes a rock face – now the limits of his physical world – on which he finds himself and organizes the means to live.

There follows a heroic, and sometimes mock-heroic, struggle for survival which, as in the Biblical account of Creation, takes six days. He forces himself to eat congealed seafood, administering an enema when food poisoning sets in, fights despair when his equilibrium is threatened and resists to the last (' "I shit on your heaven!" ' (p. 200)) the inevitability of his own death, which comes with a storm, an act of divine intervention. The narrative is characterized by a sense of concentrated effort, certainly appropriate for the bleak and arduous nature of the enterprise. But it is equally appropriate, as we might be alert enough to realize at a number of points in the course of the narrative, but are more likely to have to wait until the end to understand, for a man who is fighting to convince himself of the material and objective reality of what actually exists only in his own mind. In a final stabilizing chapter, his body is inspected by the corpse-disposal officer who, in the novel's final sentence, casually reveals that Martin lacked even the time to kick his sea-boots off; whereas in the narrative dominated by Martin's consciousness the removal of the sea-boots is one of his first acts to ensure his survival.

Although the arrival of the corpse-disposal officer, and the accompanying switch from the mind of the protagonist, does in some sense stabilize the narrative (it is comparable in effect to the final 'telling' of *The Sound and the Fury*), it de-stabilizes the reader's hold on the novel in other ways by raising as many questions as it answers. If Martin in fact died before his six-day struggle, then what is the nature of the consciousness which enables him to form a world, which for him exists in time and space and in which his physical struggle is enacted? And if that struggle (albeit confined to his consciousness, which then projects it onto the physical world) only exists for a few minutes in the 'real' world of Mr Davidson, the corpse-disposal officer, then how useful is linear time for registering such experiences? This is particularly pertinent when it comes to 'measuring' Martin's suffering, Davidson arguing that since the sea-boots are still in place, Martin had no time to suffer. This brings the reader, who has been required by the narrative form to 'share' Martin's experience, into conflict with the comfortable assumptions of the everyday world represented by Davidson. So while a dichotomy is set up in the novel between the everyday world, where the novel finally stabilizes, and the world of the mind, it does not give priority to one over the other.

The principal device for achieving this is the use of the third-person narrative voice, which makes no distinction between the separate worlds. It is also, of course, the principal source of trickery in *Pincher Martin*, in that the reader, wary of accepting first-person discourse on its own terms, allows authority to discourse in the third-person. The narrative colludes with Martin, as the narrative in *Under the Volcano* colludes with Firmin. There are in *Pincher Martin* 'clues' to the self-invented nature of Martin's world, from which Martin himself, committed for his own survival to that world, recoils with fear. The reader shares the fear and only gradually locates the source. So, thoughts of the precise shape of his own rotten molar are particularly alarming to Martin, pushed away whenever they impinge; for the reader the realization is gradual (and more likely on a second reading) that the tooth has given him the form of the rock to which he clings for survival.

The tooth is a particularly potent and resonant image in the novel, both familiar and de-familiarized by its transformation into the rock; touching a fundamental insecurity about our manner of perceiving the external world. There is a moment when Martin, absorbed by the problem of how to attract help, seems to be gaining mastery over his situation, a mastery which expresses itself in the reflection (heavily ironized by later information) that, 'Men make patterns and super-impose them on nature' (p. 108). It is a moment that, like much else in the novel, recalls *Robinson Crusoe*, as any English novel about survival from shipwreck must. Martin evokes Defoe's hero through-out – in his strategies for survival, in the precision that characterizes his description of his 'world', in his struggle to maintain sanity and an orderly routine and in his colonization of the rock face:

> If this rock tries to adapt me to its ways I will refuse and adapt it to mine. I will impose my routine on it, my geography. I will tie it down with names. (pp. 86–7)

The irony in the parallel, however, stretches much further than relative objectivity – the 'reality' of Crusoe's world by comparison with the self-created nature of Martin's. It is an ironic juxtaposition of two moments in history, two philosophical positions, two attitudes to the nature of fiction. I have already discussed *Robinson Crusoe*'s curious place in the history of fiction,[9] justifying its own claims to authenticity by the 'truth' that it embodies of the ways of Providence. If the Puritan conscience was so uneasy about the writing and consumption of fiction, it was because of a deeper certainty about what was true and what was false, what real and what unreal. Robinson Crusoe's world is real within the frame of the novel and, although fiction, is the product of a deep ontological certainty in a fundamentally Christian universe. A profound uncertainty about what is and is not real is, by contrast, frighteningly dramatized in *Pincher Martin*, giving the protagonist a pathos and an absurdity lacking in Defoe's representation of his hero. Even what may be read as divine intervention as Martin finally surrenders consciousness is open to interpretation: this too may be within his self-invented world, a dramatic closing flourish.

Robinson Crusoe is one of the great Protestant bourgeois texts. As we have already noted, Marx commented on the clear links it makes between Protestant theology, in particular a faith in Providence, and personal enterprise, in Crusoe's colonization of the island. Common to both is the belief in individual destiny. It provided a paradigm for later fictions of the eighteenth and nineteenth centuries whose plots are driven by virtuous ambition, finally rewarded. Again, the parallel with *Pincher Martin* is deeply ironic. Martin not only has a strong will to survive, but a sense of his own uniqueness ('Not me/Precious') which is sufficiently powerful to allow him to believe that he has triumphed over death. In the course of the novel, through the brief and fragmented episodes which surface in his mind from his life up until the torpedo attack, a picture builds up of the kind of man he is and has been. An actor by profession, for whom the part of Greed in a morality play was felt to be particularly appropriate, his dealings with other people have been characterized by an unwillingness ever to accept that he cannot have what he wants – other men's wives and money, the best part in a play, the best position in a bicycle race with another boy. One of those moments of fear in the narrative, provoked when he glimpses a disparity between his invented world and the 'real' world, occurs when he sees a red lobster swimming in the sea. Like the rotten molar, which serves a similar function, the red lobster is a particularly potent image, briefly opening a gap between the reader's perception and Martin's consciousness and allowing us momentarily to 'see' him. It further demonstrates that process by which 'Men make patterns and superimpose them on nature', indicating that the apparently external world of the novel owes its existence solely to Martin's will to survive; while the lobster itself, with its grasping claws, is an embodiment of the epithet 'Pincher', bestowed on Martin by one of the victims of his greed.

In their book, *William Golding: A Critical Study*, Mark Kinead-Weekes and Ian Gregor argue that the personality given to his protagonist by Golding is a necessary premise to the situation in which he then places him.[10] He is not an Everyman – a figure whom novel readers are only too eager to find when fundamental questions of survival are at issue – but the kind of man who would refuse to die in the manner demanded by the novel. This is in some senses an irrefutable argument, but one which suggests that the concerns of the novel are more marginal than one feels Golding intended them to be.

Martin is not Everyman, and his behaviour is placed within the novel beside other possible ways of being, in particular the goodness embodied in his friend, Nat, who has in the past warned Martin that he may need training in dying. But he is, somewhat in the manner of those morality plays which figure in the glimpses we have of this past, an exaggerated embodiment of one aspect of the human personality – the will – which is common to all of us. There is a sense in which *Pincher Martin* questions the unique value ('Not me/Precious') that the individual places on himself and his own desires, not only in terms of the damage that Martin does to other people, but of the suffering that he inflicts on himself by his refusal to die. To the extent that *Pincher Martin* is on one level a discourse on will, it has a bearing on the particular historical moment of the Second World War, during which the action of the novel occurs. But other historical moments are also in play. The morality drama suggests the medieval world, which had not yet invented the individual personality as we know it; while the evocation of *Robinson Crusoe* brings into play the moment when fiction appropriated the Protestant concept of the individual and confidently asserted its value.

The three novels of the Beckett Trilogy (*Molloy*, *Malone Dies* and *The Unnamable*) were first written in French in the late 1940s and early 1950s, only appearing in English in Beckett's own translation over the period 1955–59. A case can therefore be made for their belonging to both cultures, though the likelihood is that Beckett chose to write in French as a way of cutting himself adrift. Richard Ellmann, in *Four Dubliners* attributes the decision to a 'revelation'[11] which Beckett has himself described, which occurred at Dun Laoghaire in 1945 when he was visiting his mother in Ireland, after spending the war years in France.

> The label he gave to his new motive in art was poverty or impoverishment. His characters would be deprived not only of money but of youth, of health, of fortitude. I do not think that the aged, the infirm, the enervated attracted him for their own sake so much as because through them he could approach the underside of experience, go beneath pose and posture.[12]

Part of that impoverishment was linguistic:

> The linguistic decision entailed quite different modes of expression to go with the new shapes of literature that he was evolving. His boldness was almost without precedent. It freed him from literary forefathers. It was a decision only less radical than Joyce's in inventing his extravagant *Finnegans Wake*–ese. Impoverishing himself, Beckett had to forswear all those associations which a native speaker writing in his own language happily makes use of.[13]

John Fletcher, in *Novels Of Samuel Beckett*, describes Murphy, the protagonist of Beckett's first novel, published just before the war, as Beckett's 'last citizen of the world'.[14] Thereafter his 'characters' occupy 'his' world – a world where, for the reader, doubts and confusions multiply, and which demands to be taken on its own terms. No concessions are made to the comfort of readers, in terms both of form and of the conventional consolation of fiction.

The timing of the 'revelation' to which this radical shift in Beckett's art may be attributed – immediately after the war, when he had taken an active role in the Resistance, before escaping to Provence through Occupied France after his cell was betrayed – is of course highly suggestive. So is the place. Ireland had avoided the traumas of the war in Europe, and this served to intensify that division of experience which characterized Beckett's relations with his family and country. Beckett's writing – in many ways the most removed from time, place, history and society of all post-war non-realist writing – at the same time provides some of the clearest evidence we have of the effect of the Second World War on the aesthetic and formal concerns of novelists.

Within the 'Trilogy' the first novel, *Molloy*, is the most approachable. The material world inhabited by the monologuists is the most clearly realized, though unlike *Murphy*, which is specifically set in London, it is not located in the 'real' world. Molloy, and then Moran, whose voice takes over, inhabit a landscape of towns, villages, seashore and countryside reminiscent, sometimes of Ireland, sometimes of France, while the choice of names displays the same duality. The sense of place, however, far from anchoring Molloy and Moran, and providing a release for the reader from the claustrophobic experience of inhabiting the speaker's consciousness, contributes to the sense of confusion and even menace.

Molloy is an archetypal Beckett figure – a tramp, crippled and deformed, marginal to society. All his negotiations with the material world present him with immense difficulty. He responds to everything that happens to him, whether apparently benign (he is befriended by a woman called Lousse after he runs over her dog with his bicycle, and provided with every material comfort), or malevolent (the sudden and unexplained loss of half his toes), with the same minimal level of surprise; and with profound ignorance of the terms, natural or human, governing any circumstance. But while he fails to register surprise at the unusual, he cannot respond 'naturally' to 'natural' processes, as in his description of his sexual initiation by an old woman called Ruth or Edith (the name escapes him):

> I toiled and moiled until I discharged or gave up trying or was begged by her to stop. A mug's game in my opinion and tiring on top of that, in the long run. But I lent myself to it with a good enough grace, knowing it was love, for she had told me so. (p. 53)

Beckett makes extensive use, in the Trilogy, of that ironic inversion which in the last chapter I described as part of the Irish literary tradition. But what in *Murphy* seems at times a kind of verbal tic, has become by *Molloy* more deeply shocking, the expression of a vision which cannot find solace in any of those natural ties and transactions which, in orthodox systems of value, are felt to hold meaning. Molloy is locked in a relationship with his mother whom he visits, scarcely knowing why, beyond the fact that they recognize each other by their smell.

> My mother. I don't think too harshly of her. I know she did all she

could not to have me, except of course the one thing, and if she never
succeeded in getting me unstuck, it was that fate had earmarked me for
less compassionate sewers. (p. 19)

In keeping with the general inversion of values, Molloy's response
to things, as opposed to people, is often affectionate; pebbles, the
most inanimate of natural objects, having the largest claim on his
feelings. One of the novel's more celebrated comic episodes describes
the difficulties, and strategies that he has devised to overcome those
difficulties, in keeping sixteen sucking stones in circulation, so that in
sucking, he observes some kind of order. It is a spectacularly pointless
activity which he finds totally absorbing.

Molloy is a grotesque figure, his life pared down to a minimal level
of existence, a negation of human possibility. If *Molloy* were merely
about Molloy, it would be possible for the reader to dismiss his
philosophical position, with some complacency, as the product of an
extreme set of circumstances, expressing nothing, in more general
terms, of the human condition. The fate of Moran, however, whose
voice takes over from Molloy's, is nicely calculated to disturb any
such complacency. He is initially the very antithesis of Molloy, while
the material world that he inhabits must for most readers be a more
familiar one. He is a petit bourgeois, rigid in attitudes and routine
(mealtimes and church-going are observed with equal punctilious-
ness), a domestic tyrant in his dealings with his son and housekeeper.
And indeed, it soon becomes apparent that his world is one of sup-
pressed animosity and violence, held in check only by the proprieties
of the rural community in which he lives.

It's a strange thing, I don't like men and I don't like animals. As for
God, he is beginning to disgust me. (p. 97)

He spies on his son, the verger spies on the congregation and Moran
himself is controlled by a chief, Youdi, whose agent Gaber, orders
Moran to set off on a journey.

In Molloy's account of himself, no attempt is made to disguise the
absurdity of existence and his own lack of control over his own
destiny. Moran's life, by contrast, is composed of rituals and routines
whose purpose is to protect him from such knowledge. Incidents from
the Molloy account soon begin to reverberate through Moran's,
allowing us to see parallels. The circulation of the sucking stones, for
example, which is blatantly pointless, serves to expose the more
familiar (to the reader) strategies in Moran's manner of living; which
in turn allows Molloy's ritual to be seen as necessary strategies too.
Moran himself, even at the beginning, is intermittently aware of the
strategic necessity of the attitudes that he strikes. In commenting on

the unspecific, but nonetheless sinister, power exercised by Youdi over his agents, he exposes one such strategy:

> In that case it's hard for me to refuse, I said, knowing perfectly well that in any case it was impossible for me to refuse. Refuse! But we agents often amused ourselves with grumbling among ourselves and giving ourselves the airs of free men. (p. 87)

Molloy, at the end of his monologue, has come to rest in a ditch. Moran's mission, in undertaking the journey which destroys his Sunday peace, is to find Molloy. Why Molloy needs to be found and how Moran knows what to look for are again left unspecified, but the mission provokes no surprise in Moran, who is aware of a Molloy within himself:

> The fact was there were three, no, four Molloys. He that inhabited me, my caricature of same, Gaber's and the man of flesh and blood somewhere waiting me. (p. 106)

Within hours of setting out on the journey, Moran has begun to disintegrate physically, so that the seeker comes more and more to resemble that which he seeks. He loses the use of a leg and attempts, with the help of his son, whom he has forced to accompany him, to get about on a bicycle, like Molloy. Like Molloy again, he casually kills a man, scarcely registering what has happened. In time his son deserts him, taking the bicycle with him and leaving Moran all but destitute. The original antithesis of Molloy and Moran becomes a synthesis, through Moran's discovery of his physical vulnerability and powerlessness over circumstance.

Almost as soon as Moran leaves home, the terrain becomes inhospitable and hard to negotiate. All sense of time, strictly measured and observed at home, evaporates. He improvises a shelter within days of leaving home, but the return journey from that shelter takes months. He whiles away the time with theological speculation which exposes the inherent absurdity of the systems constructed by men to give 'point' to existence:

> 13 What was God doing with himself before the creation?
> 14 Might not the beatific vision become a source of boredom, in the long run?
> 15 Is it true that Judas' torments are suspended on Saturdays? (p. 154)

Moran returns to his home and his old life deeply scarred and damaged physically, but having achieved a kind of insight whose value is immediately questioned:

> And to tell the truth I not only knew who I was, but I had a sharper and clearer sense of my identity than ever before, in spite of its deep lesions

and the wounds with which it was covered. And from this point of view
I was less fortunate than my other acquaintances. (pp. 156–7)

This quotation demonstrates the disconcerting quality of much of
Beckett's prose, in creating a sense of constantly shifting ground.
There is never a last word, but he sometimes teases the reader with a
glimpse of closure, which is then withheld. The prose is unusually
flexible, capable of reversing within a sentence, or from one sentence
to the next, a stable meaning to which it appears to be drawing. In
this, it is a perfect vehicle for expressing the constant flux of human
experience.

The dislocation of time and place; the narrator's minimal physical
functioning – barely enough to sustain a life which, given the choice,
would never have been sought; the rendering of sex as grotesque; and
a persistent destabilizing of meaning and of the 'world' inhabited by
the speaker: all of these persist from *Molloy* into *Malone Dies*, with
the addition of a foregrounding of the fictional process. Malone is
confined to a room in a house, but he no longer knows how he came
there, where the room is located in the larger world or how old he is: 'I
know the year of my birth, I have not forgotten that, but I do not
know what year I have got to now (p. 171). All his senses have failed
him to the point where the outer world barely exists for him any more,
so: 'All my senses are trained full on me, me' (p. 171).

What he does have, like the other voices in the Trilogy – a self-
evident requirement for the role – is the power of language; but this,
while always abundant in Beckett's work, is felt to have little power to
alleviate the condition of living. Malone tells the story of a family
called Saposcat, who: 'had no conversation properly speaking. They
made use of the spoken word in much the same way as the guard of a
train makes use of his flags, or of his lantern' (p. 173).

Malone, who opens the novel with the statement that, 'I will soon
be quite dead at last in spite of all' (p. 165), whiles away the time
telling stories, mysteriously compelled into the role of story-teller by
some outside agency. His stories have, he suggests, reached a new
phase, which he describes in negative terms:

> They will not be the same kind of stories as hitherto, that is all. They
> will be neither beautiful not ugly, they will be calm, there will be no
> ugliness or beauty or fever in them any more, they will be almost
> lifeless, like the teller. (p. 165)

The first story is of the Saposcats – mother, father and the son on
whom they pin hopes which he is unlikely ever to fulfil. The story has
elements of folk-tale, overlaid with the middle-class values of later,
more sophisticated fictions. This narrative is interrupted by the story
of the Lamberts, a farming family; and here Malone (or Beckett)

draws heavily on stereotypes of primitive rural life. The father, Old Lambert, has no skill in rearing pigs but is valued for his relish in slaughtering and disjointing them; while the plot has elements of violence, disease and incest. This, like the Saposcat story, is never resolved, but the two narratives overlap when young Saposcat (now Sapo) appears in the Lambert kitchen to partake in 'events of no import'. Sapo leaves them to be transformed into Macmann. After an unspecified period of living rough, like Molloy, wondering whether he should feel guilty for allowing himself to be born, he passes out and then revives in a room in an asylum, to a routine and a life barely distinguishable from Malone's.

The two narratives have been interrupted, not just by each other, but by Malone, with memories of his birth and of physical sensations from his past; with expressions of weariness and disgust at his own story-telling which are in conflict with, but cannot halt, the compulsion to go on filling up the exercise books. And as the stories within Malone's story merge into his own, pulled by a centripetal force outside his control, so the nature of his compulsion to write becomes clearer. Obliged always in some sense to write about himself, the process of creating such fictions brings him no alleviation or satisfaction.

In the asylum Macmann is attended (pot of food filled, pot of excrement emptied) by an old woman, Moll. She initiates a sexual relationship with him, in the 'telling' of which the narrative focuses on what is absurd in the physical reality of sex, exaggerated to the grotesque in their case by the age, physical disabiltes and circumstances of the participants; though there is undeniable pathos in Moll's talk of love and romantic longing. Then Moll dies after an illness whose symptoms resemble pregnancy. This not only brings together the beginning and end of life but, in the grim details of Moll's death struggle, link them in a cycle of pain and squalor. Moll is replaced as 'carer' by the sadistic Lemuel who, in the course of a pleasure outing to an island arranged by a local philanthropist, murders some of the asylum party. He is prevented from further acts of destruction only when his bloody axe is transformed into Malone's pencil and Malone himself dies.

The instability of *Malone Dies*, as the initially discrete fictional worlds merge into one another and then into the 'world' of Malone himself, with the accompanying and confusing shifts from first to third person, is extended beyond this particular text to include Beckett's earlier fictions. When Malone reminisces about the old butler in London that he had killed himself with a razor (a character in *Murphy*), Malone merges for a time into Beckett himself. This is a feature of postmodernist writing that stands most in need of defending to general readers of fiction. For what is the 'point' of writing fiction at all, the common-sense argument goes, if its mechanics are to be so constantly exposed?

The answer to this must differ from one writer to another, and Flann O'Brien's reasons, for example, already discussed in the last chapter, are quite different from Beckett's, as far as one can perceive them, for unlike Joyce and O'Brien, he includes no explicit aesthetic discourse within his texts. In Beckett's world of menace and personal dislocation, where the notion of the autonomous 'character', in control of his destiny, is acknowledged to be a sham, there remain the burden of the individual consciousness and the power of speech. His fictions arise from these, but have constantly to be exposed as fictions to prevent them conferring 'point' or meaning, which is the final and, his fictions would appear to argue, illusory consolation available to suffering.

The foregrounding of the act of writing fiction, and its attendant philosophical implications, are the principal concerns of *The Unnamable*. The unnamed voice, whose extremity of physical circumstances is even more marked than that of his predecessors (his head occupies a jar outside a chop house and is tended by the proprietress because of the business he brings in), is forced 'to speak of things of which I cannot speak' (p. 267). That the unnamed should also be unnamable is partly explained by the disguises he has adopted in his fictions, stripped of which, he is as we find him:

> All these Murphys, Molloys and Malones do not fool me. They have made me waste my time, suffer for nothing, speak of them when, in order to stop speaking, I should have spoken of me and of me alone. . . . I thought I was right in enlisting these sufferers for my pains. I was wrong. They never suffered my pains, their pains are nothing, compared to mine, a mere tittle of mine, the tittle I thought I could put from me, in order to witness it. (p. 278)

The word 'unnamable' suggests something too shocking to be named; and this the text exposes as personal suffering, which can only be approached indirectly, through fictions. Suffering, which seems to the sufferer to be static, incapable of change (the head in the jar can cry, but not move), can be invested with the illusion of change, through fiction. The voice in *The Unnamable* admits to having invented his own compulsion to speak:

> in the hope it would console me, help me to go on, allow me to think of myself as somewhere on a road, moving, between a beginning and an end, gaining ground, losing ground, getting lost, but somehow in the long run making headway. (p. 288)

As an analysis of the particular consolation to be derived from linearly developed fiction (which, ironically, Beckett, since *Murphy*, has moved as far away from as the use of language itself permits), this could scarcely be bettered; though as a personal strategy it has, according to the voice of *The Unnamable*, manifestly failed. Nonetheless, the urge to continue is unabated and the voice is now considering speaking about Worm, a character who, it is felt, would more effectively carry the burden of the author's vision and suffering.

The Unnamable is the most difficult novel in the Trilogy because it is the most purely about itself. The earlier fictions, which the speaker hoped would serve as 'sufferers of my pains', not only failed in that, but served, in the time-honoured manner of all fictions, to distract the reader. Nonetheless, the concerns of *The Unnamable* are essentially those of *Molloy* and *Malone Dies*, but intensified. Philosophically, the most persistent common thread is the absence of choice. Sometimes this expresses itself as paranoia (an unidentified 'they' who govern the terms, create the compulsions); sometimes in the idea that apparent choice lies between equally appalling alternatives. For the Unnamable, speaking and silence are equally terrible, and the novel finishes with an expression of flux and instability highly characteristic of Beckett's writing: 'I can't go on, I'll go on (p. 382).

The Beckett Trilogy is so grotesque and unlocalized as to compose its own, highly unstable, world. Yet it has a power to disturb – Beckett rarely provokes neutral responses from readers or audiences – which can only come from the shock of recognition. While *The Unnamable* stops short of an identification of the 'voice' with Beckett himself, the text itself is highly suggestive of oblique personal revelation, while there is a sense of absolute personal integrity in the writing. So even as the novels outrage common sense, they carry conviction as rendering kinds of experience inaccessible to other kinds of fiction. Moran's geographical dislocation as soon as he leaves his own village, for example, is absurd in common-sense terms, but is arguably closer to the experience of living in occupied Europe than the many 'adventure' novels and films specifically located there.

Readers who cannot 'take' Beckett tend to question the value of fiction which offers no consolation or possibility of redemption. It is easy to dismiss Beckett's work as the product of a depressed mind. One possible answer to this is provided by Jean-Jacques Mayoux in 'Samuel Beckett and Universal Parody' (original title, 'Samuel Beckett et l'univers parodique'): 'He does not disturb people just for the sake of it, but because he wants to drive courage as far as it will go, without sparing himself or us or any idol, be it that of the mother (Molloy's turns your stomach) or of love (Macmann's exploits are enough to discourage the most robust).'[15] It is important to remind oneself of the courage required to write like Beckett. There is finally something exhilarating about the Trilogy which comes, not just from the quality of the prose, but from the spectacle of a writer who can face up to the bleakness of his own vision yet still 'go on'. At the same time his 'voices', while reduced to the minimum of what we are prepared to accept as human, have great pathos, and even jauntiness. Natural beauty is present in large measure in Beckett's work, gravely observed, not consoling, but registering the loss or lack of something barely articulated:

> And perhaps on my hands it is the shimmer of the shadow of leaves and flowers and the brightness of a forgotten sun. (p. 215)

4

Desire

Vladimir Nabokov: *Lolita*
Rosamund Lehmann: *The Echoing Grove*
Lawrence Durrell: *The Alexandria Quartet*

Sexual desire has been one of the principal driving forces in the plotting of the European novel since the early development of the novel form. Until our own century, however, its representation has, with a few notable exceptions, most of which were never admitted within the literary 'canon', been strictly circumscribed. This contrasts strikingly with the freedom that is available to novelists now to describe the sexual act; a freedom which, as far as the English novel is concerned, is in part indebted to the modernist movement, and the willingness of Joyce and Lawrence in particular to risk jeopardizing the publication of their novels by flouting conventional notions of decency.

Explicitness in describing the sexual act, however, is only one marker of change and, in describing the state of the art in late-twentieth-century fiction, not a particularly useful one in making a distinction between a 'realist' treatment of desire, on the one hand, and 'non-realist' on the other. Now in the late 1980s, sexual explicitness is a well-publicized feature of the popular blockbuster novel, which may be seen as the debased successor to nineteenth-century realism; while a calculated restraint often characterizes non-realist writing. John Fowles in *The French Lieutenant's Woman*, which I shall discuss in detail in the 'History' chapter, makes clever use of such restraint to chart the steady growth, and then explosion, of desire; and *Lolita*, one of the most notorious novels in English of the century, is undeniably outrageous in subject matter, but nothing like as salacious in detail as readers are led to expect.

So the difference is more than a matter of descriptive freedom. Broadly speaking, in the eighteenth- and nineteenth-century English novel sexual desire is both sublimated and linked to the quest for personal autonomy. Although the finding and winning of the beloved is central to the plots of the period, the element of physical attraction is absorbed into a more broadly defined 'rightness': the fittingness of the beloved in social and moral terms, which is disguised by a romantic insistence on the singularity and uniqueness of those individuals who are 'meant' for each other. (An exception must be made here for the novels of Charlotte Brontë, who allows her heroines strong sexual feelings, often in defiance of social norms which are nonetheless observed.) Often in novels of the period (in, for example, Jane Austen's *Pride and Prejudice* and *Emma*), the 'rightness' of the chosen individual is further defined by an earlier infatuation with someone whose attractions are both more blatant and more subversive of the appropriate social end. In novels of this period, the quest for personal happiness, culminating in marriage, is paralleled in the plot by a growing self-awareness and by the steady fulfilment of material ambition, until independence within society is achieved.

The experiments made in the English novel in the early part of this century, in the treatment of sexuality as in other matters, seem less radical in the context of the European novel, particularly the French. Joyce acknowledged an indebtedness to Flaubert, whose aesthetic required that fiction be drained of moral directives to the reader. The French nineteenth-century novel generally allowed greater expression to what was subversive of the social norm, in sexuality and worldly ambition, even if those characters who choose subversive means to attain their ends (like Julian Sorel in Stendhal's *Le Rouge et Le Noir*) eventually meet with retribution.

Twentieth-century thinking generally since Freud has been more prepared to acknowledge desire to be a powerfully subversive force, though it may be channelled in socially acceptable ways. What principally distinguishes non-realist fiction which foregrounds the sexual impulse is not its descriptive explicitness, but its willingness to allow the fulfilment of desire to be an end in itself, rather than part of a broader social process. Desire is free-floating, released from social norms. This in turn undermines the romantic ideal of the 'one and only' who is uniquely right, and allows for the part played by the imagination in transforming someone into 'the' one.

I make no claim to an exhaustive treatment of the subject in the novels selected for discussion in this chapter; while a number of the novels reserved for later discussion (David Lodge's *Small World*, John Fowles's *The French Lieutenant's Woman* and *The Magus* and Iris Murdoch's *The Sea, the Sea*, for example) also bring desire into play, at the same time illuminating a feature of British rather than American non-realist writing – the return to literary models in English older than the novel. In the case of the writers mentioned, these are the medieval and the Shakespearean romance – the former imitating, in its cyclical movement, the progress of desire, which, rather than reaching a plateau of static perfection (as in the classical realist novel) requires constant renewal; the latter acknowledging the irrational nature of love and the importance of the imagination in 'inventing' the beloved. In this chapter I have confined myself to novels which offer a diversity of approach, but were all published in the 1950s and are not, properly speaking, postmodernist. Indeed, part of their interest for us is the way that, using a range of modernist techniques, they bring the subversiveness of desire fruitfully into play against social norms, which become identified within the novels with a more 'realist' approach.

Vladimir Nabokov (1899–1977) wrote his early novels in his native Russian, as an émigré living in Berlin and Paris. It was after he moved to America in 1940 that he began writing in English; and in an Afterword to *Lolita* written in 1956, he writes emotively of the loss of his first language:

> My private tragedy, which cannot, and indeed should not, be anybody's concern, is that I had to abandon my natural idiom, my untrammelled, rich and infinitely docile Russian tongue for a second-rate brand of English, devoid of any of those apparatuses – the baffling mirror, the velvet backdrop, the implied associations and traditions – which the native illusionist, frac-tails flying, can magically use to transcend the heritage in his own way. (p. 335)

The irony for readers who come to the Afterword after reading *Lolita* is that Nabokov's disclaimers are in conflict with our actual experience of reading the novel – a tactic frequently employed by Nabokov to destabilize his readers' reading of the text, even allowing, in this case, for 'genuine' modesty about his use of an acquired language. Not only is his mastery of English stunning, but his verbal manipulation of his material is precisely akin to the skills of an illusionist. The reader is on constantly shifting ground, the victim, not only of endless games with language and narrative, but of profound moral disorientation. We are repeatedly forced to review whatever moral preconceptions and judgements we take to the reading of the novel; and the result is not so much a clear shift in moral attitude as an enforced acknowledgement of the complexity of human experience, which moral certainties fail to accommodate.

The publishing history of the English novel throughout the twentieth century has been punctuated by clashes between perceived standards of public decency, on the one hand, and bids by individual novelists for freedom to express kinds of experiences which outraged those standards, from Hardy's *Jude the Obscure* to Lawrence's *The Rainbow* and Joyce's *Ulysses* onwards. Perhaps no other writer, however, has flown so close to the wind as Nabokov in *Lolita*. Not only does the book's theme – the love of a middle-aged man for a girl barely past childhood – encompass a deviant sexuality of a kind that would find few defenders in 'real' life; but – a feature of Nabokov's endemic games-playing – he comes close to encouraging an identification between himself and his 'hero' which he then has the satisfaction of denying. The novel is written in the first person. The narrator, Humbert Humbert, is, like Nabokov, a European exile living on the eastern seaboard of the United States; tenuously attached to the academic world, he is writing a book on comparative literature, as Nabokov himself taught Russian and European literature at Wellesley College and then Cornell University. Even when Nabokov gives Humbert attributes which are a direct denial of what is known of himself – an ignorance of butterflies, for example, on which the author was expert – he is still bringing himself into play.

The deliberate outrage extends into the use of certain stereotypes which are likely to provoke a standard reaction in the reader, and against which the writer has to work to gain acceptance from his theme. Humbert first encounters Lolita when he is looking for lodgings where he can work on his book. Her attractions are immediately perceived, and powerful enough to overcome Humbert's distaste for the vulgarity of her home and of her widowed mother, Charlotte Haze. *Lolita* is not, in overall effect, a realist novel, but Nabokov skilfully deploys the conventions of realism to describe in detail the 'world' that Lolita inhabits – both its material features and the Hazes' manner of living; and in doing so, he summons up, and brings his narrator in conflict with, all the pieties of Middle America. Lurking on the edges of a narrative which is confined to Humbert's point of view is a notional Middle American one which responds warmly to the cosy detail of the house where the widowed Charlotte struggles to maintain a home for herself and her daughter; and with outrage and hostility to Humbert's 'unnatural' feelings for the daughter, lack of compassion for the mother and élite European snobbery towards the fixtures and fittings of the house and the general lack of refinement and taste. Humbert uses his position as lodger to exploit the rivalry between mother and daughter; marries the mother to secure access to the daughter; and when Charlotte is killed by a car in a blind fury after discovering Humbert's true feelings for herself and her daughter, he takes Lolita on an epic journey across America, in the course of which he exploits his role as 'father' to establish full sexual relations with her.

Despite Humbert's control over the narrative, the cards, each carrying a sacred stereotype like 'widowed mother', could scarcely be more heavily stacked against our acceptance of Humbert's point of view. Indeed, his own account of their relations finds pathos in Lolita's situation. She learns of her mother's death the morning after he has seduced her, when she is in tears, in pain and anxious to speak to her mother. Grief and loneliness enforce her dependence on him. The 'corrupting' effect of the experience is acknowledged in the constant stream of presents required to buy her continued acquiescence. In the later stages of the novel, when they have established a household again so that Lolita can go to school, the irony in his earlier descriptions of small-town American life now works against him, with the awareness of her sense of loss of a 'normal' family life. The novel never loses sight of the fact that Lolita is a child, and that the only adult to whom she can turn to for protection abuses that trust.

Nonetheless, there is a constant flux of irony in the novel which destabilizes the orthodoxies that it outrages. Indeed, one of the more disturbing aspects of *Lolita* is that it forces us to recognize that life is too complex to be rendered in fixed stereotypes, however sacred. So, the widowed mother, duped into believing in a second chance of happiness, is also jealous of her daughter and anxious to exclude her from her new establishment. And Lolita herself is not wholly an innocent victim, but actively initiates her own seduction.

The ironic displacement is not confined to our judgement of individual characters. *Lolita* is a love story, and one of its principal achievements is to de-familiarize the concept of love for us. This is done by a sequence of ironic shifts which eventually forms a circle; when complete, we are enabled to 'see' love in a new way. We are, on the one hand, morally reluctant to accept that Humbert's feeling for Lolita is love because she is a thirteen-year-old girl whom he has violated and deprived of a 'normal' family life. We become implicated, on the other hand, in Humbert's dismay that the object of his love – a commonplace girl with vulgar tastes and habits – violates his own refined criteria and is apparently indifferent to the emotions that she has aroused in him:

> There she would be, a typical kid picking her nose while engrossed in the lighter sections of the newspaper, as indifferent to my ecstasy as if it were something she had sat upon, a shoe, a doll, the handle of a tennis racket, and was too indolent to remove. (p. 174)

He calls her 'my Lolita', not just to indicate possession and love, but because she is to a large degree his own imaginative invention.

By acknowledging the transforming role of the imagination in love, *Lolita* appears to reject the romantic concept of the unique 'meantness' of the beloved, the singular aptness of that particular one. Humbert's account of his European childhood, and in particular of his abortive adolescent love for Annabel, who died as a young girl before he could possess her, suggests that his taste for 'nymphets' (the category in which he places girls of Lolita's age) was fixed by early trauma, however insistently he denies Freudian explanations for human behaviour. So the emotions that are focused on Lolita are intimately bound up with feelings of loss, exile and nostalgia, not just for childhood and Annabel, but for a whole world. At the same time, the very transience of the nymphet stage, as Humbert defines it, in itself a reminder of loss and mortality, sharpens the sense of the ephemeral, and connects the search for love with a human need to deny the power of time.

However, *Lolita* does not stabilize a definition of love in a quest for an 'Ur'-beloved who might briefly, with the help of the imagination, be found in one individual or another – a quest, moreover, which has more to do with the experience and history of the lover than with what is specific to the beloved. Humbert loses Lolita, and when he discovers her again a few years later, married, pregnant and with all traces of the nymphet gone, he finds that he still loves her:

> there she was with her ruined looks and her adult, rope-veined narrow hands and her goose-flesh white arms, and her shallow ears, and her unkempt armpits, there she was (my Lolita!), hopelessly worn at seventeen, with that baby, dreaming already in her of becoming a big shot and retiring around AD 2020 – and I looked and looked at her, and knew as clearly as I know I am to die, that I loved her more than anything I had ever seen or imagined on earth, or hoped for anywhere else. (p. 292)

Nabokov's biographer, Andrew Field, quotes a conversation that the writer had with his English publishers, George Weidenfeld and Nigel Nicolson, in which Nabokov made what Field claims to be 'the most direct statement made by Nabokov about the novel':[1] 'The tragedy of the book is that having started the affair from purely selfish motives, he falls in love with her when she is beyond loving.'[2]

Certainly. Humbert's expressions of a more altruistic tenderness towards Lolita in the latter stages of the novel confound the reader as much as anything that has gone before, forcing us to reconsider Humbert and the novel's discourse on love. But Nabokov's ability to discompose, to have always up his sleeve unsuspected cards, is most pronounced in the plotting of *Lolita*. Humbert's account is prefaced by a short Foreword by a psychiatrist, John Ray, who edited the manuscript: a framing device borrowed by Nabokov from nineteenth-century fiction, but used by him as a tool in the process of sequential destabilization. Ray 'refers' 'inquisitive' readers to newspaper accounts of Humbert's crime, but it is not until near the end of the novel, when it occurs as an event in the narrative, that we learn that the crime for which Humbert is imprisoned (his manuscript, we are told, was produced in custody) was murder, not child molestation. Humbert's own view, that he should have received thirty-five years for rape and nothing for murder, is in itself an ironic comment on the workings of justice. The victim of the murder is Clare Quilty, and his unidentified presence in the novel throughout Humbert's journey through America with Lolita, and then during their apparently conventional residence in Beardsley, alerts the reader to the limitations of Humbert's vision.

In relation to Lolita, Humbert is a predator, stalking his prey, planning his moves. In relation to Quilty, he is himself outmanoeuvred and outwitted. Quilty first enters the narrative at the hotel, 'The Enchanted Hunters', where Humbert's seduction of Lolita (or hers of him) takes place. Thereafter Quilty is a presence throughout the journey – trailing them in a car, leaving coded messages in hotel registers. Humbert, for all his sophistication, never breaks the code; and there are a number of moments within that narrative over which he has absolute control, when he is himself the victim of somebody else's plot. All Nabokov's novels have a self-referential quality, and in *Lolita*, where Quilty is a dramatist and Humbert is the author of his own story, there is an implied pun on 'plot' as a literary contrivance and 'plot' as an instrument of trickery between individuals.

When in Beardsley Lolita wants to take part in a school production of a play called *The Enchanted Hunters*, Humbert is reluctant to permit an activity which would expose her to outside influence; and while the resonance of the title is not lost on him, he fails to make a connection with the author, Clare Quilty, whom he takes to be a woman.

The ironies here are again circular, doubling back and shifting the ground at a breathless pace. The sexual ambiguity of Quilty's name (he is later revealed to be homosexual) reminds us that Humbert was once classified as a repressed homosexual by a psychiatrist – a diagnosis in which he takes a perverse pleasure, in proving his own skill at outwitting a profession that he despises. His own outwitting by Quilty is of a similar order. Then, Lolita's school is anxious for her to take part in the play because it is a 'healthy' activity, promoting 'healthy' social attitudes. But Humbert's fears, which are dismissed by the headmistress as those of an over-protective father, are in the event prophetic, since Lolita is abducted by Quilty and subjected to grosser sexual indignities than any inflicted by Humbert. Humbert has been Lolita's lover, using his role as father, sanctioned by society, as a convenient mask for his activities. When he finally learns Quilty's identity, however, after both sexual associations have ended, he becomes fully the outraged father, and in that role he murders Quilty.

In the course of their confrontation before the murder, Quilty, with a display of great verbal dexterity, appeals to Humbert through the common ground that they share: 'We are men of the world in everything – sex, free verse, marksmanship' (p. 317). There is a sense in which Quilty is Humbert's alter ego, and this has been

at the root of his failure to recognize him. The encounter between them, ending in the murder, not just of Quilty, but of that
part of Humbert embodied in Quilty, takes place after his final meeting with Lolita (she dies in childbirth shortly afterwards), when he
finds that his love has survived the physical changes in her; when she is
'beyond loving'. The greatest irony in the novel is the transformation
of an eroticism which begins by violating the principles of the society
in which it occurs, into a love which meets the highest requirements of
the humanist tradition, in showing itself not to be 'Time's fool'.

The presence of Quilty in the narrative, as well as helping Humbert
to realize the side of his personality – outraged father and altruistic
lover – which is dominant at the end, acts also as a caution for the
reader. The existence of another plot, in which Humbert loses his
status of manipulator to become the manipulated, opens up the possibility of infinite regression, where roles are determined, not by the
actors, but by whoever is in control of the plot. In *Lolita*, the resulting
instability goes beyond warning the reader of the unreliability of the
narrative voice – de rigueur in late-twentieth-century non-realist fiction and scarcely needed when the narrator is a child molester and
inevitably under suspicion of trying to justify himself. In Nabokov's
1956 Afterword to *Lolita*, he attributes the slow progress he made in
the writing of the novel to 'the task of inventing America' (p. 329).
The task of inventing an already existing reality, however, is not
confined to the writer in exile – 'It had taken me some forty years to
invent Russia and Western Europe' (p. 329) – but multiplied for the
writer by the experience of exile. So realities themselves are not fixed,
but re-invented in terms of individuals' experience of them. *Lolita*,
like other of Nabokov's novels, exposes us to the process of the individual inventing his own reality; and in so doing, forces us to decon-
struct the realities which we take for granted.

Rosamund Lehmann's *The Echoing Grove*, published in 1953, is on
the face of it an unusual choice to be included in a discussion of non-
realist fiction. Born in 1901, Lehmann wrote most of her fiction in the
1920s and 30s, gaining a reputation (which has been revived recently
with the reissue of her novels by Virago) for her honest exploration of
women's feelings. But while there is much in those early novels that
her early readers found shocking – the whole treatment of female
sexuality and a grim account of an abortion in *The Weather in the
Streets* – they are nonetheless written within the conventions of
realist fiction. *The Echoing Grove*, which is her last major work of
fiction, is also her most experimental. It is a long way from *Lolita* in
terms of its capacity to outrage and confound the reader but is none-

theless an interesting example of the way a conventional genre – in this case, the romantic novel, with a particular bias towards the expression of womens' feelings – may be modified by theoretical and formal developments in the novel. The relationship of *The Echoing Grove* to those developments is a pragmatic one, in that the element of formal surprise works more towards refreshing an existing genre than towards altering or subverting it. In this chapter, as in those that follow, it will be apparent that English versions of non-realist fiction are a good deal less radical than American and Irish, quite apart from those in languages other than English which fall outside the scope of this book. Some of the reasons for this should emerge from a discussion of individual texts.

The Echoing Grove takes as its setting that section of English society – the upper-middle professional and landed classes – which was most vocal about the erosion of traditional values in the years between the two world wars, whether narrowly perceived in terms of the difficulties in maintaining a certain style of living, or more broadly in terms of the loss of a role conferring function and worth. The principal male character, Rickie, who is seen entirely through the refracted vision of the female characters, is cast by the author in the role of victim of social change. Left after the death of his father in the First World War heir to the family estate in Norfolk, he suffers the emotional dependence of his mother; and then feels obliged to sell the family home, now heavily encumbered by his mother's debts, to meet the requirements of his young wife, Madeleine, for a glittering life in London. He works unsatisfactorily 'in the City', until the war briefly offers him a 'real' role in some vaguely defined area of intelligence, before his early death from a perforated duodenal ulcer. The death of his brother-in-law in the Spanish Civil War and of his son in the Second World War are further elements in a picture of destruction and personal fragmentation, for which the Blitz provides a metaphor, as well as narrative background.

In structure, *The Echoing Grove* conforms to the principle established in *Ulysses*, that the whole of a lived past is recoverable by memory, albeit in a fragmented and partially understood form. This is realized in the novel through the framing device of a weekend reunion of two sisters – Rickie's widow, Madeleine, and Dinah, who was for a time his mistress. Although the weekend heals the breach between the sisters for which Dinah's relationship with Rickie was responsible, this is not achieved by picking over the past, sharing memories, pleas for understanding or self-justification. Indeed, secrets between them are retained: Madeleine never learns, though the reader does, that Dinah gave birth to a still-born son by Rickie, or that Dinah attempted suicide after the first break in her relations with him. The suggestion is rather that the women they are now can meet on common ground – Dinah's presence helps Madeleine through the end of an affair with a young lover, Jocelyn; while what they were to each other in the past was determined by a relationship which is itself in the past, of wife and other woman. For Dinah, Madeleine was 'not real'; for Madeleine, Dinah was manipulative and egotistical. These are, of course, clichéd responses to an adulterous situation, and part of Rosamund Lehmann's achievement in *The Echoing Grove*, like Nabokov's in *Lolita*, is to demonstrate that clichés are both true and not true; that the individual's sense of his or her singularity is modified, in the perception of others, by the stereotypes imposed by a situation. It is a kind of writing that achieves an ironic interplay between two principles – that plot determines character, and that character determines plot.

The technical strength of *The Echoing Grove* is the extraordinary fluidity of the narrative voice, enabling shifts between present and past, between third and first person, between one and another character's point of view, without any sense of strain. In one sense it is closer to *Ulysses* than to later modernist developments (which would include Virginia Woolf's *The Waves* (1931), as well as Faulkner's *The Sound and the Fury*, discussed in the previous chapter) in that the narrative voice is not restricted to a series of 'speakers', each confined to a point of view, with the baton of narrative passed from one to the other by a concealed 'organizer'; like *Ulysses* it has a minimal third-person voice which effortlessly absorbs the voices of individual characters into itself. Where it extends the possibilities of *Ulysses* is in allowing a voice, through a sleight of hand, to characters who died before the narrative present: not Rickie himself, but Georgie Worthington, an American woman with whom he had a brief affair after the break with Dinah, and Mrs Birkett, Madeleine's and Dinah's mother. Their voices, too, have a place in that echoing grove of the past which weighs on the present. The title suggests a place, and part of Lehmann's achievement is to give 'the past' a spatial quality.

I have already quoted Faulkner's preference for an oblique treatment of events as more 'moving' and more 'passionate'. In the same way Lehmann's extension of the principle of memory to include the memories of the dead appears to be in the service of greater poignancy – experienced by the reader as a kind of dramatic irony – at a time when 'serious' writers were nervous of the direct representation of emotion. The struggle for meaning over the past may now be confined to Madeleine and Dinah, the survivors, each of whom is the central figure in her own story. But there are others with a place in the story. There is one particular day to which the narrative keeps doubling back, and which, each time, accumulates further meaning: the day of

Rickie's final meeting with Dinah, which makes him late for a dinner party with Madeleine, given by friends to celebrate their reunion, where he meets Georgie and after which his and Madeleine's third child is conceived. So a day to which all the characters attach a different meaning both retains its fragmented state in the novel (in that it only exists in the discrete memories of individuals), but takes on a more complete form in the mind of the reader.

In that sense – the achievement of a narrative stability by the reader which is denied to individual characters – *The Echoing Grove* is a modernist work. It is, moreover, firmly in the tradition of romantic novelists like Charlotte Brontë in validating women's feelings – not just the wife's but the other woman's. It departs from the romantic tradition, however, in its rendering of sexual desire, which has links with other late-twentieth-century non-realist approaches to the subject. The fragmented time scheme suggests not the once-and-for-all singularity of objects of desire and growth of feeling of linearly developed fiction, but a pattern of repetition. Desire is seen as cyclical and rooted in needs which are independent of whoever for a time fulfils them.

Rickie's disorientation in the world is fully charted. (It must be said that this is rendered in such a way as to recall the romantic hero of popular fiction, whose appeal lies in some inner remoteness which cannot be fully reached by any woman. The structure of *The Echoing Grove* allows Lehmann to avoid direct expression of such clichés, but they may nonetheless be recovered by the reader.) The two sisters whom he serially loves are distinct in personality, suggesting the unlikeliness of all needs being met by one person; while Georgie resembles Dinah in looks, independence and in a calculated distance from social values which are shared by Rickie and Madeleine. Madeleine's lover, Jocelyn reminds her of another young man, Rob, once Dinah's lover and whom she met once. The book has a number of encounters and incidents which are only completed at another time, with another person.

The Echoing Grove is the first of a number of English novels – by which, in this instance, I mean novels by British writers – that I shall discuss which have been modified rather than transformed by the pressure of both historical event and theoretical change to which the response of novelists elsewhere has been more radical. Not only is it indebted to the English romantic novel, but in the precise registering of class and manners and nostalgia for a vanishing way of life (rooted in rural rather than urban values), *The Echoing Grove* is recognizably within the tradition of the English novel, from Jane Austen onwards. We are told of the effects of two world wars, and Rickie's relationship with Georgie is conducted during the Blitz, but we experience the novel through the emotional and social concerns of the characters. In a later chapter on war, I shall be considering in more detail the effect of the Second World War on fiction; but it is relevant here, since Rosamund Lehmann has used the war as background to the emotional lives of her characters, to consider a statement made recently by George Steiner about post-war British culture. In a review of Primo Levi's *The Drowned and the Saved*, Steiner suggested that only those Britons who were imprisoned by the Japanese experienced 'systematic inhumanity', and that:

> this is the single most profound dissociation of current feeling and perception, as between on the one hand the Soviet Union, the European continent and American Judaism (so influential in post-war culture and sensibility) and Britain on the other.[3]

It is in a sense unarguable that the British, having escaped the horrors of the death-camps, of Occupation, of Revolution and of imposed exile, have been more able to retain traditional habits to thinking, perhaps at a cost in terms of radical creative initiatives. It also seems to me likely that, as far as the novel is concerned, the great vitality and continued popularity of the eighteenth- and nineteenth-century English novel have fuelled resistance to change. This issue – of the perceived parochialism of so much twentieth-century English writing – is raised intermittently throughout Lawrence Durrell's *Alexandria Quartet*. Not only is his central character, Darley, a novelist (and in that capacity the first-person narrator of three of the four novels), but the *Quartet* is haunted by the presence of another novelist, Pursewarden; they between them generate a good deal of writerly self-reflexiveness, as well as allowing within the novels expressions of opinion about the reading public and related matters.

Pursewarden, we are told, is a 'great' writer who will only be fully recognized by posterity. He is characterized in a way that suggests a parody of a 'great' romantic writer – solitary childhood in Ireland, an incestuous relationship with his beautiful, blind sister, heavy drinking and a brief involvement in Middle East intelligence work. He turns a mocking but vaguely tortured face to the world and eventually dies by his own hand. He sees the timidity of English writing as a response to the tyranny of the reading public, a monolith which he dismisses as still bearing the legacy of Puritanism (an unlovely brew of prurience and philistinism, suspicious of both pleasure and ideas).

Since Pursewarden is admired by every other character within the *Quartet*, and an identification is encouraged between Darley, who is placed by the structure of the novels in the role of community spokesman, and Durrell himself, through the similarity of surnames and the identity of initials, the supposition is that Pursewarden's views are regarded favourably by the author. And while the *Quartet* itself makes no claim to the 'greatness' attributed to Pursewarden, the British reader whose reaction to the *Quartet* is less than favourable feels condemned by the novels themselves as puritanical, prurient and philistine – in short, a victim of British cultural values. Durrell himself (who was born in 1912 in India) has chosen to live most of his life abroad, and his novels have in general met with more enthusiasm in the rest of Europe than they have in Britain. His work might, therefore, be expected to illuminate for us that 'dissociation' perceived by Steiner between Britain and continental Europe, though leaving aside for the moment the particular historical context of the war in which Steiner's argument is framed.

There is, however, an element of posturing about the *Quartet*, which appears to lay claim to a position in the avant-guarde which it has not really earned. Its literariness is partly (though not, as we shall see, entirely) a matter of insistent stylistic elaboration, a self-conscious use of language which lacks as a balance the element of self-parody, thus exposing it to the charge of self-indulgence. A comparison between *Lolita*, another intensely literary novel, and *The Alexandria Quartet* reveals this difference – that while both works include extended passages of highly sensuous writing, Nabokov will often deflate his own effects with an obvious pun, for example, which opens up a gap between himself and Humbert, allowing us for the moment another perspective; whereas in Durrell's writing, despite the play on refracted angles of vision, and the parodic characterization of Darley in *Mountolive*, the third-person narrative, there is no such stylistic distancing. When the reader is forced to supply the irony, it must be at the expense of the text.

One or two brief examples of the *Quartet*'s sumptuous prose will have to do. When Darley says of the womanizing Capodistria that he 'has the purely involuntary knack of turning everything into a woman; under his eyes chairs become painfully conscious of their bare legs', (*Justine*, p. 34), it is not clear whether we are to take it as a joke, or whether it is a kind of nervous tic from a writer who can leave no thought unembellished. When in the same novel, *Justine*, Darley describes the kisses of his mistress, Melissa, as being like an 'early form of printing', the image is decorative, but not illuminating. Much of what the characters say and write (considerable use is made in the *Quartet* of diaries, journals and letters) is self-consciously 'profound', as though intended for quotation.

To criticize Durrell for 'fine writing' is inevitably to expose myself to the criticism of judging him by the standards of realism or naturalism. If I have one overriding criticism, however, it is that Durrell has absorbed a theory of fiction, but fails to convince the reader (or this reader) that he is practising it. That theory is, as we shall see, structured into the four novels; but it is also argued at a more discursive level throughout, as though in response to doubts about the reader's ability to grasp that theory without constant nudging. So although we are to a degree shown, we are too often 'told'; and this in itself suggests a pull towards realism in Durrell's writing, which he is anxious to distance himself from. Part of my reason for including *The Alexandria Quartet* is that this dichotomy, though not the ornate language in which it is expressed, is present in much British non-realist writing.

There are four writers in the novels, including Darley, and each contributes to the theory. There is Arnauti, who in the past wrote a book about Justine, the subject of the fist novel in the *Quartet*:

> He maintains . . . that real people can only exist in the imagination of an artist strong enough to contain them and give them form. (*Justine*, p. 66)

Then there is Keats, a minor character who in the course of the *Quartet* makes the transition from journalist to 'real' writer when he becomes aware of the instability of the medium in which he works:

> 'Truth is double-bladed, you see. There is no way to express it in terms of language, this strange bifurcated medium with its basic duality! Language! What is the writer's struggle except a struggle to use a medium as precisely as possible, but knowing fully its basic imprecision?'(*Clea*, p. 160)

Pursewarden's comments on fiction, quoted or reported, punctuate the *Quartet*, but tend always to give priority to the imagination over reality:

> He was at that time deeply immersed in the novel he was writing, and as always found that his ordinary life, in a distorted sort of way, was beginning to follow the curvature of his book. He explained this by saying that any concentration of the will displaces life (Archimedes' bath-water) and gives it bias in motion. Reality, he believed, was always trying to copy the imagination of man, from which it derived.(*Balthazar*, p. 96)

And finally Darley labours through the *Quartet* to arrive, near the end, at a broadly similar conclusion:

> I began to see that the real 'fiction' lay neither in Arnauti's pages nor Pursewarden's – nor even my own. It was life itself that was a fiction – we were all saying it in our different ways, each understanding it according to his nature and gift. (*Clea*, p. 154)

The four novels all serve to illustrate this, variously expressed, thesis, *Justine*, *Balthazar* and *Mountolive* covering the same period of time, *Clea* advancing the action forward. Great importance is attached in the novels to Alexandria itself –

> We are the children of our landscape; it dictates behaviour and even thought in the measure to which we are responsive to it. (*Justine*, p. 36)

which provides a setting for the serial love affairs, public lives and underground political activity of a group of characters who are all, even those who in some sense belong to the city, exiles. Nessim, a wealthy Egyptian businessman, 'belongs', but as a Copt is an outsider. He is married to Justine, a wandering Jewess, who has affairs with the Englishmen, Darley and Pursewarden. Greeks, Syrians and French are also in the foreground of the novels, while the traditional life of the Arabs forms a world apart, encountered by the central characters in brothels, at religious festivals and as part of the general street life. So in the *Quartet* a correlation is suggested, as it is in *Lolita* and *The Echoing Grove*, between desire as a kind of quest and a state of exile.

The first three novels return to the same sequence of events, each providing, through the commentary of individual characters, meanings for those events which in some sense displace each other; and that sequential displacement, from a different perspective in time, continues into *Clea*. As a justification for this technique, an image is introduced early in *Justine*, to recur throughout the *Quartet*, of mirrors; though as so often in these novels, the 'point' of the image is made so insistently that its effect is swallowed up in explanation:

> I remember her [Justine] sitting before the multiple mirrors at the dress-maker's, being fitted for a shark-skin costume, and saying: 'Look! five different pictures of the same subject. Now if I wrote I would try for a multi-dimensional effect in character, a sort of prism-sightedness. Why should people not show more than one profile at a time? (*Justine*, p. 23)

The reasons for characters' behaviour are unstable because 'character' itself is slippery, a concept invented by other novelists but rejected by Durrell; and the foregrounding of this is in a way the motor that drives the *Quartet*. The suspense, from novel to novel, is generated by the expectation of further explanations and interpretations which will displace those already offered.

In *Justine* Darley tells the story of his affair with Justine, which is adulterous on her side and on his runs parallel with his relationship with Melissa, a young dancer. The affair ends with Justine's disappearance after a duck-shoot, organized by her husband, Nessim, at which one of the guests, Capodistria, is killed. The murder is blamed on a servant, but Darley suspects Nessim himself. Although Nessim has shown no jealousy towards Darley, the latter's interpretation of Capodistria's death is that he was the displaced victim of conjugal jealousy. Nessim, meanwhile, has an affair with Melissa, who has a daughter by him before her death from tuberculosis. Darley attributes this relationship to the need of each partner to draw closer to the original object of love by a process of de-familiarization:

> Just as my own experience of Justine had illuminated and re-evaluated Melissa for me so he looking into Melissa's grey eyes saw a new and unsuspected Justine born therein. (*Justine*, p. 183)

Because Nessim is embarrassed by Melissa's child, Darley takes care of her, withdrawing with her to an island where he works on his book about Justine.

Justine is a highly self-absorbed account of Darley's feelings for the two women he has loved. He speculates on why a woman like Justine – rich, sophisticated and a partner in an envied and glamourous marriage – should have chosen him as a lover; and generally interprets events in a way that gives him a central place in the story. Beyond that, he puzzles over the mystery of Justine, turning to the novel written by her first husband, Arnauti, for clues to her often neurotic behaviour. Justine too had a daughter by her first husband, who was spirited away under mysterious circumstances; and her intermittent search for her daughter seems to be either a factor in, or the cause of, a larger personal quest. One possible reason for her marriage to Nessim is the money he was able to provide to allow her to search more effectively.

Still on his island (a location which symbolizes the self-absorption of *Justine*), Darley in the following novel is forced by Balthazar, a Jewish doctor and homosexual, to question all his earlier assumptions. It is in this novel that Pursewarden grows in importance, not only in terms of his place in the story, but as another writer who provides a standard by which Darley might measure himself. Darley's pride is wounded on both fronts. The duck-shoot, described as a narrative event in *Justine*, assumes metaphorical significance, taking on a striking resemblence to the use made of the 'Enchanted Hunters' motif in *Lolita*. There is of course a time-honoured link in art between hunting and the pursuit of love, which in these two narratives is pushed further to exploit the instability of role of the participants, by playing with the separate elements in the configuration of hunter, hunted and decoy. The difference is that where Durrell through Darley explains the metaphorical significance, Nabokov builds an element of gamesmanship into the narrative structure, thus drawing the reader into the configuration.

Darley knows that Justine had an association with Pursewarden, but while he assumed that the letter was used by Justine as decoy to disguise her relationship with him, he is now told by Balthazar that he was himself the decoy for Justine's relationship with Pursewarden; and that Pursewarden himself was indifferent to the woman that they shared. The instability of the decoy role is given a further twist with Balthazar's information that Capodistria had perfect teeth, but a set of false teeth was seen to fall from his mouth as he died.

The blow to Darley's status as preferred lover is compounded by a growing conviction of Pursewarden's superiority as a writer. As mediated through Balthazar, Pursewarden is seen to have reached a state of enlightenment about the process of fiction and the role of the imagination in that process. While Darley's imaginative enterprise has been to reach the 'real' Justine in order to write about her, Pursewarden has already grasped the priority of the imagination over reality, and the futility of a search for the 'real': 'Personality as something with fixed attributes is an illusion' (*Balthazar*, p. 12).

While the shift from *Justine* to *Balthazar* is designed to expose the subjectivity of all interpretation – Darley had given himself a more central role in the emotional drama than was alloted him by any of the other participants – *Mountolive* supplies a new frame of reference within which interpretations might be made and meanings found. Mountolive himself is an English diplomat who, as a young man, had an affair with Nessim's mother, Leila; he has now returned to Egypt as ambassador to find his once beautiful mistress transformed by a particularly savage form of smallpox. With this, his second posting to Egypt, and entry into the *Quartet* as a character, a hitherto neglected area of the characters' lives is exposed – their public, working lives which, in some cases, serves to mask undercover political activity.

In keeping with this shift, *Mountolive* is structured as a conventional, realist novel, with a third-person narrative voice supplying information. Time, which in the earlier novels has obeyed the laws of the imagination – memory, desire and the writer's mind re-working experience all have the power to dislocate time – now unfolds in a linear development which includes a sense of historical time. *Justine* and *Balthazar* are not historically placed, but in *Mountolive* Alexandria, like the rest of the world, is preparing for World War Two. Implicit in the realist structuring of *Mountolive*, which sets it apart from the others, is the notion that different areas of experience require to be inscribed in fiction according to different principles.

The plot of *Mountolive* – it is the only one of the four which has a linearly developed plot – recalls other 1950s realist fiction (the novels of C.P. Snow or Angus Wilson, for example) wherein men of principle and importance in the world face a moral dilemma involving a conflict of loyalties. The relationship of *Mountolive* to contemporary realist fiction is opportunistic rather than parodic, in that it supplies Durrell with models – which may be recognized by readers – for fictionalizing this kind of material. Before taking up his post as intelligence agent, Mountolive has been warned by intelligence agents that Nessim may be supplying arms to Palestine. This suggestion is dismissed by Pursewarden, a friend of Mountolive's and himself working for British intelligence. Mountolive himself, because of his old ties of friendship with the Hosani family, is only too willing to see Nessim as innocent, but the evidence accumulates against him to the point where action must be taken. Pursewarden's suicide, which the earlier novels hovered on the brink of attributing to sensitive artistic temperament, occurs in *Mountolive* as the net is closing in on the Hosanis, so that the inevitable choice between rival claims – of friendship and public duty – is forestalled by death. The novel ends with the mysterious death of Nessim's brother, Narouz, who has become a charismatic figure in a subversive anti-imperialist movement, and as such has been attracting too much attention to the family.

So *Mountolive*, to use the persistent 'mirror' imagery of the *Quartet*, exposes a side of the characters' lives – the side not driven by desire and imagination but by position in society, in the broadest sense – which was left concealed by *Justine* and *Balthazar*. And in doing so it displaces a number of the meanings of the earlier novels. Nessim's involvement in Palestine is a response to the marginal role given to Copts in Egyptian society; and his marriage to Justine has ensured his acceptance by Palestinian Jews. Her affair with Darley was not only known to Nessim, but part of a larger strategy – to deflect suspicion of anti-British feeling and a route to Melissa, once the mistress of the Jewish arms-dealer, Cohen. Pursewarden, too, as part of British intelligence, was a useful tool in their political activities. Other more peripheral mysteries are cleared up, suggesting that problems are solved, not through the epistemological inquiry of non-realist fiction, through different modes of perception, but by acquiring new information, in the manner of realist fiction. The mystery of Capodistria's teeth, for example (real or false?) is solved by giving him a place in the Palestinian plot: a substitute Capodistria was killed and he himself is now in hiding. Even Balthazar's cabalistic group, which Justine from time to time consults, comes under suspicion of being an intelligence network.

If *Mountolive* were the final novel of the sequence, it would not only stabilize specific meanings, but mark a devaluing of the imaginative life, including desire and the writer's insistence on mysteries which are imaginatively penetrated, in favour of life lived in the world and the intelligence officer's decoding skills. But *Clea*, besides pushing the action forward in time, represents a return to the values of the first two novels. Clea herself is an artist and in this novel she becomes Darley's lover, while Darley himself, now back in Alexandria, resumes the role of first-person narrator. *Clea* reintroduces the idea that, while desire is stable, personality, through which desire must express itself, is not.

Although to nothing like the same degree as *Mountolive*, *Clea* too displaces some of the interpretations of the earlier novels, in particular through the journals of Pursewarden, to which Clea has access. These record his passionate love for his sister, Liza, now in Egypt as the prospective bride of Mountolive, whom she met in London; and suggest a convincing motive for his suicide – that he wanted to 'free' his sister and enable her to marry. The journals also provide further possible ways of 'seeing' Justine, by claiming that she knew that her daughter was dead – had actually seen the body – but preferred to maintain the fiction of not knowing, of still searching.

Although *Mountolive* stabilizes certain meanings which remain in place, paradoxically its presence within the *Quartet* pushes the whole sequence in the direction of the ontological instability of post-modernist writing. In rendering an effectively separate world, but with the same set of characters, it suggests not worlds which cancel each other out, but coexisting worlds between which characters move. There is also a degree of regressiveness in the ending, which shows Darley at the beginning of a creative enterprise:

> Yes, one day I found myself writing down with trembling fingers the four words (four letters! four faces!) with which every story-teller since the world began has staked his slender claim to the attention of his fellow-men. Words which presage simply the old story of an artist coming to age. I wrote: 'Once upon a time. . . .' (*Clea*, p. 246)

Four words, with four faces, must also imply the four titles of the *Quartet*.

The sense of incompleteness (and of infinite possibility) is present in a theme which is explored throughout the *Quartet*, but gathers momentum in *Clea*: metamorphosis, albeit that Durrell's expression of the concept, a central one in postmodernist writing, is nothing like as radical as may be found in later magical realist writing. Objects of desire become their opposite when the lover abandons the task of imaginatively re-inventing the beloved; desire is then replaced by disgust. (This inverts the common-sense logical sequence, which has the lover withdraw once the beloved object has become disgusting.)

This happens to Justine in relation to Darley and Nessim, to Darley in relation to Justine, and in a number of subsidiary couplings throughout the sequence.

Physical transformations are legion. Leila after her smallpox is no longer a sophisticated European in Mountolive's eyes but an old Arab woman; the despised journalist Keats returns to Alexandria from reporting the desert war, a Greek god in appearance. Sometimes physical transformations are achieved by an alliance of technology and imagination. An Egyptian doctor, Amaril, falls in love with a veiled girl, Semira, before discovering that she has no nose. Clea helps Amaril design a nose and the couple are set for wedded bliss. Clea loses a hand in an accident, and then finds that the artificial hand transforms her achievement as an artist. But perhaps the most curious example of transformation is Scobie, a seedy British intelligence officer, who seems to be lifted, both in type and manner of presentation, from Evelyn Waugh. After his death he becomes an object of religious veneration to the Arabs, his house a shrine, his remembered words (commonplace at the time) profound thoughts to be pondered. Perhaps above all else, *The Alexandria Quartet* is a celebration of the endlessly dynamic power of the imagination, whatever reservations one may have about the level of Durrell's achievement.

After 1960

5

Breakdown

Doris Lessing: *The Golden Notebook*
Saul Bellow: *Herzog*
D.M. Thomas: *The White Hotel*

The opening sentence of Saul Bellow's novel, *Herzog* – 'If I'm out of my mind, it's all right with me, thought Moses Herzog' (p. 7) – signals the theme of the novel at once, and is as good an introduction as any to this chapter, which aims to explore the creative uses made in late-twentieth-century fiction of states of mental illness. The very fact that Bellow chooses to alert the reader at the outset of a likely intention to give a central place to mental breakdown in *Herzog*, suggests a reading public prepared to find the subject of absorbing interest; willing to accept that fictional explorations of madness, neurosis, hysteria, breakdown, might yield 'truths' about the human condition of equal value to those that the novel has traditionally offered. And *Herzog*'s acceptance of his own mental state is some indication of the status given to mental disorder in late-twentieth-century non-realist writing. The three novels that I shall be discussing in this chapter record individuals' experiences of pain when the mechanisms enabling those individuals to function 'normally' in society fail. At the same time, the awareness of historical circumstance, and the sense of global as well as personal apocalypse are acute in these novels, carrying at times the implication that mental breakdown may be the only appropriate response to the condition of living in the twentieth century.

The centrality of mental illness to the novel is a relatively recent phenomenon, but it is not new to western literature generally. English dramatists of the early seventeenth century[1] showed considerable curiosity about 'abnormal' mental states; while Shakespeare in *King Lear* (which has become a key text for the twentieth century) showed a willingness to invert the common-sense ordering of priorities in favour of madness, when the apparently 'sane' world, given enough power to create its own premises, and then arguing with impeccable logic from them, can flout every human value. The applicability of this to twentieth-century history, from the First World War onwards, scarcely needs stating; and Lessing, Bellow and Thomas between them address themselves to most of the forms that man's inhumanity to man (and to women!) have taken in our own times.

The idea of madness as a response to history, of course, does not in itself account for the interest shown by novelists in mental breakdown. *The White Hotel* includes Freud as a character within the novel, as well as a case study which is a clear parody of Freud's own writing. Indeed, Thomas appears to have conceived his novel, at least in part, as an expression of homage to a man whose influence on creative writing and on critical theory has been at least as far-reaching as on the treatment of the mentally ill. Freud is now arguably more venerated by writers and theoreticians than by doctors, in that the former are not so obliged as the latter to subject Freud's findings, and the advances made on them by post-Freudians, to scientific inquiry and clinical trial.

An exhaustive account of the influence of Freud and his disciples (and apostates) is not to be attempted in a book of this length, though examples of that influence will emerge through textual analysis. What is beyond doubt, however, is that for the twentieth-century novel the mind has become a new frontier to explore. Thomas, using just such imagery, writes in an author's note to *The White Hotel* of 'the landscape of hysteria – the "terrain" of this novel'; and within the text of 'The soul of man' as 'a far country'. He goes on to state that it 'cannot be approached or explored' (p. 220), but this disclaimer, coming towards the end of a text which has attempted just that, appears to be little more than a rhetorical flourish. At the same time, that 'landscape of hysteria' which is identified as the ' "terrain" ' of the novel, marks an important shift from explorations of the mind in novels of the high modernist period. Joyce, as I have already noted in Chapter 2, absorbed what was idiosyncratic in the workings of Bloom's mind into some kind of universal vision or humanist statement, but since the last war novelists have focused increasingly on the pathology of the mind.

This is of course in line with the general development of fiction from modernism into late modernism and postmodernism, and each subject discussed in this book records just such a shift. More specifically there is the fact that within society at large both the terms of reference and the procedures of psychoanalysis have become more familiar, to a degree blurring the distinction between the 'normal' and the 'pathological'. At the same time, not just the theory but the procedures of psychoanalysis have come to infiltrate the structures of fiction, in much the same way as the establishment of a police force in Britain had by the close of the nineteenth century generated a new literary genre, the detective novel.

Indeed, the procedures of detective work and of psychoanalysis might be said to interest the novelist in similar ways. I have already noted the useful distinction made by Russian Formalist critics in narrative analysis between *fabula* and *sjužet*, *fabula* being the order of events referred to by the narrative, and *sjužet* the order of events as presented in the narrative discourse.[2] The detective novel preeminently, for purposes of suspense, exploits this distinction – a distinction which is also present in the procedures of psychoanalysis. The analyst is presented with a narrative which is structured by the memories and pathology of the analysand, from which another narrative sequence may in time be recovered. All three of the novels that I shall discuss in this chapter make some use of the meetings between analyst and analysand as markers in the narrative.

An interesting paradox presents itself here. The initial influence of psychoanalytical theory on the novel, felt in the work of Joyce and Woolf, was to reduce the importance of the material world in favour of the inner world of the individual. This in turn served to undermine plot. It has been noticed already, however, that part of the project of late modernist and postmodernist novelists has been to reclaim some of the traditional pleasures of the novel, in a changed world. In exploring the workings of the mind the novelists that I shall discuss here have chosen to 'plot' its development, sometimes by bringing the procedures of psychoanalysis within the narrative, though Lessing and Bellow continue to reveal the mind in arrested moments of time, in the modernist manner.

Doris Lessing's *The Golden Notebook* is, like *Herzog*, such a colossal book in every sense, and so representative of its particular cultural and historical moment, that one hesitates to 'contain' it by tying it to a particular theme like 'breakdown'. Published in 1962, it has come to be seen as a key feminist text, prophetically anticipating a number of the issues – particularly of women's sexual freedom – which became matters of wider debate over the next ten years. Lessing (born 1919), in a Preface to the novel published in 1972, expresses sympathy for feminist aspirations, but places them in a context of those wider political concerns which are also in the foreground of the novel. Early in *The Golden Notebook*, in the course of some despairing reflections on the role of fiction in an increasingly fragmented society, the heroine Anna suggests that novels are now read, like journalism, 'for information about areas of life we don't know'; 'they report the existence of an area of society, a type of person, not yet admitted to the general literate consciousness' (p. 79). Although Anna laments what this reveals about contemporary (to *The Golden Notebook*) fiction, that it has lost 'the quality of philosophy' (p. 79), it has to be said that anybody who is curious about the concerns of the British Left in the 1950s – nuclear weapons, Stalin's purges, McCarthyism in

America, the political lethargy of post-war British society, continued anti-Semitism and anti-black racism – would be advised to read *The Golden Notebook*.

Beyond that, there is a continuing discourse in *The Golden Notebook* on the question of form in the writing of fiction, at both a dialectical level and implicitly, through the self-reflexiveness built into its structure. Anna is a blocked writer still living off the royalties from a highly successful 'realist' novel, *Frontiers of War*, which drew on her own experiences in Rhodesia during the war. Anna's continuing debate with herself throughout the novel about *Frontiers of War* exposes her anxiety about the evasions and distortions of the truth which are the price paid for turning her experience into a commercially successful novel. So *The Golden Notebook* also marks a moment of crisis in the writing of fiction, Anna's anxieties providing us with a useful model of the anxieties that have fuelled postmodernism.

If, nonetheless, I have chosen to place *The Golden Notebook* in a chapter on 'Breakdown', it is, as it were, with Lessing's own authorization, since in the 1972 Preface she describes 'breakdown' (p. 7) as the novel's central theme, overlooked at the time of publication when, in the wake of the *Lady Chatterley* trial, its sexual frankness attracted most attention. Lessing also suggests in that Preface that the structure of the novel, which is integral to its statement, had been overlooked by English reviewers who, as Lessing sees it, are less preoccupied with form than their European counterparts (p. 14).

The business of finding a form in fiction for the experience of mental breakdown presents the novelist with major problems and major opportunities, and both *The Golden Notebook* and *Herzog* address the question of form; in Lessing's novel, in relation to a wide range of subject-matter besides breakdown. I have already mentioned what Anna sees as the failure of realism in describing racial problems in Rhodesia. A criticism of realism emerges in another context when Anna, as an active member of the Communist Party, critically evaluates the social realism of Eastern European literature as disguised myth and fantasy. The displacements and rearrangements forced by a realist structure on the experience of mental illness, however, is demonstrated rather than 'told'. Within the considerable bulk of *The Golden Notebook* there is contained in serial form a novel of standard length, *Free Women*, which deals in conventional fictional terms with experiences which Anna tries to write about more truthfully elsewhere.

The structure of *The Golden Notebook* is both an expression of Anna's mental fragmentation and an attempt to come to terms with it, to re-integrate herself; and the ironies generated by this dichotomy weigh on the novel at every point. *The Golden Notebook* is divided into six parts, the first four being further subdivided. Each of the first four opens with an 'episode' of *Free Women*, which is concluded in the final section; like *Mountolive*, the third part of Durrell's *Alexandria Quartet*, it draws heavily on, without parodying, realist fiction of the period, whose limitations are exposed once the part can be seen in relation to the whole. *Free Women* evokes that flats-and-bedsitting-room world of a rootless bohemian sub-culture encountered so often in novels of the 1950s. It is about Anna and her friend Molly, both disillusioned ex-Communist Party members, both divorced (Anna more scarred by a relationship subsequent to her marriage, to Michael, which has also now ended), each with a child. Anna has written a successful novel and either cannot or will not write again; Molly is pursuing an unsatisfactory career as an actress.

Each 'episode' of *Free Women* is followed by entries in four note-books, 'as if' the gloss for the first entries informs the reader, 'Anna had, almost automatically, divided herself into four' (p. 75). The entries in the Black Notebook re-tell the personal experiences on which *Frontiers of War* drew, and record Anna's subsequent dealings with film-makers about a possible film. The Red Notebook records Anna's political life – her work for the Communist Party, and then her disillusionment and decision to leave once the Party has retreated into evasive fantasy with the growing certainty of Stalin's purges. The Yellow Notebook is a fictionalized account of her relationship with her ex-lover, Michael, followed by the subsequent sexual encounters of Ella, Anna's fictional alter ego. The Blue Notebook is closest to a diary, parts of it recalling Anna's four years' experience of psycho-analysis with Mrs Marks (or Mother Sugar, as she and Molly call her), elsewhere an attempt to record the day-to-day events of her life as flatly as possible. Here and there Anna's writing is interspersed with newspaper cuttings reporting incidents of violence, disaster and persecution.

Part of the function of Anna's division of experience in the Note-books is to separate aspects of her personality which are in conflict with each other – Anna the writer, whose impulse to write is fed by her, often morbid, emotional states, from Anna the committed socialist, whose political philosophy rejects self-absorbed art. But in practice, division does not resolve the tension.

> And so this is the paradox: I, Anna, reject my own 'unhealthy' art; but reject 'healthy' art when I see it. (p. 344)

The strategy fails because any division of the self along these lines is necessarily artificial. Because Anna is a writer, she cannot use the notebooks to mediate other facets of herself in a non-writerly way; and various incidents from her life are, in the notebooks, 'made over' into fiction. At the same time, her political consciousness, her sense of herself as living at a historical moment, make it impossible for her to accept the separation of a personal self from an historically and socially determined self.

The root of Anna's dissatisfaction with psychoanalysis is Mother Sugar's insistence on treating a personal self within the Jungian framework of mythological archetypes which are outside history – which is at variance with what Anna takes to be the context of her neurosis:

> 'I'm going to make the obvious point that perhaps the word neurotic means the condition of being highly conscious and developed. The essence of neurosis is conflict. But the essence of living now, fully, not blocking off what goes on, is conflict. I've reached the stage where I look at people and say – he or she, they are whole at all because they've chosen to block off at this stage or that. People stay sane by blocking off, by limiting themselves.' (p. 456)

The structure of *The Golden Notebook* takes on particular meaning in the light of Anna's statement. The division of experience into the separate notebooks, and the implied division of self, may be seen as a way of 'blocking off' to be made whole; but the effect is to embody fragmentation. Moreover, not only can absolute divisions not be made, as we have seen, but there is a remarkable unity of preoccupation running across the notebooks. As a writer, Anna is concerned with the inevitable falsifications which attend any attempt to give fictional form to experience; and I shall consider shortly the widening gap between *Free Women* and the notebooks. Her dissatisfaction with Mrs Marks, whom she nonetheless concedes to have enabled her to function better over the period of psychoanalysis, turns, as we have noticed, on the inadequacies of Jungian myths – in themselves, types of enabling fictions – in describing and explaining experience. Her decision to leave the Communist Party is provoked, not so much by the failure of the ideal under Stalin, but by the attempts of the British comrades to keep the ideal alive by myth and fantasy. And Anna's relations with men are embittered by a sexual stereotyping which is comparable to Communist fantasy and Jungian myth in being false but (to the consumers) necessary fictions which can exercise a dangerous power. In the Ella/Paul story, her unashamed sexual response, welcome at the time, allows him to dismiss her to a third party as 'flighty', and when he eventually leaves her, to suffer no qualms of conscience; as if in response to the stereotype, once the affair is over Ella becomes promiscuous.

In one of the Red Notebooks, the Party members discuss a Stalinist pamphlet on linguistics. Partly arising from the pamphlet itself, partly from Anna's reflections on the formulae the comrades feel obliged to use when speaking about Stalin, Anna describes as part of the contemporary condition, 'the thinning of language against the density of our experience' (p. 301). This serves very well as a description of the common crisis to which the discrete crises recorded in the Notebooks contribute.

Free Women, as one would expect of a realist novel, is not overtly preoccupied with language, though it is a concern which surfaces at the level of social interplay. The irritation that Molly's ex-husband Richard feels towards Molly and Anna is in part provoked by the women's insistence om 'truth-telling', or naming things as they see them to be, which for him borders on bad taste; as though the act of naming what one would prefer not to exist summons it into being. But Richard is a successful businessman; and in the larger context provided by the Notebooks, the implication must be that the 'wholeness' necessary for success has been bought at the price of 'blocking off' what he would prefer not to see.

Although it is only peripherally part of the discourse of *Free Women*, the interplay between the fiction and the more amorphous Notebooks exposes a 'thinning' in *Free Women* against the 'density' of experience expressed in the Notebooks, at the level of plot. *Free Women* is both more sensational and less deeply shocking than the parallel entries in the Notebooks. The Notebooks show an Anna who, having never fully recovered after being abandoned by Michael, disintegrates when her daughter Janet, on her own insistence, goes away to school and Anna is left with no routine to support her. This process of disintegration is intensified by her affair with a new lodger, a young American called Saul who is a refugee from McCarthyism, is himself a blocked writer and on the verge of madness. The passages in the Notebooks describing their time together are the more frightening because nothing actually happens. They are becalmed, locked into a relationship which offers no solace, only the reflection that each finds in the other of his or her own mental state.

Anna, who has come to see her own breakdown as a response to the particular historical moment, has a similar diagnosis confirmed of Saul by a psychiatrist whom she consults about him. Nonetheless, while she and Saul both recognize that their inability to write is a symptom rather than a cause of breakdown, to treat the symptom seems to offer the only hope of cure, or at any rate amelioration. They decide to part, each giving the other as a parting gift the first sentence of a novel. Saul gives Anna the opening sentence of *Free Women*, while the novel that Saul writes, the opening supplied by Anna, is précised in the final Notebook, 'The Golden Notebook', which describes the circumstances of their parting.

The despair and violence of Anna's and Saul's breakdowns are internalized, conveyed to the reader through descriptions of physical sensations and the quality of their life together. In *Free Women* the despair and violence are projected onto Molly's young adult son, Tommy. Unable to reconcile the conflicting messages he receives from the adults in his life – from Molly and Anna, the sense of the value of an ideal, albeit a failed one; and of the worthlessness of most available forms of social engagement; from Richard, the importance of work, ambition and a place in society – he shoots himself, not fatally, but the wound leaves him blind. Blindness gives him the power to manipulate his elders and to become a force for change in their lives. Richard's neglected, alcoholic second wife, Marion, leaves Richard (who will later re-marry) to devote herself to Tommy, who has given her a new sense of purpose. Tommy, meanwhile, joins his father's business empire, on his own terms. Molly marries a rich Jewish businessman and goes to live in Hampstead. Anna has a brief affair with an American which is altogether less sinister than the 'other' Anna's relationship with Saul; joins the Labour Party and takes up good works.

Between *Free Women* and the Notebooks, the relative centrality or importance of Tommy and Anna is inverted. In *Free Women* Anna's inner life is left largely unexplored (though she keeps Notebooks, the reading of which has been a factor in Tommy's attempted suicide); while the 'Tommy' of the Notebooks settles himself in life without any of the drama of his fictionalized self. He marries a girl, greatly disliked by Molly, who combines a fashionable young socialism with an interest in mortgages and insurance policies. So his skill in both flouting and observing the principles of both his parents makes a cynical contribution to *The Golden Notebook*'s discourse on the 'wholeness' required for success. The implication carried by the gap between the two 'Tommy' stories is that the type of linear fiction to which *Free Women* belongs demands crisis followed by resolution. 'Real' life, on the other hand, as the Notebooks attempt to chart it, is more often cyclical: Anna works her way through her breakdown by re-telling her story in a fictionalized form. That account, while in many ways a falsification of her own experience – and in that sense helping to explain the original writer's block – nonetheless has a therapeutic value in shaping events into a pattern of crisis followed by resolution.

The Golden Notebook, apart from being one of the most powerful accounts of breakdown in late-twentieth-century fiction, also makes a significant contribution to the discourse of the period on the nature and importance of fiction. *The Golden Notebook* may be described as postmodernist in terms of the kind of relationship which it establishes with the reader, requiring constant adjustments in the way it must be read. Meanings are displaced as the narrative voice moves from one mode to another (in addition to *Free Women*, there are other fictions, and purportedly factual accounts which are organized like fiction, within the Notebooks), sometimes without a firm line being drawn between the fiction and, within the terms of the novel, the 'real'. Moreover, the many distortions of experience that are required by the plotting of *Free Women* may be taken as a criticism of realism, in line with orthodox post-modernist thinking on the subject. On the other hand, since the act of writing *Free Women*, unlike the act of filling the Notebooks, has a therapeutic effect on Anna, it may be described as a necessary fiction: the kind of fiction, to use Frank Kermode's distinction in *The Sense of an Ending*, designed to 'know by', though not to 'live by'.[3] Lessing's dualism on the subject gives *The Golden Notebook* a particular value. It should be said that her fiction since *The Golden Notebook* has included realist works and futuristic fantasies.

The Golden Notebook, as I have already suggested, might be seen as required reading for anyone interested in the preoccupations of the British Left during the 1950's. Similarly, a case could be made for *Herzog* by Saul Bellow (born 1915) as required reading in ways that extend beyond its status as fiction. Published in 1964, it is a paradigmatic text in helping us to understand the nature of the contribution made by Jewish writers to American culture in the years since the last war. The protagonist, Moses Herzog, is an archetypal Jewish intellectual, an academic who has been engaged in writing a book of enormous scope:

> Herzog tried to explain what it was about – that his study was supposed to have ended with a new angle on the modern condition, showing how life could be lived by renewing universal connexions; overturning the last of the Romantic errors about the uniqueness of the Self; revising the old Western, Faustian ideology; investigating the social meaning of Nothingness. (p. 45)

Novels 'about' brilliant men or women are often unsatisfactory because, while it is easy enough for a novelist to state that a character is brilliant, intellectual qualities often prove as difficult to render in a novel as goodness. (Iris Murdoch's novel, *The Book and the Brotherhood*, published in 1987, which explores the pivotal importance of an intellectual giant on his immediate circle, is a recent example of the difficulties posed by such a theme.) *Herzog*, by comparison, is strikingly convincing on this point. By using a narrative voice which moves easily from third to first person – and is on as intimate terms with the mind of the protagonist in the third as in the first person – Bellow draws the reader into Herzog's mental processes to an extraordinary degree. Herzog is described as 'this little demon' who is 'impregnated with modern ideas' and is to be found 'down in the mire of post-Renaissance, post-humanistic, post-Cartesian dissolution, next door to the Void' (p. 99). The principal device used to render his intellectual life is his compulsive habit (a symptom of his nervous breakdown) of writing letters – to friends and family, other academics and famous men, living and dead. Here his easy familiarity with a wide spectrum of ideas may be seen as illustrating the particular contribution of the Jews to American intellectual life, their access to a cosmopolitan culture helping to weaken that English dominance, particularly of the East Coast intelligentsia, which applied throughout the nineteenth century and into the twentieth.

In addition, the particular experience of the Jews, especially in our own times but throughout history, has left them uniquely placed to express a number of the twentieth-century's dominant issues. What was an outsider position has become central:

> Well, for instance, what it means to be a man. In a city. In a century. In transition. In a mass. Transformed by science. Under organized power. Subject to tremendous controls. In a condition caused by mechanization. After the late failure of radical hopes. In a society that was no community and devalued the person. (p. 208)

Most of these conditions of twentieth-century life, and a few more besides, have a bearing on Herzog's palpable unease in the world. Malcom Bradbury has described *Herzog* as 'a tale of two cities',[4] New York, where the hero is trying to resist the generosity and charms of the seductive Ramona; and Chicago, where he grew up and where his wife Madeleine now lives with their daughter and her lover, Valentine Gersbach, once his closest friend. In neither is he at home, but uses the anonymity of urban life for disguise and flight. He flies from New York to Chicago to escape Ramona and with the vague intention of confronting his domestic problems, but he proves himself to be quite incapable of manipulating events. He abandons, without explanation, the home of some friends he is visiting in Martha's Vineyard; is involved in a minor car accident with his daughter June in Chicago and is booked by the police for possession of an unlicensed gun (his father's), with which he had considered shooting Madeleine and Gersbach.

The novel is punctuated with aborted actions, and when Herzog at the end of the novel finds peace, it is by retreating from the world to the house in New England which he bought for his married life with

Madeleine. However, this is not because the country allows him more control over his fate. As a country dweller, he remains uncompromisingly urban, unable to subdue the natural life around him. But while this incapacity had marred his married life with Madeleine, the peace he later achieves is by allowing nature to encroach, even into the house itself, where owls nest in the bedroom. He has surrendered control, given up the unequal struggle.

His lack of control over the material and natural world, however, is reversed in the narrative structure which, despite its intermittent third-person voice, is shaped by his mental processes and memory. His name is borrowed from a character mentioned in *Ulysses*, and the influence of Joyce is apparent throughout. The motif of adultery and betrayal is appropriated by Bellow, as it was by Lowry in *Under the Volcano*, just as both later novels share with *Ulysses* the conviction that the whole of an individual's life may be recovered, through memory, at any moment. *Herzog* begins where it ends – in the country, peace newly achieved through Herzog's acceptance of his own mental state. The intervening novel may be seen as a series of Chinese boxes, in terms of the periods of his life uncovered by the narrative, except that the process of uncovering them is not managed in an ordered and sequential way. The immediate period of recall covers the events – his time as a divorcé in New York, flight from Ramona, disastrous return to Chicago and retreat to the country – contributing to what his brother Will sees as a complete mental breakdown. Beyond that are his memories of his married life with Madeleine, and of his first marriage to Daisy, and finally of his childhood. Indeed, his compulsive remembering is part of his neurosis, as the following commentary on a memory of his mother makes clear:

> All children have cheeks and all mothers spittle to wipe them tenderly.
> These things either matter or they do not matter. It depends upon the
> universe, what it is. These acute memories are probably symptoms of
> disorder. To him, perpetual thought of death was a sin. Drive your cart
> and your plough over the bones of the dead. (p. 39)

This idea – of effectiveness in the world being achieved by moving on from the past – is comparable to the connection made in *The Golden Notebook* between 'wholeness' and 'blocking off'. Both novels see neurosis as a late-twentieth-century condition afflicting the best and most sensitive, and the price of that sensitivity as failure in worldly terms. In *Herzog* the protagonist's fate is given a further dimension by his Jewish heritage, and its dualistic ambivalence concerning relative value of success and failure. Herzog's immediate family and friends are success-oriented, but he is nonetheless seen as a kind of luxury item, a reminder of traditional values, and their response to his needs is generous. His lawyer Simkin 'had a weakness for confused high-minded people, for people with moral impulses like Moses' (p. 35). Another lawyer, Himmelstein, admires his capacity for suffering:

> 'Well, when you suffer, you really suffer. You're a real, genuine old Jewish type that digs the emotions. I'll give you that. I understand it. I grew up on Sangamon Street, remember, when a Jew was still a Jew.'
> (p. 90)

And for Ramona, Herzog's capacity for suffering confers on him a certain distinction, even glamour.

So the dualism present in the Jewish ethos, and expressed through various subsidiary characters, ensures that Herzog's suffering is both valued, and viewed with a certain measure of irony. *Herzog* is usually seen as a late modernist work rather than postmodernist. I would not dispute that, but it nonetheless seems to me that while Herzog's vision and judgement dominate the novel's structure, they are to a degree destabilized from within by the suspicion, communicated to the reader by other characters, that neurosis weakens the reliability of his judgements. This is particularly marked in the rendering of Madeleine's character. She is on one level a brilliant comic creation of a kind which is rare in late-twentieth-century non-realist fiction, disinclined as it has been, on theoretical grounds, to celebrate human difference. At the same time, Herzog's view of her acquires an extra cutting edge from the post-Freudian insight that is brought to the task. Beautiful and intelligent, all her actions are seen as part of a self-dramatizing game. So she embarked on her relationship with Herzog – a Jew and a married man – when she had recently converted to Catholicism, to spectacular effect, in terms of drama, guilt and tension. But in the end, 'Catholicism went the way of zithers and tarot cards, bread-baking and Russian civilization. And life in the country' (p. 125).

This quotation is a good example of the complicity of the third-person narrative voice with Herzog's point of view, but not everybody in the novel shares Herzog's opinion of Madeleine, though he looks repeatedly for confirmation, and when he fails to find it, senses a plot. So the paranoia that colours his point of view opens up the possibility of deconstructing it, difficult though it would be to resist such a compelling narrative voice.

Although *Herzog* seems to encapsulate a certain kind of late-twentieth-century angst, it has to be admitted that, of the major American writers of the period, Bellow is in many ways most at odds with the spirit of his time. The 'little demon' Herzog, who is 'impregnated with modern ideas', and who argued, in his abandoned book, for a recovery of principles which had been lost through romanticism, is actually a last-ditch humanist of a particularly romantic sort:

> But of course he, Herzog, predictably bucking such trends, had characteristically, obstinately, defiantly, blindly but without sufficient courage or intelligence tried to be a *marvellous* Herzog, a Herzog who, perhaps clumsily, tried to live out marvellous qualities vaguely comprehended. (p. 100)

Malcolm Bradbury astutely notices in the resolution of *Herzog* the influence of New England Transcendentalism of the mid-nineteenth century[5] – Herzog's retreat to the New England countryside, with its healing powers, being a kind of re-enactment of the lives and ideas of Emerson and Thoreau. *Herzog* ends in a spirit of affirmation which helped qualify Bellow for the Nobel Prize for Literature (awarded in 1976), but which to a degree modifies his standing among other American writers. A useful introduction to what is a continuing debate is *The Novel Today*,[6] a collection of pieces edited by Malcolm Bradbury. Philip Roth, in 'Writing American Fiction',[7] attacks the continuing note of affirmation and celebration in American writing, singling out Bellow, among others, for failing to address the gross realities of American life. Bellow's 'Some Notes on Recent American Fiction'[8] pre-dates Roth's attack, but is nonetheless pertinent and may be read as a general defence of his position. He writes of the 'unearned bitterness'[9] that characterizes the response of many of his contemporaries to late-twentieth-century life, and of the continuing need to explore 'the mystery of mankind',[10] even as 'Symbolism or Realism or Sensibility' are 'wearing out'.[11] Most interestingly, perhaps, he suggests that those writers who release their anger on 'this already discredited and fallen individualism'[12] are in some sense colluding with 'the masters of the Leviathan'[13] – the civil and military powers whose actions in the course of this violent century have provoked the philosophical shifts which underpin so much contemporary writing.

The issues raised by Bellow in this piece are of critical importance to later chapters in this book, on war and society, while D.M. Thomas's *The White Hotel*, to which I turn now, provides a bridge between the personal themes which have dominated this and the two previous chapters, and the public concerns of the three chapters to follow. Published in 1981 and shortlisted for the Booker prize that year, it provoked a storm of controversy at the time. Two criticisms in particular were made. The first was that in combining an account of the slaughter of thousands of Russian Jews by the Germans at Babi Yar with pornographic material elsewhere in the novel, Thomas was guilty of sensationalizing Jewish experience. The second criticism was of plagiarism: that he had drawn heavily on a first-hand account of Babi Yar without acknowledging his source.

Both criticisms raise important questions in any study of post-modernist writing, a category into which *The White Hotel* undoubt-edly falls. The Jewish Holocaust occupies such a central place in twentieth-century history and experience that it demands to be addressed, and has indeed occasioned radical revision of moral and political philosophy. But is it an appropriate subject for fiction? If Thomas's treatment of the subject is indecorous, then what standards of literary decorum should apply? It seems to me right to question the motives of writers, since there is that in the historical material itself – of brutality and degradation – which can be used for pur-poses of titillation under the cloak of moral outrage. Moreover, the subject matter itself is so emotive as to require more than usual restraint; George Steiner, in a review of Primo Levi's *The Drowned and the Saved* already quoted in the last chapter, dismisses as 'elo-quent kitsch'[14] unspecified American treatments of the theme.

Primo Levi was himself a survivor from Auschwitz, and there is a case to be made for reserving fictional representations of the Holo-caust, if not to the dwindling numbers of survivors, then to Jewish writers. In any other hands it smacks of appropriation, of claiming something unearned for the individual imagination. Ironically, Thomas could have avoided this by acknowledging his source for Babi Yar, since his account of that event is the extent of his exploita-tion of the Holocaust.

The issue of Thomas's culpability or otherwise on this specific issue, however, should not distract us from the more general point of the blurring of fact and fiction to be found in much postmodernist writing. In the same novel, *The White Hotel*, Freud appears as a character and mingles with fictional characters, while his writing is parodied in a supposed casebook record. In *Ragtime*, a novel that I shall be discussing in a later chapter, Doctorow mingles fictional with historical figures, awarding them the same status in the narrative; while for his central plot he draws heavily on a story by the German writer, Kleist, who, writing at the turn of the eighteenth and nine-teenth centuries, was himself using historical material from the six-teenth century. The intention in both novels, *The White Hotel* and *Ragtime*, seems to be to destabilize the reader (in ways and for purposes which I shall attempt to describe later); and to give the unsung and anonymous masses of history a place in the story. The theory (ironically, since the charge of plagiarism carries the imputa-tion that the writer is bent on acquiring unmerited glory) is of a common pool of material, whether historical, mythic or the works of earlier writers, which limits the status of the individual writer. In practice – and *Ragtime* and *The White Hotel* are cases in point – the writer attracts notoriety and his book large sales.

The White Hotel is divided into seven sections, if we include the Prologue, the first four – letters, a long poem, a journal, a case study – markedly different in form; the remaining three employing a third-person narrative voice. The novel focuses on the fate of a woman referred to by 'Freud' as Anna G, and later, when she is not mediated by 'Freud', as Lisa Erdman. The period covered is from 1920 until she is slaughtered at Babi Yar. In terms of national affiliation, location and family alliances, she is made a representative figure of the European turmoil through which she lives. She has a Russian Jewish father and a Catholic Polish mother and lives in Vienna until she moves to Russia as the third wife of a Russian Jew whose first wife and son were killed in the Revolutionary period; her own first husband was a soldier in the German army during the First World War.

Frau Anna G as a young woman is referred to 'Freud' by her physician suffering from weight loss, hallucinations and pains in her left breast and pelvis for which there is no organic explanation. She returns from a holiday in the mountains in improved physical health and with a poem of pornographic fantasy in which her lover is Freud's son, newly returned from the war. Apart from the light it throws on her own case, her poem is of interest to 'Freud' as an illustration of the theory developed by himself in *Beyond the Pleasure Principle*, that the death wish is at least as strong as the libido. The poem, written on a score of *Don Giovanni* (Frau Anna is pursuing a musical career) juxtaposes highly erotic images with a series of disasters occurring in and around the white hotel where the affair is conducted. What is remarkable is that the disasters are shrugged off, creating bonds of warmth among the survivors – 'no one was selfish in the white hotel' (p. 30) – and releasing new sexual energy.

At 'Freud' 's request for a gloss on the poem, Anna produces instead a prose elaboration of it, 'The Gastein Journal'. In this the white hotel emerges even more defiantly as a place of pleasure, where the grief of the bereaved – for those who drown when the lake floods, burn in a hotel fire, are crushed by an avalanche at the funeral for those already dead, or fall to their death in a cable-car accident – is stifled in the interests of those not yet afflicted with loss. After each disaster, the work of rebuilding immediately begins, to accommodate further guests who are unperturbed by the bad luck of their predecessors. Indeed, the guests are more disturbed by harmless natural phenomena (falling stars, lightning on the lake, the seasonal falling of the leaves) than by the multiple disasters; while explanations offered from the personal histories of individual guests – a recent mastectomy, an abortion – are readily accepted for the genuinely bizarre phenomena of a floating disembodied breast and foetus. In the most bizarre incident of all, Frau Anna feeds the hotel guests from her own over-flowing breast – the central image for the hotel's lack of selfishness, which she displays also in her willingness to share her lover with a recently widowed older woman. The style throughout 'The Gastein Journal' is deliberately banal and matter of fact, minimizing the importance of the multiple deaths and providing a linguistic frame-work within which the irrational is accepted.

'Freud' 's case study of Anna G both explores the symbolism of the white hotel at a primal level –

> All who have hitherto, in a learning capacity, had the opportunity to read Frau Anna's journal have had that feeling: the 'white hotel' is known to them, it is the body of their mother. It is a place without sin, without our load of remorse. (p. 105)

– and makes the connection between specific elements in the dream and events in Anna's past which have been revealed through psycho-analysis: her mother's death in a hotel fire, for example, and her own loss of a child after a fall. The specificity of Anna's symptoms is seen to have no particular significance, but the time of their onset (coin-ciding with the emotional withdrawal from her of her father) and of their subsequent recurrence (during intercourse with her husband, from whom she now lives apart) are seen as significant. She suffered from a recurring hallucination during the sexual act – of people falling from a great height and mourners being buried by a land-slide – which not only has direct bearing on the 'white hotel' fantasy, but is interpreted by Anna as a warning that she should not have a child.

'Freud' 's view is that latent homosexual feelings have contributed to her hysteria – a view based on the strong attachments she forms with other women and embodied in the 'unselfish' triangular sexual relationship in the 'white hotel'.

An aspect of Anna's personality which emerges in the case study is her belief in her own powers of telepathy. Such powers 'Freud' admits to be possible, but does not take account of them in the development of her neurosis. (A curious feature of the relationship between analyst and analysand is that, while he takes an interpretative role in her life, she has a kind of visionary grasp of his destiny, foreseeing a number of personal losses.) Nonetheless, the telepathy indicates a special sensi-tivity which 'Freud' acknowledges her to possess:

> I began to see Frau Anna, not as a woman separated from the rest uf us by her illness, but as someone in whom hysteria exaggerated and high-

lighted a *universal* struggle between the life instinct and the death instinct.[36] (pp. 116–17)

So Thomas, using his fictionalized 'Freud' as a mouthpiece, gives his neurotic central figure a similar status to that given to Anna Wulf by Lessing and to Herzog by Bellow – that of the representative figure. However, while 'Freud' sees Anna's status in 'universal' terms, as defined by the writings of the 'historical' Freud, *The White Hotel* proceeds to demonstrate her centrality in terms of the particular historical moment.

The following section, 'The Health Resort', pushes the time covered by the narrative forward by some ten years, to the early 1930s. Through the altered perspective provided by a more 'neutral' third-person narrative voice, we met Lisa Erdman travelling in a train to Milan where she is to sing a lead role in *Eugene Onegin* as replacement for a Russian singer who has broken her arm in a fall. Lisa is now virtually recovered from the neurotic symptoms which blighted her youth and enjoying some late success after the delayed start to her career. In Milan, she forms an immediate friendship with Vera and Victor Berenstein, the singer whom she has replaced and her husband, who is taking the male lead in the opera; and after Vera has returned to Russia, Lisa spends an affectionate (but asexual) holiday with Victor at a hotel on Lake Como.

Where 'Freud' 's analysis had interpreted 'Anna' 's poetic fantasy in terms of her past, 'The Health Resort' retrospectively endows it with predictive powers. The train journey, the triangular relationship between two women and a man, the hotel by a lake in the mountains and Vera's fall were all anticipated by the poem. At the same time, however, new material from her past, which was either withheld by Lisa during her analysis, or made known to her later by her aunt, is revealed to the reader in 'The Health Resort' and strengthens the link between the poem and Lisa's past. We learn that Lisa's mother died in a hotel fire with her brother-in-law, who was also her lover, which provides a paradigm from Lisa's childhood for triangular relationships. Other information gives Lisa's individual destiny a wider historical context. In her dealings with 'Freud' she minimized the importance of the Jewish heritage on her father's side. Now we learn of her sexual harrassment during adolescence by Russian sailors, which was fuelled by anti-Semitism; and of the vehement anti-Semitic feelings displayed by her husband. This 'explains' the link between sexuality and hallucinations of violence for which she was treated by 'Freud'.

By the close of 'The Health Resort', Lisa may be seen as having completed a cycle, the particular configuration of which reclaims elements from her past which contributed to her neurosis. Returned from her operatic engagement in Milan, she learns of Vera's death in childbirth. Within a few years she has made her home in Russia as the wife of Victor who is, like her father, a Russian Jew. She now has the care of Vera's son, Kolya, the 'motherhood' from which she shrank as a young woman.

In the following section, 'The Sleeping Carriage', *The White Hotel* explodes with horror. Lisa, now in sole charge of her stepson (Victor is in a Russian camp for crimes against the state), shares with him the fate of other Russian Jews in the slaughter at Babi Yar. At the end it is a fate that she chooses, to the extent that her German name (Erdman) and Christian upbringing offer her immunity. But it is also the fate that has been waiting for her:

> Now she knew why she ought never to have had children. (p. 216)

The injuries she sustains – to her left breast and womb, by means of a horrific rape by bayonet – provide a further piece in the jigsaw, by explaining the specificity of her physical symptoms.

The description of Babi Yar is not the end, however. The Jews were lured to their deaths with promises of being transported to Palestine; and *The White Hotel*'s closing chapter, 'The Camp', is a utopian vision of healing, redemption and reunion which brings together all those whose deaths have been recorded in the novel (including those which pre-date the narrative time sequence, like her parents' deaths), together with 'Freud', who died shortly after the outbreak of war, in a camp resembling the early state of Israel. The camp also recalls features of Lisa's 'white hotel' fantasy – the selflessness, co-operation and instant re-building after devastation, together with the sexual freedom and the breast as a symbol of solace and altruism.

It is perhaps easier to explain the purpose of 'The Camp' in relation to the overall structure of *The White Hotel* than it is to justify it to those many readers who have found it inappropriate, if not offensive. Throughout the novel the 'meaning' of the 'white hotel' fantasy is subject to a continuous process of being found and then displaced. For a time it seems that the Freudian explanations for the neurosis which generates the fantasy are perceived as inadequate because of the limitations in the psychoanalytical process. This concentrates on what is known (the past), at the expense of exploring the mind's tele-pathic potential, from which science tends to shrink. Beyond that, patients may not know or remember all that needs to be known of the past, and may withhold what they do know. By the end, however, the Freudian interpretation has not so much been displaced by the tele-pathic, as absorbed into a 'meaning' which encompasses both – that the individual's life can be seen in terms of an endlessly recurring pattern in which he or she is locked. 'The Health Resort' seems to complete the pattern, but then there is Babi Yar; and then 'The Camp', which suggests not only that we can never know ourselves that completion has been achieved, but that death itself may not be the final closure. The pattern carries the power of repetition, but also the possibility of renewal and promise.

Whether the glib 'sunshine after tears' atmosphere of 'The Camp' is an appropriate afterword to the historical events of Babi Yar is another matter, whatever cloak of respectability is conferred by the novel's undoubted technical expertise. There is moreover, the further question of whether the novel's theme – of the recurring and binding pattern in which the significance of the individual life may be found – needed to be worked through the Jewish Holocaust. The use of Babi Yar is not only exploitative, but if, as *The White Hotel* suggests, Babi Yar was Lisa's appointed destiny, then it must carry the same implication for all the real Jews who perished in the Holocaust, to a degree absolving of responsibility both the individuals and the larger culture which perpetrated it.

If 'The Camp' seems flimsy and ahistorical in its promise of renewal, then it must be said that a real sense of human possibility is present in the novel in the figure Freud, who has in a sense presided over this whole chapter. Himself a Jew, suffering personal losses and ill-health, his attempts to alleviate largely ignored forms of human misery while the world around him is moving towards mass destruction, have the power to move as 'told' in *The White Hotel*, as they do in other accounts of his life.

6

Society

Thomas Pynchon: *The Crying of Lot 49*
Kurt Vonnegut: *Breakfast of Champions*
David Lodge: *Small World*

One of the great achievements of the nineteenth-century classical realist novel, in Europe, Britain and, towards the end of the nineteenth century in the United States, was its embodiment of some concept of society. The length alone of the novels of the period allowed for large numbers of characters to be drawn from a broad social canvas, the mechanics of plot establishing a chain of connections between them. It has, in the intellectual climate of the last couple of decades, become commonplace to dismiss the nineteenth-century British novel for what one might describe as its intellectual naivety, as Doris Lessing, does, for example, in her Preface to *The Golden Notebook*, already quoted in another context in the last chapter:

> it was not possible to find a novel which described the intellectual and moral climate of a hundred years ago, in the middle of the last century, in Britain, in the way that Tolstoy did for Russia, Stendhal for France. (pp. 10–11)

Yet it has to be said that it is principally to the novelists of the period that we owe our sense of the teeming masses of industrialized urban society in England and of the real but unacknowledged bonds between discrete social groups, however simple the framework of ideas in which this was achieved.

Dickens, George Eliot, Mrs Gaskell and Trollope to a lesser degree, all helped establish a social function for the novel in English. But it is perhaps Dickens's rendering of social structures which has most bearing on later twentieth-century approaches to the subject. Imaginatively fired by the modern city as a place that could absorb and hide individuals and their secrets, Dickens took on the task (in *Bleak House, Our Mutual Friend, Little Dorrit* and *Great Expectations*) of exposing and uncovering and, through elaborate plot-contrivances and highly developed symbolic structures, of establishing connections between the powerful and the dispossessed. In that fiercely individualistic phase of high capitalism – which his novels reflect by pushing human difference into the regions of the bizarre and grotesque – he nonetheless proselytized the idea of the individual as a unit in a larger structure.

'Society' in British writing remained the preserve of realist writers through the experimental early decades of this century, as the modernist writers focused on the inner life and individual consciousness. It is beyond the scope of this book to attempt a summary of twentieth-century British realist writing about society, but it may be broadly stated that until the last decade or so, the social canvas of serious realist novelists has been narrower than that of their Victorian counterparts. The journalistic reporting of social conditions in the 1930s (Orwell's *The Road to Wigan Pier*, for example), the calculated provincialism of 1950s fiction (the early novels of Kingsley Amis, John Wain, Malcolm Bradbury), the retreat to outposts of empire (by novelists like Paul Scott and John Masters) and into social comedies of class and manners (Evelyn Waugh, Anthony Powell, Angus Wilson and at least one of each year's Booker prize short list): all testify to that narrowing of social vision.

That British novelists in the 1980s have shown themselves prepared to broaden their scope is in itself a response to social change. It was not until late in the decade (1988) that the British Prime Minister, Margaret Thatcher, began to argue that 'there is no such thing as society',[1] only individuals and their families, but her government's respect for the 'Victorian values' of personal responsibility, initiative and wealth creation was already well established by then, with, as Mrs Thatcher's critics have argued, an accompanying Victorian disregard for the dispossessed and exploited. Ten years of unbroken rule by a government with a clear ideological position have generated not only discernible and widespread social change (always a spur for the novelist) and panic in some quarters at the prospect of those ten years indefinitely lengthening, but a politicizing of serious fiction. The challenge for the realist novelist has been to revive the Victorian novelist's concept of society and to uncover the invisible networks (sometimes, like Margaret Drabble, invoking the name of Dickens in doing so). Drabble's *The Radiant Way* (1987), Doris Lessing's *The Good Terrorist* (1986), Piers Paul Reid's *A Season in the West* (1988) and David Lodge's *Nice Work* (1988) are among recent examples of what has become almost a sub-genre of the 80s, the 'state of the nation' novel.

The link between fictional realism and social reality – undoubtedly an obvious one – has until recently been taken for granted in British writing, though not, as we shall see, in American, or South American. However, the very complexity of twentieth-century society – one possible reason why, until recently, British novelists have concentrated on small and clearly defined areas of it – invites a non-realist approach, and there are now signs of change in British writing in this direction. David Lodge's *Small World*, which I shall be discussing, is a non-realist romance on the social effects of technological change; while Salman Rushdie in *The Satanic Verses* has used magical realism to expose 'Thatcher's Britain'. Despite its obvious relevance here, I am reserving a consideration of Rushdie's novel, and the controversy that it has provoked, until the final chapter.

American fiction's foregrounding of society has a rather different history from British, though there has recently, and over a longer period, been a revival of interest in the novelist's role as broad social critic. In the nineteenth century, while English novelists were drawing their readers' attention to conditions of living in their own country which they might prefer to ignore, American writers were helping to 'invent' America. The conceptualizing and theorizing of America, the use of America as theme rather than setting, have always been features of American writing, which began to acquire a distinctive voice in the decades following Independence and matured over the period of the Civil War – events which inevitably helped clarify the nation's idea of itself. Melville, Whitman and Twain all helped to shape that idea and tell America what it was, or could be – a free, open and democratic society. That frontier, pioneering ideal is a powerful one, and still part of what we know as 'the American Dream', still the standard by which American writers measure their own country's failures; and throughout the twentieth century that 'dream' has more often than not generated irony in literary discourse. In Arthur Miller's *Death of a Salesman* (1949) for example, the mythologizing of America is part of the process by which the citizen is betrayed by society at large. So while, in British writing, the frame of reference for social criticism has been 'universal' concepts of justice and decency, in American writing the frame has been a specifically American one.

If American writers have always, to a degree, seen themselves as guardians of the ideals on which America was founded, and sorrowful chroniclers of the lapses from that ideal, then post-war American society has provided material for writers on a scale to encourage fresh techniques to do that material justice. The silencing of political dissent under Senator McCarthy in the 1950s; the neo-imperialism of the Vietnam War in the following decade; the continuing political marginalization of the black community; the standardization of a richly diverse country, through technology and the power of large corporations: all can and have been seen, not only as part of America's failure to live up to its avowed ideal, but in the context of American leaders', and the American public's, continued insistence on the vitality of that ideal, as part of a sinister conspiracy to disguise from the people the reality of the situation in which they live.

Since the McCarthy era, the spectrum of opinion represented by organized American politics has been narrower than in any other western democracy. There has been a striking reminder of this recently, in the Presidential campaign of 1988, when the incumbent President Reagan denounced the Democratic candidate Michael Dukakis as 'that dreaded "L" word, Liberal.' However, as the campus unrest of the 1960s, the organized opposition to the Vietnam War, the Civil Rights and the Women's Movement have demonstrated, dissent was not abandoned but sought other outlets. Moreover, the subversive critical and philosophical theories developed in post-war France, which have been slow to gain ground in Britain and have been resisted as assaults on common sense, have been welcomed in American universities and continue to flourish, despite the noticeable return to conformity in the 1980s, in American society and art.

I have selected for discussion three novels, Thomas Pynchon's *The Crying of Lot 49*, Kurt Vonnegut's *Breakfast of Champions* and David Lodge's *Small World*, which have in common with the Dickensian model for 'realizing' society, the tracing of unexpected connections which reveal for the reader what was there but not seen. They all of them employ postmodernist techniques and mannerisms, but the differences between the American writers Pynchon and Vonnegut and the British Lodge are striking. Lodge (born 1935), like others of his generation of British writers (most notably Malcolm Bradbury (born 1932), with whom he is often coupled), has achieved a kind of compromise between postmodernism and realism which engages rather than disturbs: the reader is allowed to feel a party to the games played within the novel, rather than their victim. This is of a piece with the generally benign world view which the novel proposes. Lodge takes us on a voyage of discovery which has the effect of containing the world, of revealing the 'smallness' achieved by technological advance. The voyaging in *The Crying of Lot 49* and *Breakfast of Champions* covers smaller distances, but by exposing a substratum of American society, reveals what is sinister in the familiar.

Thomas Pynchon (born 1937 in Long Island) is an exemplary figure in any discussion of postmodernist writing. Living at a time in which the publicity attracted by successful writers in America is at a peak – when they are invited to reveal all to the nation at large through the information media, and to participate in the academic process by teaching and by offering insights into their own work to hungry PhD students – he has chosen to cloak himself in near total anonymity. There is apparently only one photograph of him in public circulation, and known biographical details come to an abrupt halt in the early

1960s; such as there are include a degree at Cornell University in English and engineering sciences and a brief period of employment with the Boeing Company – both of relevance to *The Crying of Lot 49* and *Gravity's Rainbow* (to be discussed in a later chapter on war), which display more than an outsider's knowledge of engineering and large corporations. Since the publication of his novels coincided with the disappearance from public life of J.D. Salinger (another American writer who has chosen to distance himself from the intrusive publicity machine) there has even been speculation that Salinger is the author of Pynchon's novels.[2]

It is perhaps inevitable that one should read into this calculated anonymity a deliberate withdrawal from certain aspects of contemporary American society, but more seems to be at issue. In his novels he creates mysterious worlds which invite decoding; yet the process of decoding reveals deeper ambiguities and the ultimate meaning that seems to be promised becomes more and more elusive. Tony Tanner opens his study of Pynchon's work with a quotation from Roland Barthes's 'The Death of the Author';[3] and there is no doubt that Pynchon's calculated withdrawal from the field, leaving his novels to exist through their play with the reader, implies at the least a common philosophical position with certain strands of contemporary critical theory. Barthes wrote of the need to banish the author from his own text,[4] but Pynchon seems to have taken the unusual step of self-imposed exile. Then there is the further, and in some ways more intriguing possibility, that the manipulated secrecy of the life is intended not to allow the novels free play, but to be brought into play by the reader. At the very least the life reflects the secrecy and withholding of the texts allowing the suspension of meaning to be carried over from the novels into the world.

The Crying of Lot 49 is set in California, and while Pynchon's evocation of place owes nothing to the realist novelist's painstaking accumulation of detail, he does exploit the element of realized fantasy in contemporary California. The 'heroine', Mrs Oedipa Maas, eats fondue at a tupperware party and shops for ricotta in Kinnaret-Among-The-Pines to the sound of Muzak ('the Fort Wayne Settecento Ensemble's variorum recording of the Vivaldi Kazoo Concerto, Boyd Beaver, soloist') (p. 6). She is married to a used-car salesman turned radio announcer, and is seduced by Metzger, a one-time child actor, now lawyer, after watching one of his old films on a hotel bedroom television set. The 'real' California is defamiliarized, but in such a way as to suggest that California itself outstrips anything that may be imagined about it.

California is further refracted through the Californian detective stories of Raymond Chandler, which are part of *The Crying of Lot 49*'s frame of reference. Chandler's characteristic narrative formula has his private detective hero, Philip Marlowe, stumbling across linked pieces of information which initially seem to belong to a different plot from the object of his own immediate inquiries; he later finds that the two plots are in fact linked and that the primary quest can only be completed through the secondary one.

Oedipa Maas learns when the novel opens that she has been named executor of the estate of a former lover, 'one Pierce Inverarity, a California real estate mogul who had once lost two million dollars in his spare time but still had assets numerous and tangled enough to make the job of sorting it all out more than honorary' (p. 5). In the course of sorting out Pierce's affairs, Oedipa stumbles across evidence of an alternative postal system, The Tristero or WASTE, which has as its symbol a muted post horn and is used by the disaffected and dispossessed: 'those of unorthodox sexual persuasion' (p. 75), anarchists, inventors who are stifled by large corporations and the poor and marginalized generally. Evidence of WASTE's existence gradually accumulates, then becomes overwhelming when she wanders the streets for a night and finds another world of bizarre and pitiful apparitions, society's 'normal' face inverted. In the course of the night the WASTE symbol and its army of users confront her at every turn and she is forced into a complete revision of her own society:

> Last night, she might have wondered what undergrounds apart from the couple she knew of communicated by WASTE system. By sunrise she could legitimately ask what undergrounds didn't. (p. 86)

Faced with the denial and hate of orthodox society and 'indifference to the power of their vote', 'this withdrawal was their own, unpublicized, private' (p. 86). And since evidence of the existence of WASTE is present in the Inverarity estate – not least, in her former lover's stamp collection – she is forced to wonder whether, in her role as executor, this is not what she was meant to find:

> She had dedicated herself, weeks ago, to making sense of what Inverarity had left behind, never suspecting that the legacy was America. (p. 123)

Oedipa's disorientation is matched by the reader's, which is further intensified by the novel's evocation of the 'crime thriller' world of Raymond Chandler. In the latter, confusions multiply as the plot progresses, only to give way to a final satisfactory conclusion. In *The Crying of Lot 49* the confusions remain. This is not just a matter of the ominous and inconclusive ending, to which I shall return, but is a feature of the narrative technique throughout. Ambiguities abound and promises of enlightenment at various points in the text either yield nothing or generate new confusions. Early in the novel, before evidence of WASTE's existence begins to multiply, Oedipa plays strip poker with Inverarity's lawyer, Metzger, the one-time child actor. His goal is sexual congress, which she delays by putting on all the clothes in her suitcase until she looks like 'a beach ball with feet' (p. 23).

Keeping within the literary frame of reference already established for this chapter, the episode recalls Barthes's essay on 'Striptease'[5] (an analysis of the art of the Parisian stripper) which is developed into a deconstructionist approach to text by David Lodge's fictional American academic, Morris Zapp, in *Small World*. (If I am confusing the boundaries between 'real' and 'fictional' academic discourse, then I am, as we shall see, taking my cue from Pynchon himself.) Ultimate revelation is, in Barthes's terms, a disappointment, in Zapp's finally impossible. Oedipa and Metzger abandon the strip poker and the sexual act, when it does occur, scarcely impinges on Oedipa's consciousness:

> She awoke at last to find herself getting laid; she'd come in on a sexual crescendo in progress, like a cut to a scene where the camera's already moving. (p. 27)

The incident works like a metaphor for Pynchon's narrative approach throughout.

Teasing, with the expected ultimate revelation withheld, is undoubtedly part of Pynchon's strategy. Oedipa wonders at one point whether she is not the victim of a hoax – the last joke of Inverarity who, the last time that she spoke to him on the telephone a year before his death, had masked his identity with a sequence of voices (p. 6): comic Negro, Slavic, Hispanic, Gestapo, a cocktail of the racial mix in America which is to acquire significance with the growing theme of dispossession. The reader too occupies constantly shifting ground as verifiable historical fact is woven with fiction in such a way as to confuse the status of the fictional element. The Thurn and Taxis postal monopoly in late medieval Europe, the violent history of Wells Fargo in America, the disaffection of Puritans in seventeenth-century Europe – these, being 'known', lend plausibility to the possible existence of Tristero which, being essentially secretive in its operations, is unlikely to have a place in orthodox accounts of history.

There is, within the novel, a lengthy summary of a 'Jacobean play', *The Courier's Tragedy*, by 'Richard Wharfinger', which alerts Oedipa, a member of the audience when it is being performed, to the wider implications of the WASTE symbols. Pynchon's parody, reinforced with the odd quotation, draws so accurately on the known corpus of Jacobean drama as to provoke feelings of paranoia in the reader: a paranoia which matches Oedipa's and that of the other characters in the novel who see the Tristero as a conspiracy born of another conspiracy, the monopoly of power. We the readers are either, like the characters in the novel, victims of a conspiracy to suppress *The Courier's Tragedy* (complete manuscript kept under lock and key in the Vatican), with its proof of the existence of the Tristero; or we are the victims of Pynchon, who creates a world – including a completely believable example of Jacobean Tragedy – which gives such a thesis plausibility.

The treatment of the Tristero in the novel is deeply ambiguous, depriving the reader of a unified response which might help to contain the idea. On the one hand, it is seen as the last refuge of the dispossessed, who use it, not so much to communicate information, as to keep some kind of alternative system going. On the other hand, it is associated with darkness, death and secrecy, its postage stamps subverting the orthodox in sinister ways. A number of characters in the novel with knowledge of the Tristero die in mysterious circumstances; and when Oedipa goes driving on the freeways drunk, openly inviting death, the possibility presents itself that it is the knowledge that kills, rather than agents of Tristero or those bent on suppressing it. At the end of the novel we are teased into the expectation of Tristero revealing itself, when Inverarity's stamps come up for auction. Oedipa attends the auction and sees 'The men inside the auction room' who 'wore black mohair and had pale, cruel faces' (p. 126), but the novel ends abruptly before the relevant lot – lot 49 – is 'cried'.

Readers whose expectations of novels are conditioned by the conventions of realism are likely to feel cheated by this untimely final withholding. However, *The Crying of Lot 49* not only perfectly exemplifies a certain kind of postmodernist writing: it also suggests reasons why a writer might choose to write in this way. Closure completes the experience of the novel for the reader, but *The Crying of Lot 49* continues to reverberate, leaving open in the world around us the possibility of 'Another mode of meaning behind the obvious' (p. 126). As with Pynchon's deft use of *The Courier's Tragedy*, we are left uncertain as to where the frame should be placed, separating the text from the world; even on which side of the frame to place ourselves, sharing or rejecting the novel's paranoia. Pynchon makes great play, here and in *Gravity's Rainbow* (see Chapter 8, where I shall discuss the concept in more detail) with 'excluded middles'. Closure is itself exclusive, and would be inappropriate in a novel which purports to reveal the excluded, and therefore invisible.

The number of the Lot – 49 – is suggestive, linking it with the moment in 'history' to which *The Courier's Tragedy* 'belongs' (1649, the period of the English Civil War) and the moment in American history (1849), shortly before the American Civil War, when, we are told, Tristero arrived in America from Europe. Implicit in the reverberation of the novel on the world is the possibility of the disinherited and dispossessed, the 'excluded middle' of contemporary America, claiming their own.

The novel's title is not only a sophisticated play on numbers: like other American postmodernist novels (*Catch 22* and *Slaughterhouse 5*), *Lot 49* uses the occult suggestiveness of numbers both to mystify and to imply processes of mystification at work in society or particular social groups. There is also a pun on 'Lot'. The title only acquires its full significance at the end, when the action moves to the auction room, where 'lot' has a particular connotation. Until then, the novel has been haunted by a different 'lot', the car lot, which figures in the past of Oedipa's husband Mucho, the ex-car salesman, who is anxious to distance himself from his previous identity. The used car haunts him as a 'futureless, automative projection of somebody else's life' (p. 8). For the blacks and Mexicans who brought in their cars for trade, those cars were:

> motorized, metal extensions of themselves, of their families and what their whole lives must be like, out there so naked for anybody, a stranger like himself, to look at, frame cockeyed, rusty underneath, fender repainted in a shade just off enough to depress the value, if not Mucho himself, inside smelling hopelessly of children, supermarket booze, two, sometimes three generations of cigarette smokers, or only of dust. (p. 8)

There is a sense in which the soundless crying from the car lot sounds through the novel, along with the crying of the disturbed bones from the cemetery which was bulldozed to make a freeway and of the bones of the forgotten GIs, killed in Italy, which were used in cigarette filters. The pun in the title links known realities of American life – the supremacy of the automobile and of commerce – with Pynchon's invented world of the Tristero; while the poignancy of the writing about the poor and dispossessed victims of progress validates the fictional games-playing. The 'real' America proposed by the novel, in which so much that is absurd is acceptable, can only be rendered through the fantastic.

Of a piece with the persistent ambiguity of *The Crying of Lot 49* is the employment of comic devices on potentially tragic material. Oedipa's Christian name evokes the world of Greek tragedy – aptly, in the context of her being forced to 'see' what was invisible – but otherwise the names are jokes, in the manner of classical, Renaissance and Restoration comedy. Dr Hilarius the psychiatrist, Genghis

Cohen, 'the most eminent philatelist in the LA area' (p. 65), Mike Fallopian, Oedipa's surname, 'Maas', the possible readings for which are summarized by Tony Tanner:

> Maas has been read as suggesting Newton's second law of motion in which 'mass' is the term denoting a quantity of inertia. So the name suggests at once activity and passivity. But this will not do. . . . One critic, Terry Caesar, is probably nearer the mark when he suggests an audible joke in the name: 'Oedipa my ass'; she is no Oedipus at all.[6]

All have the effect of flattening character and distancing sympathy, in the comic manner. The names also, of course, as Tony Tanner goes on to elaborate, represent a rejection of realism, and of 'character', and indeed, of the whole process of naming, which is another form of closure and exclusion. If that rejection takes in humanism itself, then it is in the context of the world as proposed in the novel: a society which deprives its citizens of human value is only truly mediated and 'shown' to the reader by such means.

Kurt Vonnegut's *Breakfast of Champions*, published in 1973, opens with a dedication – to Phoebe Hurty – which nostalgically recalls the lost America of the author's adolescence (he was fifty at the time of writing *Breakfast of Champions*), where certain convictions were still possible:

> She believed what so many Americans believed then: that the nation would be happy and just and rational when prosperity came.
>
> I never hear that word anymore: *Prosperity*. It used to be a synonym for *Paradise*. And Phoebe Hurty was able to believe that the impoliteness she recommended would give shape to an American paradise.
>
> Now her sort of impoliteness is fashionable. But nobody believes anymore in a new American paradise. I sure miss Phoebe Hurty. (p. 12)

Breakfast of Champions reflects on American society by way of a continuous discourse on fiction, giving fiction priority over the world by considering ways in which it mediates, influences and invents it. Vonnegut's own fictional preferences are apparent, through both discourse and technique. He persistently undermines the stability of his created world by revealing to the reader the autobiographical sources for the fiction – the physical similarity between one of his characters, Kilgore Trout, and his father; the mental instability and subsequent suicide of his mother, which are re-enacted by the wife of his other principal character, Dwayne Hoover. Vonnegut makes an appearance within his own novel, drinking scotch and water in the lounge of the Holiday Inn as the narrative crisis approaches, and raises the possibility that the nature of his involvement with his fictional world might be symptomatic in him of the same schizophrenia as drove his mother to suicide. At the same time, however, he rejects the false assurances offered by more conventional novelists, a breed represented in *Breakfast of Champions* by a Gothic novelist called Beatrice Keedsler.

> I thought Beatrice Keedsler had joined hands with other old-fashioned storytellers to make people believe that life had leading characters, minor characters, significant details, insignificant details, that it had lessons to be learned, tests to be passed, and a beginning, a middle and an end. (p. 194)

The claims that Vonnegut makes for the dangers of this kind of fiction are large ones: no less than that it has contributed to the crisis (as he would see it) in contemporary America:

> As I approached my fiftieth birthday, I had become more and more enraged and mystified by the idiot decisions made by my countrymen. And then I had come suddenly to pity them, for I understood how innocent and natural it was for them to behave so abominably, and with such abominable results: They were doing their best to live like people invented in story books. This was the reason Americans shot each other so often: it was a convenient literary device for ending short stories and books. (p. 195)

It would be misleading to suggest that there is no irony in Vonnegut's attribution of the violence in American society to the conventions of realist fiction, or certain popular genres within it. Nonetheless, his concerns are identifiably those of postmodernist thinking. The priority that he gives to fiction over reality might seem to many a violation of common sense, but it is placed in a context where the centres of power within society are perceived as themselves producing fictions by which they govern and suppress. In the course of deconstructing his own fiction (and discoursing on the fictions of other novelists), he is also deconstructing and exposing those fictions by which he sees his own society to be operating.

That Vonnegut has, in *Breakfast of Champions*, taken America itself as his theme, in a tradition that is as long-standing as the American novel itself, is apparent in the title, the dedication and throughout the novel. 'Breakfast of Champions', as he explains at the beginning, is a registered trademark for cereal products. Using the terms of reference of his indictment of Beatrice Keedsler's novels, it might be said that the slogan carries the suggestion that the cereal will enable its consumers to be 'leading' rather than 'minor' characters. The novel's alternative title, 'Goodbye Blue Monday', is explained later. As the slogan for 'Robo-clean' washing machines, whose early advertisements carried a picture of a black domestic help who has been replaced by the machine, the title is semiotically linked to an equation of people, particularly black people, to machines. The fact that the titles are trademark and advertising slogan identifies large manufacturing corporations, and their advertisers, as producers of meaning – or fictions – within a consumer society; while the paradox inherent in the double title – of a society which, on the one hand, encourages its citizens to aspire to the highest limits of what is humanly possible, and on the other hand reduces them to machines – forms one of the principal themes of the book.

For a society to operate, as Vonnegut suggests that America does, on a paradox of this kind, requires some degree of mystification to disguise the sinister implications of the way that paradox is reconciled. Vonnegut's response to this is not directly to 'de-mystify' America but, by employing a variety of metafictional procedures, to expose the process of mystification in the writing of fiction. His interventions into the narrative to discuss the decisions that he will make over the fate of his characters lay bare for the reader the power and control of the novelist. As well as affirming the fictional nature of his own fictions, the authorial intrusions can be seen as an 'interrogation' (to use Barthes's term for the way self-reflexive writing mediates the world) of the reality of American society. The novelist's power raises, in the world, the question of free choice – the concept by which American society justifies those inequalities which are inherent in the paradox of the novel's double title. One of his characters, Kilgore Trout, offers an insight into his own status as a character in a work of fiction, which has implications beyond that somewhat rarified situation, to include all individuals whose terms of living are in the control of others:

> all I can think of is that I'm a character in a book by somebody who wants to write about somebody who suffers all the time. (p. 221)

Vonnegut also responds stylistically to those processes of mystification, in society and in fiction, by using a naively explicatory authorial voice.

> Everybody in America was supposed to grab whatever he could and hold on to it. Some Americans were very good at grabbing and holding, were fabulously well-to-do. Others couldn't get their hands on doodly-squat. (p. 22)

The naivety of his own style – which, it has to be said, often sounds a note of condescension – registers his distance from those who use language to mystify and humiliate:

Most white people in Midland City were insecure when they spoke, so
they kept their sentences short and their words simple, in order to keep
embarrassing mistakes to a minimum. . . .

   This was because their English teachers would wince and cover their
ears and give them flunking grades and so on whenever they failed to
speak like English aristocrats before the First World War. (p. 132)

Breakfast of Champions follows the fortunes of two emblematic
characters. Dwayne Hoover is the richest man in Midland City, the
sources of his wealth a reflection of American consumerism: cars, car
washes, drive-in movies, a radio station, a Holiday Inn and a burger
parlour, and a shared interest in the Miracle Cave, a Disneyesque
tourist spot with, among other attractions, a simulated Moby Dick.
Yet he and his enterprises are being destroyed by the waste products
of the industrial growth which has contributed to his own prosperity:
the Miracle Cave is being polluted by industrial waste and his own
behaviour is becoming increasingly erratic and violent as the result of
an undiagnosed chemical imbalance.

   Kilgore Trout, who is the unwitting agent of crisis in Hoover's life,
is a science fiction writer. (Vonnegut himself began his career as a
writer of science fiction, and has returned to it again recently.) Prolific
but hitherto unknown – Trout's work has only achieved publication
as the irrelevant text in books of pornographic photographs – he is
unexpectedly invited to the Midland City Arts Festival as a celebrity.
There his destiny converges with Hoover's. In the lounge bar of the
Midland City Holiday Inn, Hoover, overlooked by his creator,
Vonnegut – the author, as it were, of his impending misfortunes
– reads one of Trout's novels. This takes as its theme the thesis that
human beings are no more than machines, which authorizes Hoover,
already in a deranged state, to run amok. He wounds eleven people,
some known to him, others not (including Trout), with varying
degrees of severity. As a result of the denouement, the fortunes of the
two men are to a degree reversed: Trout achieves celebrity as a writer
(although all he really craves is to be young again); and Hoover, when
he is finally released from custody, is beggared by law suits for
damages.

   Throughout *Breakfast of Champions*, paraphrases of Trout's
novels provide a further source of commentary on the issues
addressed in the novel. Some of these – there is one about a planet
whose only form of life is the automobile, now itself on the verge of
extinction because it has used up all the resources necessary to sustain
it – may be read as parables of late-twentieth-century, particularly
American, society. Others are more metaphysical, seeing the universe
as the work of a malevolent creator. In the novel that falls so
disastrously into Hoover's hands there is a Creator of the Universe

responsible for the making and programming of human machines; and when Hoover, under the influence of this novel, has his own violent outburst, his own 'creator' is sitting by, watching.

Vonnegut himself – or at any rate the authorial voice that he adopts in the novel – proposes a kind of scientific determinism for human behaviour which runs parallel to the critique of American society. The effect that illness – syphilis, thyroid and brain disorders – can have on behaviour is indicated, though one wonders how seriously the suggestion is intended that the Jewish Holocaust may be attributed to widespread chemical disorder among the Germans at the time. The devastation of the planet he sees as partly man-made, partly beyond the control of human beings. When it comes to the causes of human misery, Vonnegut may be said to be hedging his bets. There is, of course, no reason to expect a writer to offer answers to such large questions, but the simple, explicatory, sometimes didactic voice seems to hold just such a promise; and it acknowledges complexity through contradiction rather than ambiguity – the penalty paid by the novel for the complicity of the narrative voice with bewildered and oppressed humanity.

On the question of humanism, however, *Breakfast of Champions* is productively ambiguous. Throughout the novel, an equation between human beings and machines is reiterated – partly on biological grounds, partly seen as a result of the particular form of social organization which is under scrutiny. The narrative is interspersed with lists of statistics which are at their most bizarre in quantifying sexual activity (through lengths of penises and numbers of orgasms). The use of statistics is double-edged, having, on the one hand, a reductive effect on one of the more mystified areas of human activity, and on the other taking the spirit of competition in America to its ultimate point of absurdity.

The anti-humanist stance of postmodernist writing (and of related philosophical positions) is one of the most alienating and least understood of its features as far as the general reading public is concerned. *Breakfast of Champions*, however, is not only a valuable example of the anti-humanist position, but lucid about the conditions that have produced it. Humanism (in this case, in America) has both failed to produce a just society and is indirectly used to justify the injustice. In the America of *Breakfast of Champions*, the rhetoric of humanism is used to blind people to the fact that they are treated like machines. Vonnegut, while rejecting traditional humanism, is nonetheless insisting on human value; and recognizes a part of every human being which is not mechanical and which he describes as 'an unwavering band of light', the 'sacred' faculty of awareness and reflection (p. 208).

David Lodge, the author of *Small World*, has since the early 1960s successfully combined two careers, of novelist and university teacher of English. In his essay, 'Modernism, Antimodernism and Postmodernism', first presented as an inaugural professorial lecture in 1976 at Birmingham University, Lodge describes his own fictional orientation as 'basically antimodernist, but with elements of modernism and postmodernism.'[7] Two of the novels written since then (*How Far Can You Go?*, published in 1980, and *Small World*) demonstrate further shifts towards postmodernist writing, which have coincided with his growing interest, as an academic critic, in modern critical theory. Nonetheless, his continued commitment to some form of realism in his writing, however ironized, as it is in *Small World*, is illustrative of the continued pragmatism of British novelists towards available modes of fiction. The same pragmatism characterizes his approach to critical theory (as a title like 'Working with Structuralism' demonstrates), which is characterized by a lucidity and good humour rare in the field – qualities which have done much to gain acceptance for difficult, and for British readers, often alien concepts.

Small World, which Lodge describes as a 'kind of sequel' (Prologue) to an earlier novel, *Changing Places* (published in 1975), concerns the activities of a group of academics, all teachers of literature or critical theory, together with assorted novelists, translators and publishers. They meet at international conferences and festivals, the siting of which has, by the end of the novel, taken the reader around the world; while the range of positions adopted by the academics – traditional humanist, structuralist, deconstructionist, Marxist, feminist and phenomenological – is inclusive of the currently available ways of approaching a text. *Small World* can, up to a point, be read as a 'realist' account of academic life: Lodge has an acute sense of place, of dialogue, of human difference and of the pleasures of the quotidian. And if he brings metonymic equivalents of 'real' places (Rummidge for Birmingham) into the same frame as Tokyo and New York, then that is still part of the classical realist tradition.

The joke – the whole novel is on one level a highly elaborate joke – is that *Small World* is an astonishingly detailed and comprehensive parody of the medieval romance, a form which was never intended to be read mimetically. The novel's Prologue invites a reading of the modern conference in terms of the medieval pilgrimage, 'in that it allows the participants to indulge themselves in all the pleasures and diversions of travel while appearing to be austerely bent on self-improvement.' The novel begins by quoting T.S. Eliot's 'The Waste Land', which uses echoes of romance to provide an ironic commentary on the modern world; while the form of Eliot's opening is an ironic inversion of the beginning of Chaucer's 'Prologue' to

The Canterbury Tales, with which Lodge, in his own translation, opens his 'Prologue'. So the inter-textuality of Lodge's project is signalled immediately, establishing a distance between the world of this and earlier texts, and the real world.

The hero is a young Irishman – the medieval romance was itself an imaginative reconstruction of an idealized Celtic past – called Persse McGarrigle, whose progress through the novel is similar to Sir Percival's in the Grail Legend. Persse is an English teacher at the University of Limerick (where, in the 'real' world, there is no university) who at a conference in Rummidge meets and falls in love with the beautiful Angelica, a postgraduate student preparing a doctoral thesis on romance. Angelica is unknown to the other conferees, and her appearance at the conference, and subsequent disappearance, are equally mysterious. Persse then begins a quest to recover her, his journey taking him from one international conference to another, until he finds her at the MLA conference in New York, where he learns that she is to marry another academic in his own field, Peter McGarrigle. His successful rival in love, it emerges, was unwittingly the agent of his own professional advancement, in that Peter McGarrigle had been intended to fill Persse's place at Limerick.

In New York, Persse, defeated of Angelica, wins fame professionally when he asks a symposium of eminent theoreticians the question:

> 'What follows if everybody agrees with you?' (p. 319)

Persse, like Sir Percival, is chaste and innocent (necessary conditions of romance which are given plausibility in the late twentieth century by Persse's Irish Catholic background); and just as Sir Percival, by asking the right question, unlocks the curse on the Fisher King (who is sexually impotent and ruling over a barren land), so Persse, whose question exposes the self-perpetuating, and therefore ultimately pointless nature of academic debate, unwittingly restores to sexual potency and intellectual vigour Arthur Kingfisher, the doyen of literary theoreticians.

The plot offers the kinds of pleasures to the reader described by Angelica in Rummidge when she applies the metaphor of striptease to romance:

> the endless leading on of the reader, a repeated postponement of an ultimate revelation which never comes – or, when it does, terminates the pleasure of the text. . . . (p. 29)

Most surviving medieval romances, however, are unfinished, and therefore without closure. Lodge avoids closure by ending his novel with Persse embarking on another quest – for Cheryl Summerbee, an employee at London Airport who has witnessed Persse's comings and goings and fallen in love with him; who has been converted by Angelica – also encountered in transit – from Mills and Boon novels, debased heirs of romance, to *The Faerie Queene*; and who by the end of the novel has embarked on a journey to become herself the object of a quest.

Apart from the shape of the plot, with its reliance on the Arthurian legends, and the equation of knights with travelling academics and of conferences with pilgrimages, Lodge employs a number of other romance motifs. Angelica has an identical twin, Lily, whose sexual availablility is the reverse of Angelica's withholding. They are, moreover, foundlings, and in the atmosphere of harmony and reconciliation which follows Persse's question at the MLA conference – a harmony which magically includes a brief spell of halcyon weather in the depths of the New York winter – they are reunited with their natural parents, Arthur Kingfisher and Sybil Maiden, a retired Cambridge don who is a devotee of Jessie Weston's *From Ritual to Romance* (one of the sources drawn on by Eliot in 'The Waste Land').

There are bad knights (the German von Turpitz who appears permanently and sinisterly black-gloved and who plagiarizes Persse's work) and good knights (the American deconstructionist Morris Zapp, who helps Persse on his way). A number of the characters, creative writers and critics, suffer from blocks – spells from which they, too, are released by Persse's question. The central narrative is interrupted at various points by further narratives – lengthy stories told by one character to another, like the tales told by the pilgrims in *The Canterbury Tales*. These stories too conform to the conventions of romance. Philip Swallow tells Zapp a thrilling tale of escape from death (by air), followed by a night of unrivalled passion with the wife of his host from the British Council.

One could go on indefinitely listing the correspondences; and indeed, much of the pleasure of Lodge's novel is its clever play with other texts. The creation of pleasure is, of course, an end in itself, but the question nonetheless arises of whether *Small World* is other than a highly inventive game; whether, as an intransitive and self-reflexive work, it still succeeds in mediating the 'real' world.

Some of the comedy of *Small World*, particularly in the opening, Rummidge, episode arises from the discrepancy between the imaginary landscape of romance and the perceived squalor of the contemporary world. In the course of Persse's early (and as it transpires, only) dealings with Angelica at the Rummidge conference, she suggests that they re-enact Keats's 'Eve of Saint Agnes' – a product of early nineteenth-century English romanticism, a movement which was, at least in part, a reaction against the industrial revolution. Persse, in anticipation of his sexual initiation, wanders off into Rummidge in search of Durex:

> He . . . eventually found, or rather lost, himself in the city centre, a bewildering labyrinth of dirty, malodorous stairs, subways and walkways that funnelled the local peasantry up and down, over and under the huge concrete highways, vibrating with the thunder of passing juggernauts. (p. 47)

Lodge's descriptions of contemporary urban life lack the sinister quality, and the paranoia, of Pynchon's. In the realist manner, they confine themselves to mediating the familiar; but within the context of *Small World*, they obliquely suggest reasons for the continued vitality of the romance genre, which offers release and liberation through the imagination.

To see romance as an escape from the mundane (Cheryl reading Mills and Boon behind her desk at London Airport) is hardly novel, but Lodge goes further in celebrating the power of the imagination to renew and revitalize the material world. At the same time, *Small World* is comically alert to the inevitable failures of human aspiration: experience never lives up to the ideal. When Persse finds a chemist, his Irish accent, further thickened with embarrassment, causes confusion, and he is given Farex, a baby food, instead of Durex; and when he conceals himself in a cupboard, as instructed by Angelica, to watch her undress, he realizes he has been the victim of a hoax as he sees another man prepare for bed. At the end of the MLA conference, he finally takes 'Angelica' to bed, only to discover later that it is Lily who has stolen his virginity.

The pleasure of romance, as Angelica explains, lies in its unfolding: a final revelation cannot do other than disappoint. Romance, which is cyclical in shape, gives priority to the process over closure, to means over ends. It bears on the world by suggesting that the point of life is none other than the process of living, though in medieval romance the Christian overtones imply a linear plot and final closure outside the cyclical form of the romance itself. In *Small World* Persse is still engaged in the quest for what will give his life meaning and transfers his attentions from Angelica to Cheryl to that end. His older colleagues, however, Philip Swallow and Morris Zapp, have reached an awareness, though Philip tries to disguise the fact from himself, of the ultimate pointlessness of life. What is left to them are strategies for living, of which they represent the Freudian poles of sex (Swallow) and work (Zapp). Swallow's escape from death and affair with his host's wife, Joy (who reappears in Swallow's life, having been presumed dead, at a conference in Turkey), give him a renewed appetite for life; the irony is that Joy is a younger version of his own wife, Hilary, and life with Joy would only produce the same gradual diminishing of desire. Zapp throws himself enthusiastically into an endless round of conferences, academic intrigue and publications, but since all his lectures are variations on the theme of 'Every decoding is another encoding' (p. 25) no ultimate revelation or meaning is envisaged.

The philosophy underpinning *Small World* is not so very different from what we encounter in Beckett's novels and plays. The difference is that Lodge's writing communicates great zest for life. The strategies and processes are not so much all that are left, features of heroic and lonely struggle, as what make life worth living, manifestations of human resilience and elasticity.

There is another aspect of *Small World* which invites more direct comparison with *The Crying of Lot 49* and *Breakfast of Champions*. The novel addresses itself to society through the changes effected by technology. It is technology that has made the world 'small' and created an international community of academics (along with international communities in other fields); so that the action of *Small World* is almost confined to airports, aeroplanes and conference centres. Specifically, technological advance is registered in the working lives of university teachers. Zapp tells Persse (to whom all this is new) that the concept of a hierarchy of universities has become obsolete:

> ' Because . . . information is more portable in the modern world than it used to be.' (p. 43)

He goes on to list 'jet travel, direct-dialling telephones and the Xerox machine' (p. 43) as instruments of change. To these might be added, as they figure in the lives of the characters, credit cards and computers. A minor character, Ronald Frobisher, a once angry young novelist of the 1950s, dates his writer's block to seeing a computer breakdown of the vocabulary of his novels and learning from that that his most used word was 'grease' and its variants.

The humour arises here from the conflict between technology and a more mystified system of values: in this case, 'poetic' inspiration. They serve to ironize each other, as do the medieval pilgimage and the technology required for its modern equivalent, the conference. The framing device of the romance, while generating irony, nonetheless carries the suggestion that human nature has not changed very much. In this, Lodge differs from American postmodernist writers like Pynchon and Vonnegut, who see, not just the world, but the view we must take of human beings as radically altered by recent history and technological advance. There is no sense of apocalypse in Lodge's work, nor of a crisis undermining humanist values. Persse is an embodiment of traditional values, and an instrument of benign transformation at the MLA conference because of them. More telling is Morris Zapp's loss of absolute faith in deconstruction following his experience of being kidnapped by a group of radical Italian activists. Persse questions Morris about his altered philosophical position:

> 'You mean every decoding is not another encoding after all?'
>
> 'Oh it is, it is. But the deferral of meaning isn't infinite as far as the individual is concerned.'
>
> 'I thought deconstructionists didn't believe in the individual.'
>
> 'They don't. But death is the one concept you can't deconstruct. Work back from there and you end up with the old idea of the autonomous self. I can die, therefore I am. I realized that when those wop radicals threatened to deconstruct me.' (p. 328)

This little fragment of dialogue tellingly illustrates British (the novelist's if not the character's) pragmatism towards theory in the light of personal experience.

7

History

The use of historical material in imaginative writing is part of the development of literary genres before the novel. The need to understand, celebrate or assess a national past is a central impulse in all epic, and contributed to the emergence of the history play in the Elizabethan theatre, while classical and Renaissance tragedy focus on the intense experiences of suffering of representative historical figures. The genesis of the English novel in the eighteenth century, however, owed less to a concern with the past than to a perceived market for a popular genre reflecting the way of life and ethos of the growing middle classes. This coincided with a new emphasis on 'original' material. Indeed, the two – the rise of the novel and of 'originality' as a criterion for judging worth – might be said to have a common root, in the centrality they both give to individual experience.

Within fifty years of the publication of Richardson's *Pamela*, however, historical writing emerged as a distinct strand in English fiction with the novels of Sir Walter Scott. The first of these, *Waverley*, was published in 1814, and this, with its successors, had considerable influence on the historical novel throughout Europe and in the United States, as well as in Britain. It seems likely that the development of historical fiction corresponded to a change in popular awareness of history throughout Europe comparable to that of the English after the defeat of the Spanish Armada, to which Shakespeare's history plays were in part a response.

Georg Lukacs, whose Marxist account, *The Historical Novel*, first published in Russian in 1937, remains the most exhaustive treatment of the development of the historical novel, locates what he calls 'the feeling . . . that there is such a thing as history'[1] precisely in history:

> It was the French Revolution, the revolutionary wars and the rise and fall of Napoleon, which for the first time made history a *mass experience*, and moreover on a European scale. During the decades between 1789 and 1814 each nation of Europe underwent more upheavals than they had previously experienced in centuries. And the quick succession of these upheavals gives them a qualitatively distinct

character, it makes their historical character far more visible than would be the case in isolated, individual instances: the masses no longer have the impression of a 'natural occurrence'.[2]

In the main, nineteenth-century novelists did not regard historical fiction as a separate genre. Most of Scott's writing was historical, but Dickens, George Eliot and Thackeray in England, Balzac in France and Tolstoy in Russia, moved from the contemporary world, to the 'lost' world of their own childhood (this is particularly a feature of English nineteenth-century fiction) to more remote periods of history, with little perceptible difference of approach or treatment.

Lukacs sees the development of the historical novel as a separate genre (which as a Marxist he deplores) as occurring when writers forsake the representation of broad historical movements through representative characters, in favour of a private, psychological, 'modern' approach to history, which is then historicized by a proliferation of historical detail. He characterizes this, by way of a discussion of Flaubert's *Salammbo* (published in 1862) as 'the appearance of reality in an external, decorative, picturesque manner by means of the conscientious application of archaeology.'[3]

One does not need to share Lukacs's Marxist viewpoint to accept the accuracy of his description of the historical novel once it becomes a popular genre, separate from mainstream fiction. Since the passing of the kind of historical writing which was directly influenced by Scott, readers have valued historical novels chiefly for 'pictorial effect',[4] and for a sense of historical distance which is 'simply negation of the present'.[5]

In the twentieth century, the historical novel has been further marginalized by the insistence of the modernist movement on the inner, subjective world and on the primacy of the writer's own experience; while serious realist fiction has been firmly rooted in its own time. The popular historical novel of today functions chiefly as escapist reading.

Alongside that, however, over the last twenty years or so the concept of historical writing, which had no place in modernist theory, has been revolutionized by the practice of postmodernist writers, who have shown extraordinary inventiveness in their treatment of historical material. Apart from the writers whose work will be discussed in this chapter, William Golding, John Berger and Peter Ackroyd have taken experimental approaches to history, and there has besides been a revival of interest among realist writers like J.G. Farrell.

This revival of interest would appear to be the product of a variety of cultural and theoretical changes. It seems likely that the Second World War, which was even more of a 'mass experience' than the French Revolution and the Napoleonic Wars, has helped to foster a new sense of history; and among writers since the war, realist and non-realist alike, there has been increasing unwillingness to concentrate on private emotional and psychological experiences as though they existed in a social and historical vacuum. In the next chapter, I shall concentrate entirely on novels written about the Second World War which register a direct response to the event. More indirectly the aftermath of war, as has been noticed elsewhere in this book, produced a philosophical upheaval as the need was addressed to re-examine traditional concepts – of goodness, human nature, free will – in the light of recent experience. One result, in Western Europe, has been a renewed interest in Marxist theory and a Marxist approach to history. In *The French Lieutenant's Woman*, for example, John Fowles uses a Victorian setting and characters modelled on stereotypes from the novels of the period; and then problematizes the whole process by explicitly and self-consciously analysing his characters' behaviour in the light of Marxist and Freudian theory, with occasional references to post-war French writers like Barthes who are more immediate influences on his own approach.

In the United States, there has always been a tendency among writers to foreground the concept of America through a continual re-examination of its founding philosophy in the light of later experience. In postmodernist writing, as we noticed in the last chapter, this has often expressed itself in parables which bring contemporary American society ironically into play with the American myth. E.L. Doctorow is foremost among those novelists who have taken critical moments in American history – the frontier days of the West in *Welcome to Hard Times*, the execution of the Rosenbergs in *The Book of Daniel* and the decades immediately preceding the First World War in *Ragtime* – when that myth has, in the perceptions of the author, been modified, debased or manipulated in ways that have a bearing on the present. Doctorow would appear, from the evidence of the novels, to share Lukacs's conviction 'that a real understanding of the problems of contemporary society can only grow out of an understanding of the society's prehistory and formative history.'[6]

Elsewhere in the world, as nations struggle into independence from a colonial past, or are only now exploring through the novel ways of expressing national identity, writers are still involved in the creation of national myths, as they were in America in the nineteenth century and in Europe at an earlier, more epic stage of writing. Some of the more exciting developments in later twentieth-century fiction have emerged through writers exploring the connections between history and fiction, personal and national myth, most notably in South

American writing (in the novels of Gabriel Garcia Marquez, Mario Vargas Llosa and Isabel Allende, among others). *Midnight's Children*, by the Indian writer Salman Rushdie, uses magical realist techniques comparable to those of the South American writers to examine the development of India in the decades following Independence from the British.

There have been changes in the concept of history – in the way that historians themselves approach their subject, in the teaching of history in schools and in universities – which match those changes in the theory of fiction underpinning postmodernist writing. In both there is a greater awareness of the unreliablility of all narratives, whether purporting to be fact or fiction, and a corresponding impulse to expose the processes by which narratives are made. They share an unwillingness to attribute too much to individuals, but instead examine the forces which shape the terms of individual action. Both novelists and historians allow more of a place in the story to those previously unsung, in history and fiction.

Of the three novels to be discussed here, *The French Lieutenant's Woman* by John Fowles (born 1926) most resembles, at least in its opening chapters, the popular historical genre novel. As elsewhere in Fowles's work, however, his use of a familiar genre (the romance in *The Magus* and the autobiographical first-person novel in *Daniel Martin*) serves ultimately to discompose the reader, as the expectations encouraged by what is familiar are later thwarted. Fowles has considerable gifts for narrative and description, and in another age – the nineteenth century, say, the setting for *The French Lieutenant's Woman* – would have been able to use them without self-consciousness; without provoking the suspicion of his readers that the game in which he involves them is at their expense – a suspicion more likely to be aroused by his work than that of Thomas Pynchon, for example, who might also be seen as 'cheating' his readers, but whose novels are at too much of a remove from the conventions of realism for those criteria to apply. Fowles has a gift for realist fiction, but is philosophically oriented towards post-war French theory (p. 85). His solution is to write the kind of novel which he no longer considers to be appropriate, but to establish his distance from it by ironizing and exposing its conventions.

The action of *The French Lieutenant's Woman* is concentrated on, though not confined to, a lovingly described Lyme Regis, where the romantic possibilities of the landscape are fully exploited. Lyme is also the scene of earlier romantic fictions (most notably, Jane Austen's *Persuasion*) and a hunting ground for naturalists because of its fossil remains. These two elements – the weight of the tradition of the English novel, bearing down on this novel, and the evolutionary chain, bearing down on the individual – provide two important frames of reference in *The French Lieutenant's Woman*.

Most of the characters are frankly derivative from nineteenth-century fiction. The hero, Charles Smithson – an upright and honourable man, sensitive to conflicts of principle, an archetypal Victorian hero – is a gentleman naturalist who has recently become engaged to Ernestina Freeman, heiress to a trade fortune; while her social aspirations, iron will and playful manipulativeness conform to the type of Rosamund Vincy in George Eliot's *Middlemarch*. Charles's feelings are then torn by the rival attractions of Sarah Woodruff, the French lieutenant's woman of the title, an object of both scandal and charitable patronage in Lyme, who recalls the 'forbidden woman' of a number of Victorian novels. There is a romantic sub-plot involving Charles's manservant Sam (explicitly compared in the novel to Dickens's Sam Weller), and a gallery of stereotypes among the minor characters drawn from Victorian fiction (kindly aunt, harsh philanthropist, free-thinking doctor). Dialogue, plot development, authorial omniscience (until Fowles chooses to expose it), the manipulation of a large group of characters are all familiar to readers of Victorian fiction.

So on one level *The French Lieutenant's Woman* is both an historical novel set in the Victorian period and a close parody of Victorian fiction. Both genres are problematized, however. Whereas in the conventional historical novel the author takes the reader into an apparently seamless past world and makes little or no use of the perspective offered by his own distance from it, Fowles maintains a constant commentary which issues from his own point in history. The research necessary for historical fiction is laid bare by extensive quotation from sources, rather than being invisibly woven into the narrative. Sexual mores, relations between masters and servants, the state of religion and culture, even the use of aniline dyes, are matters of a commentary more in the manner of the historian than of the realist novelist.

The placing of the novel in time is careful. It opens in 1867 – the year when, as we are told, *Das Kapital* was published in Hamburg; eight years after the publication of Darwin's *Origin of Species*, a gap which allows Charles, with his interest in naturalism, an awareness of evolutionary theory. Charles, like Fowles, who shares his hero's keen amateur interest in natural history, analyses society in terms of evolutionary principles; and with a self-consciousness that matches his creator's, sees the gentlemanly class, to which he belongs and which he eventually falls foul of, as an endangered species:

> he felt that the enormous apparatus rank required a gentleman to erect

around himself was like the massive armour that had been the death
warrant of so many ancient saurian species. (p. 253)

The application of Darwinian theory to fiction is not new to
Fowles, of course. French, British and American novelists at the turn
of the nineteenth and twentieth centuries – including Zola, George
Moore and Theodore Dreiser – adapted post-Darwinian naturalism
to the novel in ways that undermined the ethos and conventions of
nineteenth-century fiction; showing characters to be more at the
mercy of their environment, natural endowments and adaptability,
and less in control of their destinies, than classical realist fictions had
suggested. Moreover, the naturalist novelists often chose for their
'placing' in time and space, historical moments of profound change,
like Dreiser, who places the advancement of his heroine in *Sister
Carrie* against the background of the rapid urbanization and indus-
trialization of the American mid-West.

What is innovatory in Fowles's approach is, again, the self-
consciousness with which the naturalism is applied. Charles is aware
of being a member of an endangered species at the very moment when
Darwin's ideas are gaining ground. At the same time, Fowles in the
authorial commentary isolates two of the forces that are weakening
the 'gentleman''s position: trade, on the one hand, represented by
Ernestina's father; and on the other hand, the professional scientist,
who takes over that disinterested commitment to a common good
which the Victorian gentleman had inherited from the medieval
knight, and professionalizes it.

What actually destroys Charles's social position in the narrative,
however, is his seduction by Sarah Woodruff and the subsequent
breaking of his engagement to Ernestina. So his fate is emblematic of
another of the novel's principal themes – the public denial by the
Victorians of sexual desire and the necessary hypocrisies which
accompanied that denial. Fowles's characterization of Sarah is one of
the most interesting features of *The French Lieutenant's Woman*,
where the play between Victorian attitudes and stereotypes and
twentieth-century perspective is at its most ironic and acute. On one
level she is, like all the morally ambiguous women in Victorian fiction
(and, it has to be said, like a number of Fowles's own female characters throughout his work), the mysterious 'other', unfathomable by
the honourable male characters; but our judgement of her is confused,
as it is not in Victorian fiction, by the exposing in the novel of the
social forces and pressures to which she is responding.

Sarah is living in Lyme as companion to the fearsomely pious Mrs
Poulteney, having left a job as nursery governess after a doubtful
episode with a wounded French soldier. Shunned by respectable

Lyme, Sarah makes a confidant of Charles and confesses what is otherwise a matter of gossip and speculation, that she lost her virtue to the Frenchman. She engineers her dismissal by Mrs Poulteney, is befriended by Charles, and when he visits her at the hotel in Exeter where she has taken sanctuary, he makes love to her only to discover that she was still a virgin.

Before Charles's visit to Exeter, when she receives him, apparently unprepared for a visitor, in her nightdress and recovering from a sprained ankle, the reader has been allowed to witness the preparations for that visit. These include the buying of the nightdress and bandage for an as yet uninjured ankle. There is throughout a degree of manipulation in Sarah's behaviour, particularly towards Charles; and where Lyme generally needs little encouragement to see her as a fallen woman, the more scientifically minded Dr Grogan warns Charles off her as a hysterical neurotic. Grogan's interpretation of Sarah is an advance on Lyme's, but the reader, guided by the commentary of Fowles, who none the less refuses to 'fix' a view of Sarah, has the benefit of Marx, Freud, Darwin and French existentialism. So the undoubtedly neurotic elements in her behaviour may be seen as issuing from her social powerlessness. Poor but educated above her station, Sarah has been given the taste for a way of life which her economic situation denies her. Her hysterical management of events allows her some degree of control over her own destiny – a means of control which places her outside the moral orthodoxies governing Victorian heroes and heroines but is recognized by late twentieth-century theories of human behaviour.

Indeed, the concept of personal freedom, albeit in the greatly modified and re-defined terms of the existentialists – Sarah's attempts to control the plot do eventually gain her a more 'authentic' way of life – is important in Fowles's work and explicitly included in his own theory of the novel. In an authorly intrusion in which he comments on the god-like omniscience of the Victorian novelist, he declares that 'There is only one good definition of God: the freedom that allows other freedoms to exist. And I must conform to that definition' (p. 86).

We have noticed already, and shall have cause to again, that in American non-realist fiction the concept of personal freedom (enshrined both in the American Constitution and in its citizens' perceptions of the privileges that they enjoy) has been systematically problematized and subverted, allowing new kinds of fictions which barely conform to the conventional definitions of the novel. In Britain, however, novelists like Fowles and Iris Murdoch (whose work I shall be discussing in Chapter 9) have used philosophical principles to validate some notion of personal freedom, which in turn has allowed them to retain modified forms of realism.

Sarah's dealings with Charles – manipulative, teasing, creating confusions between truth and personal fictions – are comparable to the relationship that Fowles sets up with his reader. In the early chapters of the novel, he deploys, albeit within the frame of a twentieth-century perspective, all the familiar conventions of the Victorian novelist, only to lay bare the whole process once it might be assumed that the reader's attention is secure:

> The story I am telling is all imagination. These characters I create never existed outside my own mind. If I have pretended until now to know my characters' minds and innermost thoughts, it is because I am writing in (just as I have assumed some of the vocabulary and 'voice' of) a convention universally accepted at the time of my story: that the novelist stands next to God. He may not know all, yet he tries to pretend that he does. (p. 85)

So Fowles builds up the readers' expectations of a certain kind of novel only to violate them; and I suspect that the sense of irritation that this provokes in many readers is not just because they feel 'cheated', or suspect Fowles of writing 'fashionably', but because what is on the surface a disclaimer of power may be read as an exercise of power at the reader's expense.

Certainly we are more aware of the novelist's power in *The French Lieutenant's Woman* than in the Victorian novels that it parodies, precisely because the mechanics of that power are exposed. Moreover, the exercise of power in the creation of a novel is not necessarily confined to the novelist. 'Omniscient' Victorian novelists experienced the tyranny of the reading public – in matters like the treatment of sexuality, a moral stance that required the good to be rewarded, in the necessity for lovable characters with whom readers might identify – more than any other novelists, before or since, because of the practice of serialization. Nowhere was that tyranny exercised more rigorously than over the ending, though in at least two novels of the period (Charlotte Bronte's *Villette* and Dickens's *Great Expectations*, the only Victorian novel that Fowles admits to admiring)[7] there is a degree of ambiguity that allows the reader to 'imagine' a happy ending, while the novelists retain their integrity by suggesting gloomier alternatives which are more appropriate to the preceding narratives.

Fowles uses a double ending not so much to spare the reader while salvaging his principles, but, it seems, to establish his right not to satisfy the expectations that his use of Victorian conventions has raised. The alternative endings are introduced by a discussion on the whole question of closure. Sarah disappears after seducing Charles, and when he finds her after a few years have elapsed, along with the daughter that he fathered, she is far from being in the outcast and dejected state of the stereotyped fallen woman of Victorian fiction. Instead she is a valued member of the Rossetti household. Another important moment in social evolution is isolated as Sarah, the chrysalis of the hysterical neurotic now cast off, emerges as the New Woman, in dress, attitudes and independence; her particular qualities recognized by a community of people who have managed to distance themselves successfully from the social conventions of their time. In the first ending she is reconciled to Charles; in the second – which as Fowles acknowledges, appears to be more 'final' as an ending, simply through placing – they go their separate ways.

Fowles's metafictional interventions expose the reader to the theory of the novel within the novel itself. Since these are often experienced by the reader as intrusive, the question must be raised of whether they serve any purpose beyond establishing the author's credentials as a man of the moment, familiar with the latest theories from across the channel (for there is sometimes a note of patronage in the tone adopted by Fowles towards his English readers). The answer to this must be 'Yes', and that the further purpose of the interventions reveals itself by an analysis of the context in which they occur. The authorial interventions gather momentum as the novel draws towards its climax in the Endicott Family Hotel in Exeter, where Charles discovers that he has deflowered a virgin. Fowles exposes his own manipulation of plot, and discusses the choices open to him, as Sarah is making her preparations for Charles's arrival. Sarah, in attempting to seize control over circumstances, is in a sense becoming the 'author' of her own life. The lies that she tells Charles may be seen as necessary fictions, embodying truths if not conveying facts. Fowles's interventions, discussing the choices available to himself, help to suggest this interpretation of Sarah's behaviour, without imposing it on the reader (other possibilities, held by characters within the novel, remain). Because Sarah's behaviour is presented in a context of discourse about the nature of fiction, her example extends that discourse to include the purpose of fictions (which in certain frames of reference are labelled 'neurotic') in the lives of individuals. Sarah's behaviour has bearing too on what we mean by 'history', Fowles quoting Marx's definition of history as ' "the actions of men" ' (and of women) ' "in pursuit of their ends" ' (p. 398).

The 'ragtime' of the title of the novel by E.L. Doctorow (born in New York City in 1931) refers both to the kind of music developed by black American musicians like Scott Joplin (and the fictional Coalhouse Walker, whose story provides the novel with its central narrative thread), and to the period in American history to which that music belongs. More obliquely, we can find in 'ragtime' a description of Doctorow's technique. In a little over two hundred pages he gathers into his narrative an extraordinary number of 'scraps' (of information, historical incidents, vignettes of historical figures) with which he creates a brightly coloured and intricate pattern of connections, of a kind that is reminiscent of another American art form, the patchwork quilt.

Ragtime, published in 1974, takes as its subject a period of great vitality in American history. It opens in 1902 with the building of a house in New Rochelle by an archetypal WASP family (known simply as Mother, Father, Younger Brother, Little Boy) and ends with the Armistice Day celebrations in 1918, the First World War having effectively marked the end of American isolation from the rest of the world. It was a time when vast personal fortunes were made and converted into art collections; when Henry Ford launched his Model T car, which revolutionized both production methods and consumer expectations; when Peary took his expedition to the North Pole; when Houdini, characterized in *Ragtime* as the last of the innocently perceived mother lovers, was a folk hero, and when Freud, whose theories effectively marked the end of that innocence, visited the United States; when the American film industry was established in California; when labour was unionized but deprived of muscle as the American left was routed; when well-brought-up women discovered both sexuality and practical skills; when black leaders like Booker T. Washington were encouraging irreproachable respectability as the means of advancement for their race.

Against this richly textured historical background, the fictional stories of three families are interwoven; in all three narratives there are casualties and survivors. The even tenor of life for the WASP family is disrupted by the involvement of Father, an amateur explorer, in Peary's expedition to the Pole which is characterized in the telling by a certain pointlessness:

> He [Peary] couldn't find the exact place to say this spot, here, is the North Pole. Nevertheless there was no question that they were there. All the observations together indicated that. (p. 66–7)

Father returns from Pole confused more than enlightened by the experience, to find that the world he left behind has become unfamiliar in his absence. Mother has gained in personal authority, and lost some of her respect for his, after successfully running his fireworks factory. More than that, she has taken advantage of his absence by introducing into the house as a servant a young black woman, Sarah, and the baby whom she tried to kill in a fit of despair.

When the baby's father, a pianist called Coalhouse Walker, comes courting Sarah in a new Model T Ford, Father is further confused, both by his wife's treating the black man as a guest and by Walker's prosperity and self-possession:

> It occurred to Father one day that Coalhouse Walker Jr didn't know he was a Negro. (pp. 122–3)

Running parallel to this narrative is the story of a Jewish immigrant family who, like the WASP family, are unnamed, representative: Tateh, Mama and the Girl in the Pinafore. After a disastrous start in New York, when Tateh casts out his wife, a seamstress, because she has been seduced by her employer, there follows a period of work in a mill in Lawrence, Massachusetts, when Tateh's destiny coincides with a key moment in American history. The strike by the workers in Lawrence for more wages, supported by a children's crusade, is violently crushed, and Tateh begins to dissociate himself from his life-long socialist principles:

> From this moment, perhaps, Tateh began to conceive of his life as separate from the fate of the working class. I hate machines, he said to his daughter. (p. 101)

He is enabled by a marketable skill for which, again, the historical moment has arrived: an artistic talent which takes him from the making of silhouettes to moving picture books to the cinema.

The Coalhouse Walker story, meanwhile, moves in the opposite direction, from near triumph to disaster. Coalhouse, whose success as a musician is crowned by Sarah's agreement to marry him, is challenged on his way home from New Rochelle one Sunday by a group of white firemen who desecrate his Model T Ford: the car which is, for him, the symbol of his achievements in a white man's world, is for them an outrageous presumption. His obsession with justice – the return of his car in its original condition – , intensified when Sarah is killed while intervening on his behalf, leads to a series of terrorist acts: the blowing up of the fire station and the occupation by Coalhouse and his supporters of the Pierpont Morgan Library. After intercessions by Booker T. Washington and Father, the car is returned, cleaned and restored by the firemen's leader, and Coalhouse gives himself up to a firing squad, having allowed time for the escape of his followers.

The involvement of the New Rochelle family in Coalhouse's story goes beyond Mother's continued care of Sarah's baby. Her Younger Brother, still unhappy after an unhappy love affair with the showgirl, Evelyn Nesbit, finds in Coalhouse's obsession with justice a heroic cause in which he can channel his own unhappiness. (This makes him, in the perceptions of the Communist and feminist Emma Goldman, an historical figure who is brought into the narrative to provide a broadly Marxist commentary on events, a typical bourgeois terrorist.) It is Younger Brother's remarkable skill with explosives, acquired in Father's fireworks factory, that provides Coalhouse and his supporters with ammunition. After escaping from the Pierpont Morgan Library, he is killed in the revolutionary struggles in Mexico.

Mother, meanwhile, takes refuge from the turmoil in Atlantic City, with her natural and adoptive sons, and there she meets Tateh and the Girl with the Pinafore. Tateh, who when last seen was prematurely aged by his early experiences in America, has now, in the manner of successful immigrants, re-invented himself. Transformed by success, hair dye and a new name and title – the Baron Ashkenazy – he wins Mother's love. After Father's death on the *Lusitania*, Mother and Tateh marry and set up home in California, with their three children, one WASP, one Jewish, one black.

One of *Ragtime*'s closing images – of the multi-racial family living together in perfect harmony in the Californian sunshine – is worthy of the fast-growing Hollywood that has given Tateh a place in American society. And indeed, with an irony that doubles back on itself, forestalling and inviting criticism of the ending, we are also shown Tateh looking at his family and deciding to use that image of harmonic difference in a film. This ending, however, which leaves unresolved those tensions – between black and white, rich and poor, manufacturers and labourers – which have dominated the narrative, stands in a complex relation to the rest of the novel. On one level it is a calculated betrayal of serious issues in the manner of the American film industry which has, since the period covered by *Ragtime*, played such an important role in shaping America's image of itself. It encompasses two key elements in the American myth – of a multi-racial society, and of the man of talent and diligence who is enabled to shed a troubled past and re-make himself. On another level, the myth of the self-made, self-invented man is, and was at the time when *Ragtime* is set, part of the reality of American society. Moreover, while the form of words used to describe the achieved happiness of this 'representative' family has a fairy-tale quality: 'They felt blessed. Their union was joyful though without issue' (p. 236), the novel as a whole has not shirked from telling the cost of that happiness, in terms of discarded mates, parents destroyed by violence.

Lukacs, in his account of the historical novel, singles out for particular praise those texts of the classical realist period – pre-eminently, Sir Walter Scott's – which show an awareness of historical forces, and of the ways in which these work through individuals. He has praise too for the way that historical figures are used peripherally by

Scott, and other novelists who conform to the principles of historical writing that he established, while the main burden of the narrative is carried by fictional figures. It does not perturb Lukacs that Scott's own personal views were typical of a man of his class and time, since his rendering of history conformed to Marxist orthodoxy.

Doctorow's approach to his material comes close to meeting Lukacs's requirements, in the awareness his narrative shows of larger historical forces, and in the relationship he sets up between historical and fictional figures; while the view of history that emerges in *Ragtime* is consciously Marxist. In the many subsidiary narrative threads in the novel (too numerous for me to give an account of here), wealth is always power, and ruthless towards the lives and aspirations of the poor when vested interests are threatened. Doctorow's account of the strike in Lawrence, and of the children's crusade that was staged to draw public sympathy to the strikers, is deliberately flat and unemotive, but nonetheless leaves us in no doubt about the way the incident should be 'read':

> The mill owners in Lawrence realized that of all the strategems devised by the workers this one, the children's crusade, was the most damaging. If it was allowed to go on, national sentiment would swing to the workingmen and the owners would have to give in. This would mean an increase in wages that would bring some workers up to eight dollars a week. They would get extra pay for overtime and for machine speed-ups. They would get off without punishment for their strike. It was unthinkable. The mill owners knew who were the stewards of civilization and the source of progress and prosperity in the city of Lawrence. For the good of the country and the American democratic system they resolved there would be no more children's crusades. (p. 96)

Where Doctorow differs from early historical novelists – takes, as it were, a postmodernist approach to history – is in the confusions that he sets up between documented historical events and fiction, thereby problematizing the whole process of historical writing. The distinction between known and documented historical figures (Houdini, Henry Ford, Pierpont Morgan) and the representative fictional characters (the WASP and the Jewish immigrant families) is clear enough, though *Ragtime* is so crammed with incidental detail that it would require an exhaustive knowledge of the period to pronounce on the authenticity of each comment or episode attributed to the famous figures who move in and out of the narrative. Moreover, information about documented historical figures is often given in an anecdotal style which throws doubt on their authenticity –

He [Freud] sat in his quiet cozy study in Vienna, glad to be back. He said to Ernest Jones, America is a mistake, a gigantic mistake. (p. 36)

– Doctorow often uses formulae suggestive of orthodox historical writing ('It was widely reported', 'It is known', 'We are not sure of the exact circumstances') (pp. 138, 139, 225) for the narratives involving fictional characters.

The confusion of fiction and history is most evident in the 'Coalhouse Walker' story. Unlike the other fictional characters (Mother, Tateh), Coalhouse and Sarah are named, and historical figures – Pierpont Morgan, Booker T. Washington – are assigned roles in their story. This inevitably creates the possibility that the the 'Coalhouse' story will be read as though it were history. It is certainly given more weight by the historical detail of the context: if it did not actually happen, it could have happened. In fact, as I mentioned in the course of a discussion of D.M. Thomas's *The White Hotel* in the chapter on 'Breakdown', the central narrative in *Ragtime* was not invented by Doctorow but borrowed from the German writer Kleist, who lived at the turn of the eighteenth and nineteenth centuries. Kleist's story of Michael Kohlhass, written during a revolutionary period, uses an historical incident from the early sixteenth century which came to involve the religious 'revolutionary', Martin Luther. Kleist's Kohlhass, and the historical Hans Kohlhaas, challenged with force a system that had denied them justice, in circumstances similar to those described by Doctorow in *Ragtime*. So Doctorow's Coalhouse Walker is a paradigmatic figure, representing all those who challenge an unjust system and, because of their ultimate powerlessness, slide out of the history books.

Midnight's Children by Salman Rushdie (born 1947) is like *Ragtime* in reversing the traditional priorities of historical writing in favour of the crushed private citizen, who is given a central place in the story. But whereas *Ragtime* is a masterpiece of compression, with a flat and understated style generating multiple ironies, *Midnight's Children* is digressive and elaborately wrought, working often through extended metaphor rather than statement. In terms of the European tradition of the novel, *Midnight's Children* has clear links with the first anti-novel, *Tristram Shandy*, to which Rushdie has acknowledged a general indebtedness in his work.[9] Both begin by promising, and then withholding, the birth of the first-person narrator (Saleem Sinai in *Midnight's Children*), whose story is the novel's, before proceeding to expose the difficulty of any beginning, even one so obvious as a birth, by time shifts to uncover circumstances which help to reveal the parti-

cular significance of this birth. By this means the whole process of
story-telling is immediately problematized.

That deviant strand in the European tradition that Rushdie draws
on, however, is, fittingly, only part of the mixed ancestry of a novel
which, in a highly idiosyncratic way, tells the story of India since the
winning of Independence from the British – an event which coincides
with the birth of Saleem in *Midnight's Children*. Rushdie has made
clear his personal fondness for *The Arabian Nights*;[10] and within the
novel Saleem invokes *The Arabian Nights* through discourse on the
properties of the number 1001:

> the number of night, of magic, of alternative realities – a number
> beloved of poets and detested by politicians, for whom all alternative
> versions of the world are threats. (p. 217)

Throughout *Midnight's Children* priority is given to poetic truth
over historical fact. This is validated, if it needs validation, by
reference to the lies told by governments through the news media in
the reporting of events – government reports being an initial stage in
the process of creating historical 'fact'. During the Indo-Pakistani
War,

> on the radio, what destruction, what mayhem! In the first five days of
> the war Voice of Pakistan announced the destruction of more aircraft
> than India had ever possessed; in eight days, All-India Radio massacred
> the Pakistan Army down to, and considerably beyond, the last man.
> (p. 339)

What the reader is given in *Midnight's Children* is an alternative
history of India since Independence – a history built on the premise
that the 1001 babies born within the frontiers of India between
midnight and 1.00 a.m. on 15 August, 1947 (the hour and day of
Independence) were:

> endowed with features, talents or faculties that can only be described as
> miraculous. It was as though. . . . history, arriving at a point of the
> highest significance and promise, had chosen to sow, in that instant,
> the seeds of a future which would genuinely differ from anything the
> world had seen up to that time. (p. 195)

These children – midnight's children – are:

> only partially the offspring of their parents – the children of midnight
> were also the children *of the time*: fathered, you understand, by
> history. It can happen. Especially in a country which is itself a sort of
> dream. (p. 118)

Saleem – the oldest of the children and, as the possessor of extraordinary telepathic powers, the means of bringing them all in touch with each other – is, within the book, the symbol of his country's destiny after Independence. He is also, in his manner of telling history, keeping alive the narrative traditions of his country at a time when India is struggling and, in Saleem's judgement, failing to find her own voice and ethos. The legacy of the British is everywhere, from the skin disease that produces changes in pigmentation –

> It seems that the gargantuan (even heroic) efforts involved in taking over from the British and becoming masters of their own destiny had drained the colour from their cheeks . . . (p. 179)

to the jars of Bovril left in the houses built in Bombay by the Englishman, Methwold, who insists when the houses are transferred to Indian owners at the time of Independence that the contents be preserved, as relics of the colonial period.

This approach to the material – giving metaphorical meaning precedence over common sense, allowing weight to the trivial and absurd in the patterning of events – is everywhere evident in *Midnight's Children*. Family myth is based on metaphor which continues to generate and gather meaning as the novel progresses. Saleem's grandfather, Dr Aziz – named, presumably, in ironic reference to Forster's character in *A Passage to India*, and by that means suggesting and subverting that considerable body of novels about India by English novelists – falls in love with his wife in the course of treating her, as a patient, through a perforated sheet which allows him only fragmented glimpses of her body. He

> had come to think of the perforated sheet as something sacred and magical (p. 27)

but it takes on a significance not envisaged at the time of courtship: of the fragmented and unsatisfactory nature of the relationship between them, sexual and intellectual, which fails to fill the hole left by his loss of faith in Indian culture and in Islam dating from his time in Europe. The sheet subsequently acquires the power of a family curse:

> which doomed by mother to love a man in segments, and which condemned me to see my own life – its meanings, its structures – in fragments also, so that by the time I understood it, it was far too late. (p. 107)

Saleem's sister, Jamila, whose singing voice makes her, as an adolescent girl, a national idol in Pakistan, is seen by her adoring public through a perforated veil which masks her destructive energies.

Although Saleem shares the family fate of fragmentation, signified by the sheet, he is in fact a foundling, and mother, grandfather and sister are not his 'natural' relatives. His personal history opens up a bewildering proliferation of mothers and fathers who reflect the diversity, racial and religious, of the new Indian state. Brought up as the son of Amina and Ahmed Sinai, the latter a prosperous Muslim businessman whose fortunes later flounder, he was swapped at birth by an Anglo-Indian nurse, Catholic by faith, Mary Periera, who hoped by this act to satisfy the revolutionary zeal of her lover, Joseph. (The connotations carried by the names of this further pair of surrogate parents are entirely appropriate, Mary being the only mother left to Saleem by the end of of the novel.) His natural father is the Englishman, Methwold, who built the house where Saleem is brought up, and whose considerable powers of attraction for women are concentrated in his head of hair, which is ceremoniously and symbolically exposed as false during the drinking of the last sundowner before Independence. His natural mother is Vanita, who dies in childbirth, wife of the street entertainer Wee Willie Winkie, and as such part of a marginalized sub-culture. Meanwhile, Saleem's alter ego, Shiva, the displaced natural son of Amina and Ahmed, takes to a career of violence and destruction which eventually wins him high rank in the Indian army.

The ends to which Saleem places his remarkable psychic powers are suggestive – as Shiva's career is in another way – of the squandering of talents and resources in India in the years following Independence:

> Despite the many vital uses to which his abilities could have been put by his impoverished, underdeveloped country, he chose to conceal his talents, frittering them away in inconsequential voyeurism and petty cheating. This behaviour – not, I confess, the behaviour of a hero – was the direct result of a confusion in his mind, which invariably muddled up morality – the desire to do what is right – and popularity – the rather more dubious desire to do what is approved of. (p. 172)

One of the central conceits used in *Midnight's Children* to link Saleem's fate to that of his country is to make him the covert cause of the principal events in India in the years following Independence, thus subverting the realistic conventions of historical writing. A childhood skirmish in which his telepathic powers are brought into play transforms a demonstration about language into a riot:

> In this way I became directly responsible for triggering off the violence which ended with the partition of the state of Bombay, as a result of which the city became the capital of Maharashtra – so at least I was on the winning side. (p. 192)

Saleem is a driving force behind the military coup in Pakistan, and then, by his own account, the hidden cause of the Indo-Pakistani war in which his family, by then resident in Pakistan, perish:

> Let me state this quite unequivocally: it is my firm conviction that the hidden purpose of the Indo-Pakistani war of 1965 was nothing more or less than the elimination of my benighted family from the face of the earth. (p. 338)

This absurd and often comic combination of delusions of grandeur with paranoia serves a number of functions. In a novel which has chosen to give 'alternative versions' of India's history as a calculated affront to politicians, the presence of these qualities in Saleem, the reflector and cause of his country's history, obliquely suggests a similar combination of paranoia and delusions of grandeur among politicians, which is more than confirmed by the behaviour of the 'real' politicians, as judgement on that is implied by the novel. At the same time, the gap opened up between Saleem's perceptions of his own power, and the reader's perception of his actual powerlessness, rather than blocking readerly sympathy, becomes a focus for the pitiful powerlessness of Indians like Saleem in the face of their government's acts.

The Indo-Pakistani War is central, both to Saleem's development as a character, and as a turning-point in the way the reader 'sees' him. Conscripted into the Pakistan army, bereaved by the loss of his family, amnesiac as a result of the fighting, the only part of his body which retains some vestige of his extraordinary gifts is his nose: once vital to his now lost telepathic powers, it is now used by the army for tracking. Saleem takes part in the atrocities at the time of the partition of Bangladesh; but later, in the jungle, he and his companions learn an ancestral wisdom and personal responsibility in place of the blind obedience they have given to the army. His need to distance himself from military power is reinforced when, among a pile of 'enemy' corpses, he discovers his old playmates from the Methwold estate. He returns to India and joins a group of Communist street magicians.

From this point Saleem, still representative of his race, is more unequivocally presented as a victim of repressive government; specifically of the measures introduced by Mrs Gandhi, otherwise known as 'the Widow', who has clearly emerged as a force for evil by the end of the novel. This parallels the shift in writing mode from comic to tragic absurdity. Before joining the street magicians in Delhi, Saleem uncovers, while staying with his uncle, one of his few surviving relatives and an officer in the Civil Service, evidence of a plot to eliminate midnight's children. (The reader has already learned that 420 of the original 1001 died within their first ten years.) In Delhi he crosses paths with two of the surviving midnight's children. Shiva, with whom he was swapped as a baby, is now a major in the Indian army, and his fortunes have risen while Saleem's have been in decline: 'There is nothing like a war for the re-invention of lives . . .' (p. 407). Here the connection between violence and the deprivation of birth-right has larger implications for the whole Indian sub-continent; while Shiva's rapacious sexual appetite, which has allowed him to sire numerous babies in similarly disaffected circumstances, has sinister implications for the future.

One of the babies is born to Parvati-the-witch, another of midnight's children, whom Saleem, now impotent, marries, thus restoring the child, Aadam, to his 'natural' ancestry. Aadam, like his adoptive and natural fathers, is 'handcuffed to history'(p. 420), being born at midnight as the State of Emergency is declared, which is the government's response to being found guilty of electoral malpractice. He is a sickly child, gripped by tuberculosis, his disease:

> not unconnected with the larger, macrocosmic disease, under whose influence the sun had become as pallid and diseased as our son. (p. 422)

Saleem's paranoia and delusions of centrality are acute in the later phases of the novel, as he sees in the acts of a violent and corrupt government the specific intention to destroy him and what belongs to him; but by now they have accumulated significance from the poetic re-telling of thirty years of Indian history. The supernatural gifts of midnight's children, which in the beginning were a magical intrusion into the known facts of history, generating comedy, have acquired meaning as subversive, transformative powers alien to the processes of government because they suggest alternative possibilities. Saleem sees behind the State of Emergency the intention to destroy the remaining midnight's children, and by implication, whatever remains of that potential immanent at the time of Independence. The magicians' ghetto is broken up by government troops using Russian guns, with Shiva in command, and Parvati dies in the course of the raid. Saleem is captured, imprisoned and tortured for the names of other midnight's children. 'Handcuffed to history' as he is, his fate is paradigmatic of that of others during the State of Emergency, and a way of commenting on the situation of countless Indians:

> I was given no reason . . . for my incarceration: but who, of all the thirty thousand or quarter of a million, was told why or wherefore? (p. 434)

By government order, the children of midnight – located by means of Saleem's information – are sterilized and surgically deprived of their magic powers. Thus a hidden purpose for the government steriliza-tion programme – one of the more controversial of Mrs Gandhi's acts – is suggested. All further alternative possibilities are eliminated.

Midnight's Children ends, where it began, in Bombay, with a new party in power after the 1977 election. Saleem has been reunited with Mary Pereira and her sister Alice, who are running a pickles factory where Saleem is working. References to the pickles factory have been made throughout the novel, in the course of many digressions from the main story-line. Mary, the only mother left to Saleem, has taken charge of his, and Shiva's, son. Saleem has a new mistress, Padma, whose energies are directed to the magical restoration of his castrated sexuality. Saleem's own energies have been absorbed in telling the story of midnight's children, whose curse it has been 'to be both masters and victims of their times' (p. 463). For this project, the setting of the pickle factory has had a particular appropriateness:

One day, perhaps, the world may taste the pickles of history. (p. 461)

Midnight's Children is a fine example of magical realism, a mode of writing which has had less impact on British fiction than on fiction in parts of the world less bound by the conventions of realism. It also illustrates the way that postmodernist theory and practice have forced us to reconsider many of the assumptions that we derive from the classical realist novel of the eighteenth and nineteenth centuries, in particular about the suitability of certain kinds of writing for certain kinds of subjects. If there is one area above others where a realist approach might be held sacred, it is in mediating material which is, by common concensus, 'real': recorded historical fact which, in this case, is well within living memory. Yet *Midnight's Children* is both a highly unorthodox account of history, with deliberate errors of fact[11] which are from time to time acknowledged in the text and excused on the grounds of imaginative truth; and highly political, intended to be taken seriously, as it was by Mrs Gandhi, to whom Rushdie subsequently made an apology.

One practical reason suggests itself for a highly imaginative treatment of material which is elsewhere factually recorded: that, when attacked for his views, the writer can then claim to have written a work of the imagination which he never intended to be read as fact. Rushdie has defended himself in this way over the publication of *The Satanic Verses*, a novel which has had much more tragic consequences, for himself and others, and which I shall be discussing in the final chapter:

Literature is where I go to explore the highest and lowest places in human society and in the human spirit, where I hope to find not absolute truth but the truth of the tale, of the imagination and of the heart.[12]

The use of fantasy for political satire is an honourable tradition which includes Swift, among others, but it can hardly be said to eliminate risk for the writer. Swift, and now Rushdie, have paid dearly for what they dared to say.

The appeal to the imagination, which Rushdie is right to use, is not a form of retreat, but a way of identifying the role the writer should take in the world. The justification for Rushdie's approach to historical material in *Midnight's Children* is implicit in the novel itself. I have already quoted that distaste for magic which is attributed to politicians, 'for whom all alternative versions of the world are threats.' Politicians are often successful to the degree that they are able to impose a version of reality with sufficient conviction to gain widespread acceptance. This is not confined to contemporary politics: Swift's subversions of common sense in 'A Modest Proposal' are a way of challenging the English version of the 'reality' of Ireland. It is nonetheless the case that twentieth-century linguistic theory has, in its wider applications, alerted us to the need to 'decode' the statements made by politicians, rather than take them at face value. For example, in the 1980s in Britain under the government of Mrs Thatcher, a supremely successful politician, reverence for something called 'the real world' has become much more widespread, while the struggle for meaning has been largely played out in her terms. In such a climate, as in the more overtly repressive climate of Mrs Gandhi's India, imaginative subversions of politically imposed realities might well be thought the most effective means of dissent.

It seems appropriate to close with what was said by Rushdie in a television interview about *The Satanic Verses*, but which could just as easily have been said of *Midnight's Children*

> One of the things a writer can do is to say: Here is the way in which you're told you're supposed to look at the world, but actually there are also some other ways. Let us never believe that the way in which people in power tell us to look at the world is the only way we can look, because if we do that, then that's a kind of appalling self-censorship.[13]

8

War

Joseph Heller: *Catch-22*
Kurt Vonnegut: *Slaughterhause 5*
Thomas Pynchon: *Gravity's Rainbow*

It is a truism of a certain kind of English criticism – one that restricts itself to writing in English by British writers – that the Second World War failed to generate anything like the volume of imaginative writing that emerged from the trenches of the First World War. As a judgement, it overlooks the fact that novels about World War II, including the three that I shall discuss in this chapter, have been among the most innovative and influential in American writing in the period since 1945. Nonetheless, a comparison between the responses given by creative writers to the two world wars is instructive; as later will be a comparison between British and American responses to the Second World War.

For the West, the two world wars have been the most devastating events of the twentieth century; but whereas the war against Hitler was one that had to be fought, the military tactics employed by the opposing generals in the First World War, and the imbalance between the colossal military casualties and the objectives actually achieved by the fighting, have in the judgement of history left neither side with any credit. The real division, in our perceptions of the First World War, is not between right and wrong, aggressors and defenders, but between those from both sides who fought in the trenches and those who did not. The First World War produced, not just the effective destruction of a generation of young men, but a profound division in experience between military and civilian. Robert Graves and Siegfried Sassoon, in autobiographical accounts published more than ten years later (*Goodbye to all That* in 1929 and *Memoirs of an Infantry Officer* in 1930), record both the total ignorance of the British public of the reality of trench warfare, and an accompanying unwillingness to have that ignorance shaken. The growing outrage of those fighting in the trenches found expression in a flood of poetry. And while it is true to say that potentially major poets like Owen and Rosenberg died in the war before their full potential was realized, it is also likely that the pressure of that experience made poets of men who might not have felt the need for that kind of expression in other circumstances.

The dominance of poetry as a medium of expression during the First World War is appropriate, if for no other reasons than its brevity and concentration, which give much First World War poetry the status of dispatches from the trenches – but alternative dispatches which bypassed the military and civil propaganda machines. This brings me to a major difference between the writing that emerged from the First World War and both those novels about the Second World War that I shall be discussing and the early modernist work which was being produced at the time of the First World War itself. Those combatants of the First World War who wrote about their experiences overwhelmingly chose poetry as a means of expression, though there were prose works which emerged some years after the event; and poetry traditionally gives priority to the word over the world, a priority which, in most prose, is reversed. One of the principal characteristics of First World War poetry, however, is an insistent fixing of the relationship between word and thing; the use of language to draw attention, not to itself, but to the point of reference – the physical reality of the trenches and of the dead and maimed. And this in itself was a reaction against the abuse of language in propaganda which kept the reality of trench warfare from the civilian population. At a time when government machinery was using the rhetoric of war to destabilize the relationship between word and thing, the poets used language to mediate reality. Moreover, those writers, like Graves and Sassoon, who later produced prose works on the subject, turned their experiences into autobiography, not fiction.

The three American novels about the Second World War that I have selected for discussion – Heller's *Catch-22*, Vonnegut's *Slaughterhouse 5* and Pynchon's *Gravity's Rainbow* – all, in their different ways, reject realism as a response to war. Yet they have in common with the poetry of the First World War an acute sense of a mechanistic 'other', variously located by the novels in the military, intelligence, government and industrial hierarchies, which devalues and debases both the individual and language. Indeed, *Catch-22* in particular shows a keen awareness of the ways in which the devaluing of language assists the devaluing of the individual, as in the absurd predicament of the medical officer, Doc Daneeka, who is officially deemed dead because his name is included on the list of personnel in a plane that is lost in combat, and as a result finds that his physical presence is refused acknowledgement by the military hierarchy. Bureaucracy condemns him to a death in life. The novel's central character, Yossarian, who is aware of the manic rigidity in the bureaucratic use of language, reacts in a way that is highly suggestive of the different responses given to broadly similar phenomena by, on the one hand, the First World War poets, and on the other, these particular American novelists of the Second World War. Having failed to persuade anyone in authority of the absurdity of prevailing practices, Yossarian's strategy is to outwit the machine, and one of his games is lexigraphical: as censoring officer he signs all documents 'Washington Irvine' in order to generate confusion.

There is no one answer as to why the First World War should have produced an emphatic form of poetic realism, against the grain of early modernist innovation, while the response of these American novelists to phenomena which they perceived to be broadly similar (the British novels to emerge from the Second World War indicate, as we shall see, a different set of perceptions) was a rejection of realism just as emphatic. One possibility worth pursuing, however, emerges from a comparison between the two world wars in *Gravity's Rainbow* where, in keeping with a kind of patterning which runs through the novel, the differences are perceived in terms of different kinds of sexuality:

> an English class was being decimated, the ones who'd volunteered were dying for those who'd known something and hadn't, and despite it all, despite knowing, some of them, of the betrayal, while Europe died meanly in its own wastes, men loved. But the life-cry of that love has long since hissed away into no more than this idle and bitchy faggotry. In this latest War, death was no enemy, but a collaborator. Homosexuality in high places is just a carnal afterthought now, and the real and only fucking is done on paper. . . . (p. 616)

The poets of the First World War may have had difficulty in gaining acceptance by non-combatants for their version of the reality of trench warfare, but the poems themselves suggest that the sense of a distinct and shared reality – albeit one that was spurned by those who remained at home – created bonds of fellowship which crossed fighting lines. In the case of these American novels of the Second World War, however, the sinister and manipulative hierarchy which controls the war, especially in *Gravity's Rainbow* and *Catch-22*, has a corrosive effect on all human warmth and relationships, though representations of camaraderie are not excluded. In the paranoid manner of postmodernist writing, the destructive forces acquire a sinister character by being both harder to locate and closer to hand than in the poetry of the First World War.

Indeed, one of the principal differences between these American fictions about the war, and major British novels to have emerged from the Second World War – like Evelyn Waugh's *Sword of Honour* Trilogy and *The Valley of Bones*, *The Soldier's Art* and *The Military Philosophers* in Anthony Powell's 'Dance to the Music of Time' sequence – is that the latter lack that sense of an enemy within, debasing value. And that fundamental stability is an important precondition of the broadly realist mode in which Waugh and Powell write. Despite the potential grimness of their subject matter, and the sombreness of much of their writing, their novels remain within the dominant English tradition of 'comedy of manners'.

There are two further points in particular which emerge from a comparison between the British and American fictional responses to the Second World War. The first is that the British War novelists avoid detailed and explicit descriptions of destruction, whether of individuals or of masses, though bonbing raids often feature as background to the emotional lives of characters, as they do in Lehmann's *The Echoing Grove* and in Graham Greene's *The End of the Affair*. Since *Moby Dick* there has been a tradition in American fiction of writing about physical and material reality, and this is evident in the response given by American novelists to the experience of war. In *Catch-22* the death of the young bombardier Snowden, and the bombing of Dresden in *Slaughterhouse 5*, are at the centre of the novels, profoundly destabilizing experiences both for the characters and for readers, isolated in the 'telling' from the kind of moral framing (a certainty about the issues of war) which might soften the impact.

This brings me to the second point of difference – that in these American novels the moral imperatives of the Second World War are left deliberately unclear. In *Catch-22* the naivety of the American soldiers about the issues on which they are risking their lives is comically suggested by the values they are defending:

> The hot dog, the Brooklyn Dodgers, Mom's apple pie. (p. 15)

If this, from a European perspective, looks like reprehensible ignorance, it should be remembered that the Americans depicted in these novels are caught up in a war in Europe without themselves having been threatened from Europe.

Blicero, a sado-masochistic SS officer in *Gravity's Rainbow*, describes Europe as having moved – 'into obsession, addiction, away from all the savage innocences' (p. 722). Europe was given America as 'a way of returning. But Europe refused it' (p. 722). Instead Europe colonized America with its own degeneracy, until now 'American Death has come to occupy Europe' (p. 722). The persistent ambiguity of Pynchon's approach does not allow us to dismiss theories which come from a morally dubious source; and indeed one possible reading of *Gravity's Rainbow* is as a postmodernist reanimation of a dominant theme of earlier American novels like Henry James's – of the innocent American disorientated among the corruptions of an older,

European civilization. It is a theme that Vonnegut, too, makes play with in *Slaughterhouse 5*. The city of Dresden is described as it appeared to a group of American prisoners-of-war who are taken there by train shortly before the bombing:

> The boxcar doors were opened, and the doorways framed the loveliest city that most of the Americans had ever seen. The skyline was intricate and voluptuous and enchanted and absurd. It looked like a Sunday school picture of Heaven to Billy Pilgrim. (p. 100)

When the prisoners-of-war are released after the bombing, the city, so ravishing to the senses as to have appeared scarcely real, has been reduced to a heap of rubble.

The central character in *Gravity's Rainbow*, Slothrop, is an American who moves from London through newly liberated Europe during the last year of the war. His ancestor, William Slothrop, was a Puritan who crossed the Atlantic in the seventeenth century in defence of the Word. Considerable play is made in the novel with breaches and horizons, both metaphorically – the only truly tender love affair is seen by its participants as:

> the breaking of the wave. Suddenly there was a beach, the unpredict-able . . . new life. Past and future stopped at the beach . . . (p. 126)

and as a site for significant meetings. A sunset on the French Riviera is described as:

> a 19th-century wilderness sunset, a few of which got set down, approximated, on canvas, landscapes of the American West by artists nobody ever heard of, when the land was still free and the eye innocent, and the presence of the Creator much more direct. Here it thunders now over the Mediterranean, high and lonely, this anachronism in primal red, in yellow purer than can be found anywhere today, a purity begging to be polluted . . . of course Empire took its way westward, what other way was there but into those virgin landscapes to penetrate and to foul? (p. 214)

There is a persistent metaphorical association in *Gravity's Rainbow* of the frontier ideal with the primitive and pure and of Europe with pollution and corruption. That corruption is in part a feature of complexity, further compounded by war. Slothrop, who has returned to the Europe of his ancestors, seeks for meaning among the devasta-tion – a Puritan quest which is overlaid by a postmodernist awareness of the slipperiness of the text itself. In London:

> Ruins he goes daily to look in are each a sermon on vanity. That he finds, as weeks wear on, no least fragment of any rocket, preaches how indivisible is the act of death . . . Slothrop's Progress: London the

secular city instructs him: turn any corner and he can find himself
inside a parable. (p. 25)

Amidst the devastation of Hamburg, the question is whether this is
'The Real Text'. The task is 'decoding the Text, thus coding,
recoding, redecoding the holy Text . . .' (pp. 520–1).

Gravity's Rainbow in particular yields clues, if not answers, to the
perceived need of these American novelists to adopt a rigorously anti-
realist approach to material which, for the poets of the First World
War, demanded an emphatic poetic realism, and which the British
novelists of the Second World War did not see as requiring radical
modification of traditional English realism. There is a further point
about American fiction throughout its history, excellently made by
Tony Tanner in *City of Words: A Study of American Fiction in the
Mid-Twentieth Century*:

> My point is that American writers seem from the first to have felt how
> tenuous, arbitrary, and even illusory, are the verbal constructs which
> men call descriptions of reality. Again speaking of a matter of degree,
> the European writer usually seems to have felt more firmly embedded
> in his given environment than his American counterpart; to have been
> more sure of his language and his society, using the former to speak
> about the latter with more confidence and insight even if he feels
> alienated from the prevailing structures. If anything, it is the instability
> of language and society which has more often made itself felt to the
> American writer.[1]

If American writers have from the beginning shown an awareness of
the instability of language and society, then this awareness can only be
more acute in American fictions about Europe; and Europe at a time
when not only society, but the visible, material world itself was at its
most unstable.

Joseph Heller (born 1923) served as a bombardier during the Mediterranean campaign. His first novel, *Catch-22*, is set in Italy on a US Air
Force base and must, one supposes, draw on his own wartime experiences. His own military background certainly gave the novel an extra
piquancy of authority which contributed to its status among the
young in the 1960s. *Catch-22*, which employs a highly elaborate
narrative technique, took Heller eight years to write. It was published
in 1961 and shortly after became a cult novel for a younger generation
of Americans – those who felt their lives threatened by their government's involvement in Vietnam. *Catch-22* was therefore one of the
key subversive texts of the 1960s, a major influence on that revolution
in social attitudes (since reversed) which characterized the decade.

Although the two conflicts – the Second World War and the war in

Vietnam – were markedly different in cause and in the military tactics deployed, Heller's novel forms a bridge between the two by focusing not on issues, but on the absurdities perpetuated by the military machine. *Catch-22* is anyway set in the latter stages of the Second World War, when the defeat of Hitler is assumed by the characters to be certain, so that the justice of the eventual rejection of military authority at the end of the novel need not be argued.

On first reading, *Catch-22* is deeply confusing, but the form is designed to mimic the confusions experienced by the participants in the war: the labyrinthine form being in itself a reflection of military bureaucracy. Each short chapter carries the name of a 'character' (I shall deal later with the modified way in which that term must be used of *Catch-22*), or, more rarely, an event. This attention to individuals – which can include their previous history and eventual destiny in the war – allows for considerable fluidity in regard to time, so that even repeated readings may not yield up to the reader a stable chronological time sequence lurking behind the events as they are presented in the narrative. One of the effects of this is to draw the reader into the experience of the combatant, for whom 'war'time lies outside 'normal' time. The disruption of time further disrupts the chain of cause and effect on which realist fiction is so reliant for plot, and which anyway is repeatedly outraged within the novel by the workings of military bureaucracy. Most important, perhaps, in the overall design of the novel, it allows the narrative to circle round the key experience of the central character, Yossarian, which accumulates further tantalizing detail with each mention: that is, the death of the young gunner, Snowden, on a combat mission, which is witnessed by Yossarian although its significance for him is not fully stated until the death is described in detail in the novel's closing stages.

Snowden's death, although antedating most of the narrative events, becomes, through the device of deferred 'telling', the climax of a series of deaths in the novel's final quarter, of characters whose fortunes we have followed; and in these closing sequences *Catch-22* makes the transition from comedy of the absurd towards tragedy of the absurd. (This is a development that we have already noticed in *Midnight's Children* and which may be seen as a feature of certain kinds of postmodernist fiction.) The comedy – of a very grim order – arises from the way the base, and beyond that, the whole American operation, is run by those in authority – a form of management which outrages all but its own logic. The 'Catch-22' of the title is revealed to Yossarian by the base's medical officer, Doc Daneeka, when Yossarian has asked to be grounded because he is crazy:

> There was only one catch and that was Catch-22, which specified that
> a concern for one's own safety in the face of dangers that were real and

> immediate was the process of a rational mind. Orr was crazy and could
> be grounded. All he had to do was ask; and as soon as he did, he would
> no longer be crazy and would have to fly more missions. (p. 54)

Yossarian's wish to be grounded is driven both by a heightened fear
of death in the wake of Snowden's death, and by a sense of injustice.
The new base commander, Colonel Cathcart, keeps raising the
number of missions that his men are required to fly in order to gain the
favourable attention of his own superiors. Cathcart's quest for
advancement is such that, in the course of the novel, the usual priorities are overturned to the point where the war has become a means
serving the end of his own career. He considers another dangerous
bombing mission over Avignon (where Snowden was killed) because
it will provide him with the opportunity of writing a record number of
letters of condolence, when he can be photographed for the Christmas
issue of *The Saturday Evening Post*. Such is his single-mindedness that
all human impulses have atrophied:

> the colonel was certainly not going to waste his time and energy making
> love to beautiful women unless there was something in it for him.
> (p. 226)

The impoverishing effect of the military machine on personality is
suggested in the mode of characterization. Heller employs caricature,
a technique which elevates form over substance in the manner of the
military machine itself. Considerations of form govern every aspect of
army life. So the unfortunate Major Major (Christian and surname) is
promoted to the rank of 'major' (where he becomes isolated and
unhappy) because the computer cannot distinguish between rank and
name. Bombing raids are organized with a view to the formation that
will appear in aerial photographs. By the end of the novel the entire
theatre of operations is under the command of General Scheisskopf
whose passion is the military parade. He is only deterred from
achieving perfect marching order, tantalizingly possible if metal pegs
are inserted into his mens' thighs and then linked to the wrists by
strands of copper wire allowing three inches of play, because 'good
copper wire was hard to come by in wartime' (p. 84). *Catch-22*'s play
with concepts of form and substance is at its most bizarre in the
symbolic role assigned in the novel to the Soldier in White, a fellow
patient of Yossarian's during one of the latter's frequent hospital
stays. Completely encased in plaster, the only sign of life he gives is to
register a temperature, until the day Nurse Cramer sticks a thermo-
meter into a hole in the plaster and declares him dead. The unease
occasioned by his presence in the ward turns to hysteria when, at a
later date, a similarly de-personalized body appears and is assumed by
the patients to be the same Soldier in White, mysteriously resurrected:

It was, indeed, the same man. He had lost a few inches and added some weight, but Yossarian remembered him instantly by the two stiff arms and the two stiff, thick, useless legs all drawn upward into the air almost perpendicularly by the taut ropes and the long lead weights suspended from pulleys over him and by the frayed black hole in the bandages over his mouth. He had, in fact, hardly changed at all. . . . Yossarian would recognize him anywhere. He wondered who he was. (p. 387)

The inversion of common sense which is a feature of the prose throughout the novel – a reflection both of the flouting of reason by the military authorities and of the subversive strategies needed to challenge that authority – suggests here the tragic absurdity of the human condition when reduced to barely living matter. The two soldiers in white have lost individual identity, and the particular fear of death that they inspire among their fellow soldiers is of the loss of a conscious and recognizable self. They are characterized only by white, the colour, or pallor, of death; and this forms a symbolic and linguistic link with Snowden, the gunner who 'had frozen to death after spilling his secret to Yossarian in the back of the plane' (p. 180). That secret is finally 'spilled' to the reader fifteen pages before the novel's close. The description of Snowden's death is, in Tony Tanner's words: 'detailed and appalling, a scene that can only be fully looked at once'.[2] Yossarian, who had failed to notice Snowden's fatal wound in treating a minor one, can only scream at the revelation:

Here was God's plenty, all right, he thought bitterly as he stared – liver, lungs, kidneys, ribs, stomach and the bits of stewed tomatoes Snowden had eaten that day for lunch. . . . It was easy to read the message in his entrails. Man was matter, that was Snowden's secret. . . . The spirit gone, man is garbage. That was Snowden's secret. Ripeness was all. (p. 464)

This confrontation with human matter pulls the novel into particularly sharp focus. The rigid rules and disciplines of army life act as a barrier against awareness of this central fact of the human condition, especially in the case of those senior officers, non-combatants to a man, who make the rules and enforce the discipline. At the same time, however, their imaginative failure to 'see' what Yossarian has seen (the quotation from *King Lear*[3] in the full description of Snowden's death is apposite here) is in part responsible for the reduction of man to matter on the unnecessary missions that they authorize. It is Yossarian's own confrontation with Snowden's secret that sharpens his insistence on personal survival, and at the end of the novel, having exhausted every means available to expose Colonel Cathcart's injustice, he is on the point of deserting for Sweden.

The morality of the ending has been questioned, even by critics like Tony Tanner, whose response is generally favourable. This, after all, was a war which had to be fought, and it is impossible to imagine a British realist account of the war adopting such a position. Heller goes out of his way, however, to make the conduct of the military authorities less comically absurd and more sinister as the novel draws to its conclusion. Dissidents are treated with a new harshness – the chaplain is court-martialled, Yossarian's friend Dunbar disappears – and Yossarian, who is offered a deal to silence him, learns that, once complete, the terms of the agreement will be set aside and he will be court-martialled anyway to avoid disgracing Colonel Cathcart:

> 'it would be for the good of the country to have you found guilty and put in prison, even though you are innocent.' (p. 467)

Among the deepeningly sinister elements is one that I have yet to touch on – the role of the supplies officer, Milo Minderbinder, which carries implications that are also explored by Thomas Pynchon in *Gravity's Rainbow*. Playing on the senior officers' craving for fresh food, he acquires the use of military aircraft to establish what becomes a business empire spanning the Mediterranean. It is known as the Syndicate, the title suggesting collective benefit, but Milo's business practices are so arcane and mysterious – for example, buying eggs that he has already sold to the Syndicate at an apparent loss – that they are allowed to go unquestioned. Milo becomes a law unto himself and the Syndicate a kind of sacred cow, not only because of the *haute cuisine* that he takes care to supply while his supremacy is being established, but because he invokes the American god of free enterprise when challenged:

> Their alternative – there was an alternative, of course, since Milo detested coercion and was a vocal champion of freedom of choice – was to starve. (p. 391)

Protected by a principle higher than the war itself, he leaves those on combat missions without parachutes, morphine and carbon dioxide cylinders for their life jackets because these items have more value as trading commodities than as life-saving equipment. Recognizing that trade knows no boundaries, even those of war, he strikes a deal with the Germans to bomb his own camp's airstrip with American planes, charging the Germans costs plus 6 per cent; and then sells the Germans ball bearings to maintain the balance of power. The licence allowed him by Colonel Cathcart reaches its ultimate point of absurdity when other men are charged to fly combat missions on his behalf, such decorations as are awarded for their valour going to him: profit is no longer enough, he craves glory too, but not at the cost of risking his own life. Even that aspect of Milo which seems most purely comic, the extraordinary flexibility of identity which allows him universal access (he becomes Mayor of Sicily, Assistant Governor General of Malta, Caliph of Baghdad, in addition to god of rain, rice and corn in more backward regions) has sinister undertones, in suggesting how difficult it it to locate the ultimate source of corporate power, which assumes protective local colouring from one country to another. This is a major theme in *Gravity's Rainbow*.

Slaughterhouse 5 (1969), draws on its author's, Kurt Vonnegut's, own wartime experience as prisoner-of-war in Dresden at the time of the city's bombing, but the connection is more overt than in *Catch-22*. In the opening chapter, Vonnegut explains his own role in the events described in the novel – 'All this happened, more or less. The war parts, anyway, are pretty much true' (p. 9) – before disclosing the difficulties that he encountered in assimilating, and then writing about, an experience that he always intended turning into fiction. He describes a recent visit that he made to Dresden with an old army friend, O'Hare, whose wife is one of the dedicatees of the novel, the other being the taxi driver that he met on that same visit. By reporting a conversation about his work with a friend, he both prepares the reader for the kind of war novel that he has written and admits the futility of such gestures.

> 'Is it an anti-war book?'
> 'Yes,' I said. 'I guess.'
> 'You know what I say to people when I hear they're writing anti-war books?'
> 'No. What *do* you say, Harrison Starr?'
> 'I say, "Why don't you write an anti-*glacier* book instead?"'
> What he meant, of course, was that there would always be wars, that they were as easy to stop as glaciers. I believe that too. (p. 10)

The candour of Vonnegut's approach, together with the naivety of his style, mark him out as a novelist working in quite a different postmodernist mode from Heller in *Catch-22*. Nonetheless, his ingenuousness, while convincing, is part of the crafting of the novel. His opening chapter is not so much a preface in the manner of, say, Henry James, which discloses the source material for an ensuing novel which has a separate identity, but is part of the novel itself. Vonnegut appears himself at events in the novel, mingling with fictional characters like his 'hero', Billy Pilgrim; uses as a character in the novel Edgar Derby, who is part of his own recollections of the war, without apparently changing the name to mark Derby's passage from 'fact' to 'fiction'; and continues to expose the processes of his own fiction late into the novel:

> There are almost no characters in this story, and almost no dramatic confrontations, because most of the people in it are so sick and so much the listless playthings of enormous forces. One of the main effects of war, after all, is that people are discouraged from being characters. But old Derby was a character now. (p. 110)

The insistent and repeated breaking of the fictional frame, while used elsewhere in Vonnegut's work, serves the special purpose here of suggesting that the experience of the Dresden bombing defies the process of fictional transformation. In the same way, the restraint of the language implies that language itself lacks the resources to deal with such events. The omnipresent authorial voice – benign, decent, accepting, despairing – registers the response of hapless and power-less humanity when confronted with such catastrophes.

Vonnegut's 'hero', Billy Pilgrim, who as prisoner-of-war billeted in an animal slaughterhouse (Slaughterhouse 5), survives the bombing of Dresden to see what 'looked like a Sunday School picture of Heaven' (p. 100) transformed into a landscape which resembles the surface of the moon, is, as his name suggests, representative of suffering humanity. His life is punctuated by random acts of violence. Before Dresden his father is killed in a hunting accident; later in middle age he survives a plane crash, but his wife is killed by exhaust fumes driving to see him in hospital. He meets his own death at the hands of an assassin: a fellow war veteran avenging an imagined wrong done to yet another fellow soldier. The circumstances of his own death match the pointlessness of the bombing of Dresden. Before being taken there as prisoners, the Americans are told by British prisoners-of-war that they will be safe in Dresden because it 'is an open city. It is undefended, and contains no war industries or troop concentrations of any importance' (p. 99).

Billy's only defence against what he cannot help is to establish a private means of escape – to the planet Tralfmadore, whose inhabi-tants, Billy claims, captured him, just as he was captured by the Germans. Tralfmadore, however, is a wholly pleasurable site of captivity, with a particular philosophy of its own which the Tralfmadorians impart to Billy. What distinguishes the planet is that time has a fourth dimension. Every moment is recoverable, and this is reflected in Tralfmadorian literature, which is not constrained by linear narrative: 'There is no beginning, no middle, no end, no suspense, no moral, no causes, no effects' (p. 63). The pleasure of the text is in: 'the depths of many marvellous moments seen all at one time' (p. 63). Linear narrative, however, is an effect rather than a cause, and Tralfmadorians live in cheerful innocence of other laws which govern life on earth. Billy is told that "'Only on Earth is there any talk of free will'"(p. 61). And without the concept of free will there is no guilt.

It is easier to assess the role of Tralfmadore within the overall structure of *Slaughterhouse 5* than it is to decide what we as readers are to make of the insights that Billy acquires there. Billy's fantasy life, couched in the mode of science fiction, is a further rejection of realist fiction, though of quite a different order from the way the events at Dresden are presented. In retreating to Tralfmadore, Billy enters the world of Vonnegut's earlier fictions, the planet having first made an appearance in Vonnegut's second novel, *The Sirens of Titan*, published in 1959. Billy is introduced to science fiction immediately after the war, when he is in hospital recovering from a nervous breakdown, by a fellow patient, Eliot Rosewater; and in particular, to the work of Kilgore Trout. (Both Rosewater and Trout are characters in other Vonnegut novels.) The part that science fiction plays in Billy's and Rosewater's recovery is in helping them 'to re-invent themselves and their universe' (p. 70).

Billy's retreat into fantasy from the horrors of war makes perfect psychological sense: what else is the individual to do with what cannot be helped? The justification of science fiction as a genre – that imaginative transformation and re-inventions offer the possibility of change in our turbulent century – is also sustainable. But the principal lesson of Tralfmadore – that since everything is determined, conscience and guilt are redundant – presents similar problems, in the context of the Second World War, to Yossarian's desertion from the Air Force at the end of *Catch-22*.

The irony is that Billy, who is indeed guiltless, remains subject to nervous breakdowns and fits of uncontrollable weeping; whereas the one representative in the novel of the military hierarchy – a military historian, Rumfoord, who shares a hospital ward with Billy after the latter's air accident – shows the same kind of indifference to human value as the figures of authority in *Catch-22*. Rumfoord feels that Billy, his fellow patient, should be left to die:

> Rumfoord was thinking in a military manner: that an inconvenient person, one whose death he wished for very much, for practical reasons, was suffering from a repulsive disease. (p. 128)

Rumfoord, twenty-odd years after the event, is writing about Dresden, but finds it difficult to believe that Billy, who was there, has much of any substance to say about it. As a historian he admits that earlier accounts of World War II have been secretive about Dresden, but justifies the secrecy on the grounds that "'a lot of bleeding hearts

. . . might not think it was such a wonderful thing to do"' (p. 127).

Vonnegut approaches this event – one of the worst and least known of the atrocities committed by the Allies in World War II – through what are explicitly his own memories; through a fictionalized version of his own experience, with Billy at the centre; through science-fiction fantasy, references to his own earlier fictions and quotations from factual accounts of this and other wars. He gives none of these approaches priority over the others. His random choice of climax – the shooting of a fellow prisoner, Edgar Derby, by the American military for stealing a teapot from the ruins of the bombed city – features in both his own memories and the fictionalized version of them. As a climax, it makes its own point about the absurdities of military discipline, and just as importantly, exposes the whole process of selection and emphasis in any kind of writing.

Although Vonnegut steers well clear of explicit moralizing, the role he assigns to Rumfoord in *Slaughterhouse 5* implies a moral frame, a chain of cause and effect, though the vision of the Tralfmadorians, which Billy tries to maintain in his own life, may be the only tolerable one for those whom Billy represents, who are caught up in events over which they have no control. There is an emphasis on vision throughout the novel. Billy works after the war as an optometrist, correcting people's sight; the Tralfmadorians offer a new perspective on time. Vonnegut, in finally writing a novel about an event which had haunted him, and which those responsible had shrouded in secrecy, had set himself the task of extending the perceptions of his readers.

Thomas Pynchon in *Gravity's Rainbow* (1973) explores new modes of perception which release possible alternative meanings and proliferating systems of connection, but it is impossible to overstate the difficulties placed in the way of readers in pursuit of those perceptions. Brian McHale in *Postmodernist Fiction* describes *Gravity's Rainbow* as 'one of the paradigmatic texts of postmodernist writing, literally an anthology of postmodernist themes and devices.'[4] It is encyclopaedic in the manner of *Ulysses* or *Moby Dick*, displaying a formidable range of learning which includes mathematics, engineering, chemistry, Puritan theology, musical theory and every branch of popular culture. Pynchon's grasp of highly specialized (and for many 'lay' readers, if one may use such a term of fiction, arcane) areas of knowledge, while intimidating, exposes the reader to the truth, only recently acknowledged by novelists, that these are among the forces that shape and govern our lives and therefore have a place in serious fiction. Since the novel is the least clearly defined of the literary genres, and the most accommodating to non-'literary' material, we are seeing the emergence now, particularly in the United

States, of the polyglot novelist, prepared to include scientific and technological material in a work of fiction.

This is easily the largest of the novels that I have included for discussion. According to Tony Tanner, who has presumably counted, there are over 400 characters, or: 'we should perhaps say "names", since the ontological status of the figures that drift and stream across the pages is radically uncertain.'[5] The novel opens in London in the closing stages of the war, moves to Holland, France, Switzerland and then a Germany shattered by defeat; but the ontological status of the 'real' places named is as uncertain as that of the characters. London during the final bombing raids of the war is described as 'all theatre', 'a spectacle: the fall of a crystal palace' (p. 3); and what reads like metaphor at that point arguably takes on a different status by the end of the novel, when the reader becomes part of a cinema audience waiting to see (or experience?) the rocket fall. Considerable use is made throughout of cinematic technique and notation, while the boundaries separating cinema from 'life' are undermined at a number of points. One character, Pokler, who works on the V2 rockets in Germany, fathers a daughter, Ilse, after being sexually roused by a film. Ilse is later interned in a concentration camp, and the possibility is explored that the daughter who is allowed out on annual visits to her father is a kind of cinematic creation of the powers who employ him and have incarcerated her: 'the moving image of a daughter, flashing him only these summertime frames of her, leaving it to him to build the illusion of a single child. . .' (p. 422). At the same time, Ilse may be being 'played' by Bianca, the daughter of the actress, Margharita Eardmann, whose cinematic image first aroused Pokler.

Those in the War Zone of occupied Germany – which is described as swarming with refugees and displaced persons – have a particularly indeterminate ontological status:

> Ghosts used to be either likenesses of the dead or wraiths of the living. But here in the Zone categories have been blurred badly. The status of the name you miss, love, and search for now has grown ambiguous and remote, but this is even more than the bureaucracy of mass absence – some still live, some have died, but many, many have forgotten which they are. Their likenesses will not serve. Down here are only wrappings left in the light, in the dark: images of the Uncertainty (p. 303)

The chaos created by the war is of course the justification for the mode of presentation. The text's own self-defence is that 'Nobody ever said a day has to be juggled into any kind of sense at day's end' (p. 204). War intensifies the truth of this general proposition. *Gravity's Rainbow* makes great play with the phrase, 'State of

War' – a separate mode of being with its own values and its own dynamic – and with the word 'Zone'. Wars are fought over boundaries and frontiers which are then re-made. It explores, as has already been noted, the imaginative possibilities of horizons – new worlds of being which, once imagined by the mind, may be lived. So *Gravity's Rainbow* takes the reader through a kind of collage of theatre, dream sequence, fantasy, historical event, never alerting us when boundaries are crossed. This uncharted voyage of discovery reproduces both the fragmentation of war and the ability of the mind to create new horizens.

Almost any statement that one makes about *Gravity's Rainbow* demands to be problematized. The central character (to the extent that the novel has either characters or a centre) is the American Slothrop, who is in London during the final bombardment of the city by the V2 rockets. The particular fear provoked by the rocket is because 'It travels faster than the speed of sound. The first news you get of it is the blast. Then, if you're still around, you hear the sound of it coming in' (p. 7). In the course of the novel, the rocket's apparent defiance of natural law – which can be taken as a measure of human achievement – is seen as the key to its power to generate excitement. Pokler, who works on the rocket, sees in it the means of possible transcendency: 'in something like this extinction he could be free of his loneliness and failure' (p. 406). Mankind, which is bound by gravity, creates in the arc of the rocket its own rainbow:

> This ascent will be betrayed to Gravity. But the Rocket engine, the deep cry of combustion that jars the soul, promises escape. The victim, in bondage to falling, rises on a promise, a prophecy, of Escape. (p. 758)

The rocket is also phallic, not just in shape, but because of the materials used in its manufacture, in particular Imipolex G: 'The first plastic that is actually *erectile*' (p. 699). This brings us to Slothrop's special relationship with the rocket. His movements in London are being monitored by the British Intelligence Service because his numerous sexual encounters, scattered about the city, anticipate where the rockets will fall. The link between sexuality, with its potential for generating life, on the one hand, and the rocket, built only for destruction, on the other, is a highly suggestive one which is repeatedly explored throughout the novel.

The struggle for meaning within the intelligence services over Slothrop polarizes between Roger Mexico, a young statistician whose distribution maps for the rockets and for Slothrop's sexual activity coincide, but who nonetheless sees the distribution of both as random and the coincidence between the two as no more than that; and the Pavlovian behaviourist Pointsman, for whom:

'the ideal, the end we all struggle toward in science, is the true
mechanical explanation. . . . No effect without cause, and a clear train
of linkages.' (p. 89)

The antipathy between the two men goes beyond professional
disagreement:

The young statistician is devoted to number and to method, not table-
rapping or wishful thinking. But in the domain of zero to one, not-
something to something, Pointsman can only possess the zero and the
one. He cannot, like Mexico, survive any place in between. (p. 55)

In *The Crying of Lot 49*, as well as here in *Gravity's Rainbow*,
Pynchon invests in that ability, possessed by Mexico, to 'survive' in a
place 'in between' zero and one, a willingness to entertain alternative
meanings, versions of reality other than the mechanical. The only
passages in the novel which communicate states of joy and delight
concern Roger's love for Jessica, to whom he willingly surrenders a
sense of self ('there has been no way to tell which of them is which
. . .') (p. 38) and with whom he experiences something which is, to
use Pynchon's formula, between the zero and the one:

In a life he has cursed, again and again, for its need to believe so much
in the trans-observable, here is the first, the only real magic: data he
can't argue away. (p. 38)

When later he loses her to a former lover, Jeremy Beavor, who is the
embodiment of army disciplines and values:

He is losing more than single Jessica: he's losing a full range of life, of
being for the first time at ease in the Creation. (p. 629)

The antithesis to Roger, supplied within the novel by Pointsman,
encompasses and sinisterly extends the proposition that the
Pavlovians' mechanistic determinism precludes such states of being.
Pointsman is not just engaged in the war effort, he is in some sense
committed to war as such and is alarmed by the prospect of war
ending:

this war, this State he'd come to feel himself a citizen of, was to be
adjourned and reconstituted as a peace – and . . . professionally
speaking, he'd hardly got a thing out of it.' (p. 75)

While there is in the novel a kind of binary opposition between love
and war, *Gravity's Rainbow* is too complex, too aware of places
between one and zero, to admit of such neat formulations. The coincidence between Slothrop's sexual activity and the rocket falls, never
fully explained, opens up a number of possibilities. It can be decoded,

through the symbolism of the rocket itself, to suggest that (male?) sexuality and destruction are inextricably linked. On the other hand Slothrop's frenetic sexual activity (a well documented feature of human behaviour in times of war) may be seen as a way of opposing the rocket by the only means available: sex as a commitment to life in the face of death. There is also the fact that Slothrop as a baby (Baby Tyrone) was used in Pavlovian experiments of the kind to which Pointsman is committed, to discover the principles of infant sexual arousal.

Nonetheless, there is an unambiguous correlation in the novel between sado-masochistic sexual activity and the perversion of innocence, and direct involvement in the production and deployment of the rockets. Near the base in Holland from which the rockets are launched on London, the SS man Blicero has created a sado-masochistic love nest in the woods with the young Katje and Gottfried. This is described in terms of the Hansel and Gretel story, with particular play on the 'oven' which features in both the fairy story and in Blicero's attempt to reproduce it, and which has a larger resonance in terms of the war as a whole. Pokler, who works on the rocket, develops an incestuous – and violent – relationship with the 'daughter' who is allowed out from the concentration camp on annual visits. To make the point that there are no frontiers for perversion, Katje later makes herself useful to British Intelligence with her sado-masochistic skills.

This corruption – decay, rot and rancidity are marked features, both literally and metaphorically, in the description of such encounters – , while embodied in individuals and their relationships, is part of an invisible system which, like the alternative postal system in *The Crying of Lot 49*, is only partly uncovered in the course of the novel, and which may, in the end, be the creation of paranoia. The agent of discovery is Slothrop who, on the basis of the empathy that he appears to have with the rocket, is sent by the Intelligence Services to uncover its 'secret'; and who possesses the 'Puritan reflex of seeking other orders behind the visible, also known as paranoia' (p. 188).

What he partly uncovers – and this should surprise nobody with an acquaintance with Pynchon's work – is a kind of corporate international state. A file in the War Department admits as much, even before Slothrop is able to name names:

> Don't forget the real business of the War is buying and selling. The murder and the violence are self-policing, and can be entrusted to non-professionals. The mass nature of wartime death is useful in many ways. It serves as spectacle, as diversion from the real movements of the War. It provides raw material to be recorded into History, so that

children may be taught History as sequences of violence, battle after battle, and be more prepared for the adult world. (p. 105)

The late German Foreign Minister, Walter Rathenau, is described as seeing the war as:

> a world revolution, out of which would rise neither Red communism nor an unhindered Right, but a rational structure in which business would be the true, the rightful authority. . . . (p. 165)

Slothrop discovers that the headquarters of Shell – 'with no real country, no side in any war, no specific face or heritage' (p. 243) – had been used as a radio guidance transmitter for the rocket; and that British Shell had developed a mysterious insulation material which could be Impolex G, used in the manufacture of the rocket. It is suggested that Lyle Brand of Boston, who worked with Rathentau, supplied tons of currency to the Weimar Republic to ruin the Mark – thus helping the Germans to avoid paying war debt and precipitating the Second World War. His business interests include the outfit which experimented on Slothrop as a baby and, as part of the deal, paid for his Harvard education. General Electric, ICI, Siemens are all implicated, as are Oxford and Harvard.

Conspiracies, and the paranoia that they generate, are recurring motifs in postmodernist writing. If this particular conspiracy seems superfluous to the 'real' causes of the war, its centrality to *Gravity's Rainbow* is part of that climate of distrust, by no means confined to Pynchon, of the 'truth' of history, particularly of recent history, as imposed by historians. At the time of writing this (March 1989) claims are being made, and assessed, that Churchill had advance intelligence information of the Japanese bombing of Pearl Harbor which he withheld from the Americans in the belief (justified by events) that such an attack would bring them into the war. New frames are being made, and broken, all the time. The particular conspiracy proposed in *Gravity's Rainbow* may not convince the individual reader, but it is a reminder of the endless possibilities of interpretation.

One of the more interesting possibilities explored in the novel concerns Slothrop's Founding Father ancestor, William Slothrop. He is said to have taken a particular interest in the Puritan division of mankind into 'elect' and 'preterite', sheep and goats. Like the 'zero to one' option, it is a doctrine based on exclusion, an either/or on which everything may hinge; and just as the 'zero to one' formula is used in many contexts other than the mathematical, so considerable play is made in the novel, in contexts other than the religious, with the 'elect' and 'preterite' opposition. Those with power – the Nazis, the industrial cartel, the intelligence services – are the elect; the rest, who are dispensible, the preterite. In a parody of government information machines, informing us of a war which is always with us, we are told that:

> the right people are dying. . . . These are the one the War cannot use, and so they die. The right ones survive. (p. 645)

William Slothrop, we are told, wrote a tract, 'On Preterition', in which the holiness of the Preterite, the 'second sheep', the followers, it is suggested, of Judas Iscariot is argued. Tyrone Slothrop speculates of his ancestor:

> Could he have been the fork in the road America never took, the singular point she jumped the wrong way from? Suppose the Slothropite heresy had had time to consolidate and prosper? Might there have been fewer crimes in the name of Jesus, and more mercy in the name of Judas Iscariot? (p. 556)

Slothrop, considering this, wonders if 'there might be a route back' (p. 556). Meanwhile, and poignantly illustrative of the wrong way taken, the Puritan reverence for the Word has, among the latter-day Slothrops, declined to a financial interest in a paper mill. But the continuing vitality of the Word is suggested in the claim made by *Gravity's Rainbow* that the print union in Germany was alone among the unions in defying Hitler.

Whether there is a 'route back' or not, the post-war future predicted by *Gravity's Rainbow* looks bleak. Guilt:

> is becoming quite a commodity in the Zone. Remittance men from all over the world will come to Heidelberg before long, to major in guilt. There will be bars and nightclubs catering especially to guilt enthusiasts. Extermination camps will be turned into tourist attractions. . . .' (p. 453)

The novel stops short of the nuclear attacks on Japan, but there are Japanese in the novel who look forward to returning home to Hiroshima, remembered by them as:

> very pretty, a perfect size, big enough for city excitement, small enough for the serenity a man needs. (p. 480)

The rocket fall which we, as part of a cinema audience, are waiting for at the end, is presumably nuclear, a final closure of meaning which renders artificial any other closure that a novelist might select. Slothrop himself starts to disintegrate towards the end, retaining an identity only in the eyes of Seaman Bodine, a fellow paranoiac with whom he has struck up an acquaintance:

He's looking straight at Slothrop (being one of the few who can still see Slothrop as any sort of integral creature any more. Most of the others gave up long ago trying to hold him together, even as a concept – 'It's just got too remote''s what they usually say). (p. 740)

This disintegration is a reminder (should we still need one) of Slothrop's fictional status; just as, inversely, the War Zone has become a text that resists decoding. *Gravity's Rainbow*, however, as well as employing such postmodernist devices, provides its own justification for them in the world that it mediates. Slothrop is in some sense representative of the historical moment, of those who are caught up in events without having any control over them; and programmed as he has been since birth, what kind of integrity as a character could anyway be claimed for him?

The scale of *Gravity's Rainbow* is beyond the scope of a book like this to represent adequately. It is not just 'about' the war but about what will matter in the post-war world. Particularly suggestive is the fable of the black tribe, the Hereros, who live in abandoned mine shafts close to the sites where the rockets are manufactured. The tension between the black and the white races, as well as being a major factor in late twentieth-century experience, has a contribution to make to that continuing discourse in Pynchon's work on the 'zero to one' option and on the inability of both individuals and governments to tolerate a place in between. The Hereros, who were brought to Germany as an experiment in cultural engineering,

> exposed to cathedrals, Wagnerian soirees, Jaeger underwear, trying to get them interested in their souls . . .' (p. 315)

are not only responding with subversion (they, like Slothrop, are looking for the secret of the rocket), but have themselves been subverted. Committed now to racial suicide, they have become:

> prophets of masturbating, specialists in abortion and sterilisation, pitchmen for acts oral and anal, pedal and digital, sodomistical and zoophiliac . . . (p. 318)

Often compared with *Moby Dick* and *Ulysses*, and indeed resembling them in encyclopaedic scope, *Gravity's Rainbow* in other ways stands in relation to its own times as Eliot's 'The Waste Land' does to the period between the two world wars. There are at times distinct echoes, particularly in the descriptions of a collapsing and disintegrating Europe:

> What is that sound high in the air
> Murmur of maternal lamentation
> Who are those hooded hordes swarming

Over endless plains, stumbling in cracked earth
Ringed by the flat horizon only . . .
('What the Thunder Said', 'The Waste Land')

. . . . so the populations move, across the open meadow, limping,
marching, shuffling, carried, hauling along the detritus of an order, a
European and bourgeois order they don't know yet is destroyed
forever. (p. 551)
(*Gravity's Rainbow*)

They share a fragmented technique, with a variety of voices surfacing
in the text, and no stable centre; both use to symbolic effect descriptions of devitalized and dehumanizing sexual experiences. What is
disturbing about the parallels is that Eliot's vision of his times, which
was by no means unique to him, though there is a unique aptness in
his poetic expression of it, proved intolerable, and many sought
refuge in fascism as offering 'a route back'. *Gravity's Rainbow*, of
course, written half a century later, sees fascism as part of the problem
rather than as a solution: no other political philosophy, after all, has
been so bent on excluding anything between 'zero and one'. Nonetheless, one of the lessons of the period to which 'The Waste Land'
belongs is that there are real dangers in trading in despair, paranoia
and conspiracy, however brilliant the literary product.

9

The Tempest and Other Games People Play

John Fowles: *The Magus*
Iris Murdoch: *The Sea, The Sea*
Muriel Spark: *Not to Disturb*
Vladimir Nabokov: *Pale Fire*
Paul Auster: *The New York Trilogy*

The subject of this last chapter is the writerly novel. This may seem a redundant category in that all of the novels that have come under discussion in earlier chapters are writerly in ways that realist fiction is not. They all, in varying degrees, foreground both language, refusing to treat or use it as a transparent window on the world, and the activity of writing: games are played on the reader, frames broken, the conventions of fiction exposed and the ontological status of fictional characters is questioned. Nonetheless, with notable exceptions, these novels have been received by readers, and as far as one may judge, perceived by writers, as being 'about' something other than the process of writing itself. As I argued in my opening chapter, and have tried to demonstrate since, the choice of a non-realist mode of writing by an individual novelist arises partly from the intellectual and philosophical climate of the time, but also from the demands made by the subject itself, as the writer wishes the reader to perceive it.

The most notable exceptions from earlier chapters – those writers for whom a case may be made as writing essentially writerly novels – are Flann O'Brien and Samuel Beckett. Their work has been discussed elsewhere for largely historical reasons. Flann O'Brien's *At Swim-Two-Birds* (1939) subverts both language and narrative development in ways that are recognizably part of an Irish literary tradition; and I wanted to draw attention to the ways in which Irish writers – who have had their own reasons for subverting the language and narrative modes of the colonial power – helped establish a tradition of non-realist writing in English. Beckett too is part of this tradition, while at the same time his most important works of fiction – the Trilogy of *Molloy*, *Malone Dies* and *The Unnameable* – belong to a particular moment of post-war philosophical questioning about the status of the individual and his place in the material world. While this sets the Trilogy apart from writerly novels published since 1960, his work remains a clear point of reference for three of the writers whose work I shall be discussing in this chapter. *The Magus* has as a central concern the ways in which the experience of the Second World War has forced a reconsideration of the concept of personal freedom, which in turn affects modes of writing. Iris Murdoch, in her essay, 'Against Dryness', identifies Beckett as one of the few contemporary writers (the other that she names is Nabokov) able 'to animate prose language into an imaginative stuff in its own right.'[1] And Beckett's influence is everywhere apparent in the most recently published book that I shall discuss here, *The New York Trilogy*, by the young American writer, Paul Auster.

In many ways the novels selected for discussion in this chapter form a much looser group than in any of the preceding chapters, making generalizations at this stage perilous. In three of them (*The Magus*, *The Sea, The Sea* and *Not to Disturb*) it might be argued that the writerliness has more to do with the theatre than with the printed word; though as I hope to demonstrate, one of the effects of the centrality of Shakespeare to English cultural life is that writerly concerns often present themselves in theatrical terms. *Pale Fire* comprises a poem and a critical commentary on it, allegedly by two different writers. *The New York Trilogy* subverts the conventions of the detective novel, on which it is nonetheless heavily reliant.

Despite surface differences, however, what these novels share is that they are all finally more about themselves than about aspects of the real world that are being mediated through them. This in turn raises questions about the nature of reality and about the part played by fantasy – or the fictions that individuals create for their own solace – in our perceptions of reality. Moreover, since the act of creation is an exercise in power, questions of power, freedom and choice abound, though are often left unanswered.

It goes without saying that all of these issues – ontological, phenomenological and existential – have been matters of serious interest to twentieth-century philosophy (and already broached in earlier chapters), as well as seeping into fashionable cant. It is salutary to consider, therefore, that they all seem to have been anticipated by Shakespeare in his last play, *The Tempest*, albeit that readings of the play in those terms only began to appear in the twentieth century. Or perhaps one had better say that a late modernist or postmodernist age has made of *The Tempest* a postmodernist text, though that leaves out of account the fascination that it exercised over earlier writers like Dryden, as well as earlier twentieth-century writers like Eliot and Auden.

All of my own perceptions of the play are indebted to Anne Righter's insights in *Shakespeare and the Idea of the Play* (1962)[2] and in her Introduction to the Penguin *Tempest* (1968). The link between

Shakespeare himself and his central character, Prospero, had been widely noticed before, and in particular the suggestive coincidence of Shakespeare's departure from the London stage and Prospero's renunciation of his magic arts. What was not so systematically explored before Righter, however, was the hermetic, secretive and irreducible quality of the play itself. Ariel, for example, can only exist in the world of the play, having no equivalent in the 'real' world; is known only to Prospero and the audience but not to the other characters; cannot be satisfactorily reduced to a symbol but is clearly associated with the play's exploration of the nature of theatrical illusion. That it is a play about a play is suggested, for the alert, in the fact that the time spanned by the action (a single afternoon) precisely coincides with its own playing time. Moreover, the discourse on power arising from the colonial relationship of Prospero and Caliban and the family relationship of Prospero and his daughter Miranda, is part of a larger discourse on power which includes the power of the dramatist. As we shall see, *The Tempest* is a crucial point of reference for both *The Magus* and *The Sea, The Sea*.

The Magus was first published in 1966 and then reissued in a revised form in 1977 (I shall quote exclusively from the 1977 version). The revision, an unusual step for the author of an already popular work to take, indicates the importance that Fowles attaches to the novel, although in the Foreword to the revised version he stresses the imperfections which brought him back to the original text. *The Magus* nonetheless reads as very much a product of the decade in which it first appeared. In the Foreword to the revised version, Fowles characterizes the writing of the novel as 'an exploration . . . into an unknown land' (p. 5) and acknowledges the strong influence on him at the time of Jung. In the course of the novel hypnosis and drugs are used to induce heightened states of awareness and the central character is encouraged to 'cross a frontier to a new world that was half art and half science . . .' (p. 337); to surrender to a boundless experience: 'There is no place for limits in the meta-theatre' (p. 406).

In his book on Fowles, Peter Conradi identifies a contradiction in *The Magus* which is central to the criticisms that have been made of it:

> *The Magus* is an extended attack on the use of literature as sympathetic magic; and also one of its greatest exemplifications.[3]

The changes made to *The Magus* in the late 1970s were intended to shift the emphasis away from 'sympathetic magic', but for many of its more devoted readers that remains its most powerful attraction. Indeed, part of the interest of the novel now is in its curious effect of historical layering. On one level it is a distillation of 1960s attitudes overlaid by soberer afterthoughts; on another (the first version, still perceptible in the second) it is a critique of England in the early 1950s from the perspective of the mid-1960s.

The Magus is set in 1953, more than a decade earlier than its first publication, and while the long central narrative is set on a Greek island, firmly linked by direct allusion to Prospero's island in *The Tempest*, this is framed by a post-war London made familiar to readers of the English novel by writers like Spark, Greene and the Iris Murdoch of the early novels. In other words, Fowles's account of London is not so much naively realist as knowingly pastiche, designed to alert the knowing reader and to set the naive reader up for subsequent frustrations. It is a London of bed-sitting rooms, bohemian subculture and a drifting population of art students and itinerant Australians.

The first-person narrator, Nicholas Urfe, has recently come down from Oxford with a poor degree, an acquired contempt for his middle-class, military, minor public school background, a fashionable existentialism and a general dissatisfaction with what the world has to offer to him. He attributes his chilly philandering, in an insight acquired later in the novel, to 'the craving for the best, that made the very worst of me . . .' (p. 400);[7] while his greatest fear is of 'A steady job and a house in the suburbs . . .' (p. 407)[8]. At a loose end in London, he embarks on an affair with an Australian girl, Alison Kelly. The relationship is by any standards other than those of Nicholas's inflated expectations, successful, but he despises Alison both for her sexual availability and for her colonial lack of sophistication. Essential to our perception of Nicholas is that he displays all of those English attitudes that he affects to despise (at a time when it was fashionable to despise them); so that his self-conscious distancing of himself from 'Englishness' is itself a form of play – or role-playing – which links with the more overtly theatrical form of play of the Greek narrative, thus suggesting a more general link between theatre and lived life.

In flight from a desolate Alison, he takes a job as schoolmaster, in a school run on English lines, on the Greek island of Phraxos. Bored by the other masters, he is flattered to be taken up by Maurice Conchis, a reclusive millionaire who spends part of each year on the island, and who is shunned by the villagers for collaborating with the Germans when he was Mayor of Phraxos during the Occupation. From the time that Nicholas chances into Bourani, Conchis's domain, direct references to *The Tempest* abound. Conchis refers to himself as Prospero, Nicholas to his host's style of hospitality as 'stage-management' (p. 109); and since Nicholas first wanders into Bourani after being asleep on the beach, and is judged by Conchis to be 'elect' (in a psychic sense), the role assigned to him seems to be that of Ferdinand.

That sense of election, flattering Nicholas's self-importance, seems to be confirmed during the early visits. Conchis's long narrative account of his experiences at Neuve Chapelle (he claims to have had an English father and upbringing) is followed by a theatrical experience of the same events (the smells and sounds of the trenches), laid on solely for Nicholas, the mechanics of which are never fully explained. Later Nicholas is introduced to a young actress, Julie Holmes, playing the role of Lily, Conchis's first love. In the manner of romance – a genre to which *The Tempest* belongs and with which *The Magus* plays – Nicholas immediately recognizes in Julie/Lily his ideal, which conforms closely to the romance ideal and represents all that was absent in Alison:

> a breeding, a fastidiousness, a delicacy, that attracted me as fatally as the local fishermen's lamps attracted fish on moonless nights. (p. 158)

To win her would be to redeem the past:

> my selfishness, caddishness . . . could now be justified. It was always to be this, and something in me had always known it. (p. 210)

Nicholas assumes some of the status of the romance hero as the narrative seems poised for a conventional romance development. Obstacles in the quest for Julie/Lily abound: her own sexual diffidence, the appearance of a twin sister, June/Rose, further masque-like entertainments whose meanings have to be decoded as though part of a test, and above all, Conchis's ambivalence towards Nicholas. Is the older man merely an exacting task-master who, like Prospero with Ferdinand, intends Nicholas for Julie/Lily once his faith has been tested, or is he a malevolent self-appointed deity, playing with Nicholas for his own sport? As the narrative proceeds, Conchis's attitude to Nicholas becomes more unambiguously hostile, but what of the twins? Are they Conchis's prisoners on the island, forced to enact his commands; his accomplices in an elaborate test of Nicholas which will ultimately prove to be benign; or colluding with Conchis in a cruel game at Nicholas's expense? All are possible interpretations of the twins' insistent role-playing; and Nicholas, who keeps hoping for a point of stability, finds with each return to Bourani that the ground has again shifted in his absence.

Both the elaborate plot and the stress on the deceptiveness of appearance are well within the conventions of romance, a genre for which Nicholas's sense of himself as a solitary romantic hero has prepared him. The sustained interest of *The Magus*, throughout a long and sometimes repetitive narrative, is the play it makes with the limits of the genre; the violation of boundaries set by readerly expectation; and how this in turn contributes to a discourse on lived experience. And it is in this – the sense of 'life' and theatre as being separate, but related to each other in mysterious ways – more than in the exotic island setting or the explicit parallels, that *The Magus* shows itself indebted to *The Tempest*. Nicholas is both an audience to the continuing show at Bourani, and a participant in the action. As audience, he has a life outside the play which he can control and keep aloof from the life of Bourani. Or so he thinks.

During the early weeks of his stay on Phraxos, communication is maintained with Alison. She has, since their parting, become an air hostess and spends a weekend with him in Athens. For Nicholas the time with Alison is a profound emotional experience, which he then minimizes to himself, to Alison and to Julie/Lily, in the interests of what he takes to be the greater prize of the more desirable woman. Later he learns that Alison has committed suicide – a fact that he conceals at Bourani. Meanwhile he checks by letters to England all the information that he has managed to gather of the twins' lives outside the island.

Whatever unease he feels about his own lying is dispelled by the conviction that a higher end – the conquest of Julie/Lily – is being served. And when he makes his full entry into that rarified world, when the unattainable has been attained, he will become a finer person, leaving his old self behind like a discarded skin. He lies to gain control over the situation, to fulfil his destiny; while for the reader his lack of faith balances within the narrative Conchis's manipulation of him, each justifying and being justified by the other. One of Conchis's early lies to Nicholas is that Lily is schizophrenic and he is her psychiatrist. This too serves an end – the symbolic rendering of Nicholas's own divided self. In a more candid moment, which serves as a warning to Nicholas that goes unheeded, Conchis explains the principles of meta-theatre to him: 'a new kind of drama. One in which the conventional separation between actors and audience was abolished' (p. 404).

The culmination of Nicholas's involvement at Bourani is a trial scene. This brings to a close a breathless sequence of events which includes the long-delayed sexual encounter with Julie/Lily, followed immediately by Nicholas's being forced to watch a film of her making love with her 'real' lover (the black American Joe, who has participated in the masques), with 'real' feeling. (The irony is that the 'real' can be rendered in film, thus depriving of 'reality' what Nicholas felt 'really' happened between himself and Julie/Lily.) At the trial – a mixture of masque, psychiatric jargon and ritualistic enactment – Nicholas's character is stripped bare, his bad faith exposed.

This apparent closure, however, is the prelude to a series of discoveries and occurrences which allow no limit to be set on Conchis's knowledge and manipulation of the events of Nicholas's life; a control which extends to the time before they met and into the future. Conchis is responsible for Nicholas's dismissal from the school; has used one of the masters there to spy on Nicholas; and dictated an early mis-diagnosis of syphilis in Nicholas by an island doctor. Before leaving for London, Nicholas is led to a sighting of Alison in an Athens street. Alison, it appears, has been part of the main plot, in league with Conchis and the twins, not a dispensable figure in the subsidiary plot to which Nicholas had relegated her. Nicholas returns to London and takes a room with Kemp, a seedy but goodhearted Fitzrovian landlady (a clear use of a stereotype drawn from 1950s fiction): she too, it is revealed towards the end, has a role in the plot. The scale of the conspiracy against Nicholas defies every law of probability. In his book, *The Modes of Modern Writing*, David Lodge places *The Magus* in a group of postmodernist novels whose plots 'We shall never be able to unravel . . . for they are labyrinths without exits.'[4]

This conspiracy, together with the theatrical events of Phraxos, most of which are naturalized but the management of which outrages common sense, places *The Magus* firmly outside the realist tradition. Nonetheless, the novel does demonstrate the extraordinary persistence in English writing of the concept of morally resonant choice, the cornerstone of the realist tradition. The conspiracy organized by Conchis, each stage of which is justified by fresh instances of Nicholas's lying and bad faith, is designed to demonstrate the need for personal 'wholeness' or integrity. Whatever apparent diversity of plots exists in the life of an individual, there is in the end only one plot, the denial of which leads to hypocrisy and treachery. Fowles in the Foreword to the revised version, acknowledges a debt, unconscious at the time of writing, to *Great Expectations* (p. 6): Dickens's hero, Pip, like Nicholas, comes to learn that he has systematically mistaken the plot to which he is central. The moment of insight on which, it is hoped, Nicholas might be able to rebuild his life resembles other moments of acquired wisdom in English fiction stretching back at least to Jane Austen:

> They had been wrong, at the trial. It was not that I preyed on girls; but the fact that my only access to normal humanity, to social decency, to any openness of heart, lay through girls, preyed on me. (p. 608)

In *The Magus*, however, that insistence on choice is part of a discourse which includes existentialist theory. Nicholas, in the manner of the young – Fowles himself describes his work as 'a novel of adolescence written by a retarded adolescent' (p. 9) – mistakes the nature of freedom in assuming that once he has achieved his ideal state (defined by acquisition of the perfect girl) there will be no further need for uncomfortable choices. Conchis, in the long narrative accounts of his life (a number of which are assumed autobiography, to illustrate 'truths' which take precedence over facts), demonstrates the difficulty of choosing when the conditions of choice lie outside our control. Two key episodes in the narrative are placed in the contexts of the First and Second World Wars, two events which have helped to alter the bias of moral philosophy in this century. In the first (as it happens, fictional account) the young Conchis showed himself prepared to face the opprobrium of desertion after witnessing the senseless slaughter of Neuve Chapelle. The aim of the anecdote is to communicate 'the passion to exist' (p. 130): this is reinforced by some play with a cyanide capsule designed to cure Nicholas of the then fashionable existentialist toying with the notion of suicide as the ultimately 'authentic' act. In the second episode Conchis, then Mayor of Phraxos, refused to club to death a member of the Greek Resistance, knowing that eighty hostages (himself included) would be shot by the Germans as a result of that refusal. Freedom, according to Nicholas's interpretation of Conchis's meaning, is:

> something much older than the existentialist freedom . . . a moral imperative, an almost Christian concept, certainly not a political or democratic one. (p. 440)

Conchis was seen as a traitor by many of his fellow villagers, though his own survival from the episode, which he could not have anticipated, was a matter of chance. The telling of this story runs parallel, in the narrative, to Nicholas's betrayal of Alison, thus allowing the transfer of questions of freedom and treachery from the story being told to the life being lived. What Conchis gives Nicholas throughout – as he has given earlier masters at the school, and will give to Nicholas's successors, for the 'show' put on at Bourani is an annually recurring one – is an imaginative experience, comparable to that offered by Shakespeare's comedies and romances, where a willingness to submit to the experience in the theatre, to release control, carries with it the possibility of transformation. His role, like that of Prospero in *The Tempest* – they are both god-like figures in their manipulation of events – is in human terms questionable. In other words, they can only exist in a literary text, having no equivalent in 'real' life, though Conchis's behaviour is given a degree of plausibility in the narrative by the possession of great wealth. (This raises questions of power, and its abuse, that are never fully explored.) The role assumed by Conchis, as by Prospero, can only be judged by its results. Nicholas's judgement, despite his rage and humiliation, is implicit in his decision not to warn his successor at the school, who comes to Nicholas for advice when the latter is settled again in London: he is given, by Conchis, the choice of complicity in the continuing 'godgame'. Meanwhile, he shows some measure of transformation in the ordinary human kindness he shows a young Scottish waif, Jojo, and in the undemanding friendship he establishes with his landlady, Kemp. Meanwhile, he waits for Alison's reappearance.

After his return to London, he also makes contact with the twins' mother, who expresses her support for her daughters' behaviour (with which Nicholas had hoped to shock her) and her endorsement of Conchis's ultimately life-enhancing theory and practice. She refuses to supply a full explanation for events, quoting Conchis's belief that 'An answer is always a form of death' (p. 626). Fowles himself appears to have taken this to heart. After leading the reader to the brink of closure, he ends the novel with Alison and Nicholas in Regents Park, the frame frozen with Alison still undecided on the extent of Nicholas's transformation and on whether to take him back.

Early in their acquaintance, Conchis tells Nicholas that he has burned all the novels that he ever possessed: ' "Why should I struggle through hundreds of pages of fabrication to reach half a dozen very little truths?" ' (p. 96). It is a sentiment that might well be echoed by readers of *The Magus* if they are judging the novel as discourse rather than on the pleasures afforded by the text. Indeed, in *The Magus* the two are in a sense at odds. The message delivered to Nicholas by Conchis's games is that it is better to accept the 'real' (which includes one's own limitations) than to pursue an unattainable ideal. The message, however, is delivered by way of romance, which is driven by pursuit of an unattainable ideal. In *The Magus* it is the journey itself, what is irreducible in the text, that matters.

The Sea, The Sea by Iris Murdoch (born 1919), published in 1978 and winner of that year's Booker Prize, is another first-person narrative, allowing, as in *The Magus*, the progressive uncovering of the narrator's self-delusion. Her narrator, however, a retired theatre director called Charles Arrowby, is the novel's Prospero figure. Murdoch draws heavily on Shakespearean sources in her work (*A Fairly Honourable Defeat*, published in 1970, and *The Black Prince* in 1973 are the most notable earlier examples), but *The Sea, The Sea*, because of Arrowby's earlier career in the theatre, is perhaps her most revealing work for those seeking reasons for that continuing fascination. Arrowby has abandoned the theatre, as Prospero at the end of *The Tempest* abandons his magic, because of its power to deceive:

Even a middling novelist can tell quite a lot of truth. His humble medium is on the side of truth. Whereas the theatre, even at its most 'realistic', is connected with the level at which, and the methods by which, we tell our everyday lies. This is the sense in which 'ordinary' theatre resembles life, and dramatists are disgraceul liars unless they are very good. (p. 33)

We can assume that, within these terms of reference, Shakespeare is not among the 'disgraceful liars', but his work does use, often quite self-consciously, the role-playing, disguise and illusion of the theatre to expose the ways in which the conventions of the theatre 'resemble life'. Peter Conradi's recent book on Iris Murdoch, the most comprehensive study of her work to date, is called *Iris Murdoch: The Saint and the Artist*. In it, he draws attention to the way in which many of her plots (including *The Sea, The Sea*) exploit the distinction between an exemplarily good character and an artist; and then suggests that all her characters are, to a degree, artists in their own lives: ' "art" itself is an analogue of the process by which we create in life a self-serving world view in which other people figure merely as subsidiary characters.'[5]

The Tempest is a particularly suggestive play in this respect, as must already be evident from the discussion of John Fowles's appropriation of it in *The Magus*. But whereas *The Magus* is, on Fowles's own admission, an 'adolescent' novel, one in which he was learning how to write, *The Sea, The Sea* is, like *The Tempest*, a mature work and may be read as a culmination of a writing career already spanning more than twenty years. It is, as Conradi describes it, 'a tale of obsession, and in it many of its author's own writerly obsessions – the sea, the box-like enclosure, the persecuted maiden, the interaction of magic, religion, guilt and the quest for virtue – all reach some culmination.'[6] Like *The Tempest* it can be read as itself, and as a discourse on its creator's own art.

Like a number of Murdoch's other novels, before and since, *The Sea, The Sea* focuses on a small group of characters who are bound by long-standing ties and commitments and who in the course of the narrative are driven by desire to enact an increasingly bizarre sequence of events. At the centre of the group is Charles Arrowby, and a number of the subsidiary cast of characters – Gilbert, Peregrine, Rosina and Lizzie – are actors who have been directed by him in the course of his theatrical career, the women seduced by him. His use of power for sexual gratification (and of sex to demonstrate his power) in the past destroyed Rosina's marriage to Peregrine; and in the course of the narrative Lizzie's recently established platonic relationship with the homosexual Gilbert is shattered when Arrowby renews his overtures to her. Arrowby is routinely addressed by them all in terms which draw attention to the power relationship. Lizzie speaks of, 'The habit of obeying you' (p. 46); Rosina calls him 'a sorcerer' (p. 108); Gilbert, who by his own admission has 'the soul of a slave', offers himself to Charles as 'a chattel'.

Prospero in *The Tempest* has near absolute power (stopping short of the power to affect the workings of the human heart) over all the other characters in the play. The exercise of that power, however, is justified within the play by the wrongs done to him in the past, with the exception of his treatment of Caliban (a paradigm of the colonial relationship), on which the play is resonantly ambiguous. When Prospero renounces his magic arts, it is at least in part because of their limitations: he cannot make the wicked good. Conchis's power, too, serves desirable ends, though the way he exercises it over Nicholas is often apparently sadistic. There is no inwardness in Fowles's presentation of Conchis, the reader, like Nicholas, not being allowed to penetrate the masks he adopts, so that he remains an ambiguous figure. Charles, however, through the device of the first-person narrative, exposes his inner self to the reader with unusual candour – a candour born of the belief that his decision to leave the theatre demonstrates a change of heart. In terms of the parallel with *The Tempest*, Charles is both Prospero during his time on the island and Prospero after he has left the island and renounced his magic, with the surface detail reversed. Prospero returns to the world (Milan), whereas Charles, when the novel opens, has recently left London to take possession of an isolated house on the north-east coast of England. At the end of the novel Charles, like Prospero, returns to the world.

The novel's first section, 'Prehistory', gives an account of Charles's past and a description of the newly achieved simplicity of his present way of life. Of Charles's past, we learn of the virtue and comparative poverty of his parents, from which he 'fled to the trickery and magic of art' (p. 29); of his feelings of rivalry towards his wealthy cousin, James, now a retired general whose present activities are shrouded in mystery; of his adolescent love for a girl called Hartley, from which he has never recovered and of her final rejection of him, which 'made me faithless' (p. 84). The apparent candour of Charles's account of himself, however, while showing a willingness to admit his own abuses of power, is destabilized by his obvious difficulty in allowing others, particularly his cousin James, the same measure of reality as himself:

When I was young I could never decide whether James was real and I was unreal, or vice versa. Somehow it was clear we could not both be real; one of us must inhabit the real world, the other one the world of shadows. (p. 57)

An unacknowledged attraction in the role of theatre director is the power to assign reality to others; and the events of the novel, once the narrative is underway, demonstrate that he has not yet overcome whatever need that served.

The description of his current simple way of life – swimming, gathering and arranging stones, writing his memoirs – provides, in the Shakespearean manner, a comic burlesque on his need to be the arbiter of value. Considerable space is given to the meals he consumes. This attracted some critical attention when the novel first appeared, the reviewers judging much of the food, with its often bizarre combination of ingredients, to be quite unappetizing. (One of the tricks played by Murdoch in *The Sea, The Sea* is to invite reading, at a number of points, as a cookery book, a species of writing which bears quite a different relation to 'reality' than Murdoch's own novels.) Charles is insistent, however, on the value of his theory and practice in the matter of food:

> views which I hold on the subject of food approximate to absolute truths. (p. 87)

He has equally firm ideas on what he describes as 'the real me' (p. 32): his cleverness beyond the scope of the camera to capture, his appearance, or at any rate his hairline, improved by art.

The power embodied in the role of theatre director has been replaced by that control over external reality invested in the act of writing what he comes to describe as 'this novelistic memoir' (p. 239). The link between the two is the transforming power of the imagination. This is tested when his prescriptions of value are exposed to the judgement of others. He declares himself deeply attached to his new house, whose curiously inward design is at odds with its seaside location (and serves therefore as a symbol for his own mind in relation to the world), but the visitors from London who invade his retreat in the novel's long central section, 'History', find it hateful and ugly. More momentous to the action of the novel is his discovery that his first love, Hartley, is living in the village with her husband, Ben Finch.

> I saw: a stout elderly woman in a shapeless brown tent-like dress, holding a shopping bag and working her way, very slowly as if in a dream, along the street. . . . (p. 113)

The effect on Charles is immediate:

> How totally in every atom I had been changed. . . . (p. 137)

The power of love to effect sudden and dramatic change is the central dynamic in all Murdoch's plots; while the link that she makes between love and the imaginative life of the individual – on the one hand enabling the transformation of the beloved, releasing on the other the temptation to self-delusion – is the clearest evidence in her work of her debt to Shakespeare. *The Sea, The Sea* provides her most bizarre treatment of the theme, in the renewed love of Charles Arrowby for 'that funny old woman' who was his first love:

> as I worked and worked to join together her youth and her age, I so much desired to desire her. (p. 186)

This motive, grotesque to outsiders, fills Charles with a sense of his own altruism. He had, before seeing Hartley, written to Lizzie (who once played Ariel to his Prospero) to suggest that they renew their relationship; now he is happy for her to remain with Gilbert:

> Was this new detached generosity, I wondered in passing, a first symptom of that changed and purified form of being which the return of Hartley was going to create in me? (p. 138)

His first noble act, however, will be the 'rescue' of Hartley from her husband.

Once the plot is underway it moves, as always in Murdoch's work, at a breathless pace (she shares with John Fowles considerable narrative skills). More remarkable to this novel is the virtual confinement of the action to Charles's house and immediate coastline, and the neighbouring village, the house itself serving as a kind of stage set, the plot gathering momentum in the manner of farce, until it is overtaken by tragedy. Charles is joined by Lizzie (hoping for a renewal of love); Rosina and Peregrine (severally bent on revenge); Gilbert (who is in need of companionship); and his cousin James, whose motives are harder to fathom. They are forced into amused, baffled or outraged complicity in Hartley's imprisonment within the house, until such time as she voluntarily agrees to be 'rescued' from the 'prison' of her marriage.

Meanwhile Titus, the eighteen-year-old adopted son of Hartley and Ben, has appeared. He has been rejected by Ben who suspects, because of certain accidents of timing, that Titus is Hartley's son by Charles. (One of the ironies of the novel is that Ben and Charles share a violent and jealous temperament, their similarity masked only by Charles's greater sophistication.) Charles has to tell Titus that they are not father and son, but:

> He was a clever attractive boy and I was going to do my damnedest to get hold of him. (p. 261)

In the resolution of this drama, James is the key player. He gives Charles an unwelcome account of his behaviour towards Hartley which gives a new twist to the theatrical metaphor on which the novel turns. He describes Charles's obsession with Hartley as:

> 'a mental charade, a necessary one perhaps, it has its own necessity, but not like what you think.' (p. 353)

He suggests that Charles needed to re-enact his love for Hartley in order to come to terms with his past. Directed by James, Charles is finally persuaded of Hartley's misery and returns her to her husband. Later, forming the climax to a drunken evening in and in the environs of the house, Charles is pushed into the sea by (as it finally emerges) Peregrine, and is saved from drowning by James performing (as Charles's memory later reconstructs it) a supernatural act:

> One moment he was against the rock as if he were clinging onto it like a bat. Then he was simply standing on the water. (p. 468)

Then while James is confined to bed recovering from whatever effort was required of him to save Charles, Titus is drowned.

Before Charles is able to reconstruct his relationship with James in the light of his memory of miraculous escape, James too is dead. At this point in *The Sea, The Sea* James's mysterious eastern connections, the residue of his army career, are brought into play. James is described by the Indian doctor who was summoned to his body as 'enlightened' (p. 473) and the suggestion is made that he chose the moment of his own death. James had spoken to Charles of his ability – which he dismisses as a trick – to raise his body temperature at will. He had appeared to blame himself for Titus's death, but Charles by the end of the novel has settled on another explanation, one which obeys the principles of classical and renaissance tragedy:

> There is a relentless causality of sin and in a way Titus died because, all those years ago, I had taken Rosina away from Peregrine. (p. 471)

Throughout the novel Charles and James, bound by ties of family, men of influence and power, dispensers, even, of magic, signify each other's opposite. Charles's power is a matter of external control and appropriation; James's of self-discipline and internal control which allow to others their full measure of reality. His interventions in other people's lives are benign because he feels no need to impose his own reality on them. He tells Charles, in the course of advising him to return Hartley to her husband, that:

> 'she is real, as human creatures are, but what reality she has is elsewhere. She does not coincide with your dream figure. You were not able to transform her.' (p. 353)

James's function in the novel is, to return to Peter Conradi's terms of reference for Murdoch's work, that of the 'saint', the good man whose statements, we must assume, represent some kind of 'truth' within the novel. This stabilizing of meaning through a character specially privileged by the author would seem to place Murdoch's work, here and elsewhere, firmly within a realist tradition. She has on a number of occasions expressed her admiration for the nineteenth-century novel, the English and Russian particularly, and her opinion that the status allowed the individual in post-war fiction is an impoverished one, lacking a sense of human difference. Her novels all have a powerful narrative drive and are rich in detailed descriptions of individual characters and of the material and natural worlds. Charles, like Nicholas by the end of *The Magus*, is modestly 'improved' on his return to London, in terms both of self-insight and benevolence towards others. As a moral philosopher, Iris Murdoch is professionally concerned with the theory of 'goodness', which she has explored through character and plot throughout her career as a novelist; and for which the structure of the realist novel is particularly appropriate.

The question therefore arises of why one might choose to include her work in a discussion of non-realist fiction. Hers is a highly stylized world, peopled, for all the proliferation of detail – in which one sometimes detects a sense of strain, as though the author is trying to convince – by characters who are remote from social reality. Money, work and ordinary family life, touchstones of realist fiction, enabling readers to recognize their own world in the mediated world of the novel, barely figure in her novels. Released from commonplace and diurnal concerns, her characters are curiously free-floating, able to pursue their desires and philosophical concerns. Murdoch does not appear to feel herself restricted by the probability of the situations on which her plots turn. Charles's renewed love for Hartley is a case in point; and it is significant that he envisages their life together as:

> a vast plain goodness. . . . And I would join the ordinary people and be an ordinary person. (p. 371)

The 'ordinary', which he can only envisage in the most vague and generalized terms, here takes on all the charm of the exotic. Readers value Iris Murdoch's work for the richness and vitality of the writing and for the excitement generated by extraordinary characters in unlikely situations, but not, I would suggest, because they find in her work a reflection of the world that they know. Indeed, her persistent use (very marked in *The Sea, The Sea*) of the terms 'real' and 'reality' is always in contexts which suggest the difficulty human beings experience in knowing what is real.

Moreover, there are unnaturalized supernatural elements in most of her novels. James's actions – associated in unspecified ways with his 'goodness' – are an example, as is the mysterious sea creature which Charles sights from time to time. Such incidents and sightings are often associated with the sea, which is of recurring importance in her work. She herself, in the course of a critique of late-twentieth-century fiction, has written of 'a dangerous lack of curiosity about the real world, a failure to appreciate the difficulties of knowing it.'⁹ Conradi offers an explanation to the continuing fascination with the sea in her work, which is on similar lines: 'Its point, in fact, is its resistance to human devices, its miscellaneous nature, its hugeness and unpredictability.'¹⁰ The sea, along with other natural phenomena – her writing shows the same kind of tenderness as Beckett's towards inanimate objects like pebbles and shells – are reminders of 'reality' which are profoundly mystified.

Finally, while her plots are always resolved, her novels nonetheless resist final closure. Partly, this is a consequence of her method of presenting character. All of her characters, at each transitional point in their lives – most commonly, on falling in love – confer on their present state the distinction of finality. Such transitions are handled abruptly, with no perspective beyond the present moment. In the course of a novel, a number of 'final' states may come and go, generating a fruitful tension in her work between, on the one hand, the autonomous character, suggested in the way that each character is delivered by the author to the reader in a highly 'finished' form; and on the other, the individual as comprising fleeting moments of consciousness. So Murdoch, along with other English novelists of the period (including John Fowles, Rosamund Lehmann, Lawrence Durrell) artfully plays off traditional modes of writing against postmodernist innovation; allowing readers some of the consolations of realism, while leaving other possibilities open for consideration.

At the end of *The Sea, The Sea*, Charles is back in London, now living in James's flat, picking up the threads of his old life, forming new ties, beginning a new cycle, already starting the process of naturalizing and de-mystifying the picture of James that he constructed after his near escape from drowning and his cousin's death. To quote Conradi again: 'Murdoch is wholly of our time in her insistence that 'truth' cannot be secured.'¹¹

In 'Against Dryness', Iris Murdoch divides contemporary fiction into the crystalline (tightly structured fables in which everything signifies and a sense of human variety is sacrificed to meaning) and the journalistic (the debased heirs of the more openly structured nineteenth-century narrative tradition). Within these terms of reference, *Not to Disturb* by Muriel Spark (born 1918) would unquestionably be classed as 'crystalline'. Set in a mansion in Geneva, the home of Baron and Baroness Klopstock and the Baron's idiot younger brother, the action is confined to a single night – a night when the Klopstocks are closeted in the library with their secretary, Victor Passerat, having given orders to their servants that they are not to be disturbed. The outcome of the night's events is the murder of the Baroness and of Passerat by the Baron, followed by the Baron's suicide. The principal device used in telling the tale is to reverse the usual order of priorities by focusing on the servants, with only brief glimpses of the 'chief' players. In this, *Not to Disturb* resembles Tom Stoppard's play, *Rosencrantz and Guildenstern are Dead* (first performed 1966), which turns *Hamlet* inside out to allow the bit players to take centre stage. Stoppard's play provides an instructive comparison, which I shall return to later.

Not to Disturb is in fact more purely theatrical than either *The Magus* or *The Sea, The Sea*. The Klopstocks' house is used like a stage set, the unities of time and space are observed and the dialogue, particularly that of the butler, Lister, is highly stylized, naturalism firmly rejected. Its inter-textuality, however, is more diffuse, not confined to one play. The first spoken words are a quotation from *The Duchess of Malfi*; *Hamlet* and *The Tempest* are later invoked. It is not so much one play as the atmosphere and themes of Jacobean tragedy that are more generally summoned: the darkness, locked room, degenerate offspring of a noble family and the use of power and wealth to satisfy a decadent sexuality. Lister's comment on the affairs of his employers, '"How urgently does an overwhelming obsession with life lead to suicide!"' (p. 13), could be made to serve just as readily for any one of a number of Jacobean plays. Moreover, *Not to Disturb* shares with the drama of that period a sense that the lives of the rich and powerful are essentially theatrical. As Lister again observes:

> 'They take everything, like stage-companies who need their props. With royalty, of course, it is all largely a matter of stage production.' (p. 28)

There is a suggestion that the catastrophe has been provoked by the Baroness who, like the Duchess of Malfi, has allowed 'real' feeling to interfere with her role. In the words of the porter's wife, Clara:

> 'Why did she suddenly start to go natural? She must have started to be sincere with someone.' (p. 35)

The most important effect of the theatrical metaphor, however, is to suggest that the action is predetermined, the events have already been scripted, in a way that recalls Stoppard's appropriation of *Hamlet* in *Rosencrantz and Guildenstern*. Stoppard's title is a quotation from *Hamlet*, the announcement of the death of two minor characters. As a title, however, the use of the present tense carries a different resonance, of a destiny from which there is no escape. The present tense is used throughout *Not to Disturb* for the narrative voice, but in the conversation of the servants events which have yet to take place are given the past tense. Lister, who functions as chorus, is quite explicit on this point:

> 'To all intents and purposes, they're already dead although as a matter of banal fact, the night's business has still to accomplish itself.' (p. 12)

Later he dismisses as '"vulgar chronology"' any reference to the Baron in the present tense.

Rosencrantz and Guildenstern and *Not to Disturb* are both profoundly writerly texts in their assumption of a prior script which takes precedence over everyday probability. In the novel, the servants' foreknowledge of the outcome allows them to make their own detailed preparations, even though, for the party in the library, events presumably still hang in the balance. Clovis the chef has already written a film treatment of the drama; newspapers have been warned, the stories of the servants are expected to command large sums. The funeral wreath is on hand before the deaths have taken place. When something unscripted occurs – the discovery that the idiot confined to the attic is not, as was supposed, a relative of the Baroness but the Baron's younger brother and heir – the servants show themselves capable of improvisation: the Baroness's pregnant maid, Heloise, is married to him by the clergyman who has been summoned to the house to be present at the catastrophe.

Not to Disturb plays cleverly on the cliché that servants know everything that goes on in a great household. They are not responsible for the deaths of their employers, though they are more than willing to profit by them. In adopting a passive role of non-intervention, they are merely obeying to the letter the order that the party in the library is not to be disturbed. In this they show themselves to be no more nor less callous than members of the Klopstocks' own circle. When in the course of the evening the Baron's friend, Prince Eugene, arrives, on the invitation of the Baron, he accepts without question the imperative that the Klopstocks are not to be disturbed, recognizing, like the servants, the inevitable outcome of the drama being enacted. He too is prepared to profit from the catastrophe, offering Lister and Clovis positions in his own household; when day breaks, his car and those of other potential employers are lined up outside, their owners waiting to outbid each other for the servants. Throughout the night a storm rages, noises off suggesting both the climactic disturbances of stage tragedy and the divine displeasure that these represent in the theatre.

For most of the night the servants serve as audience, passive witnesses to what is taking place. With the approach of the catastrophe, however, they make preparations to assume their roles as principal actors. They have gone without sleep to reproduce the symptoms of shock and rehearse the moves they will make when the deaths are discovered. The appearance of spontaneity is artfully achieved. As morning breaks they take the stage and the future is theirs.

All three of the novels so far discussed illustrate the ease with which theatrical imagery may generate discourses on power. *The Tempest* (to say nothing of other of Shakespeare's plays) is a reminder that the link between theatrical and other forms of power is not a discovery of our own times. However, the twentieth century has seen both an increased self-consciousness about all creative enterprise and an intensified debate, inside and outside the academy, about power, freedom and destiny in every field of human behaviour. Stoppard's *Rosencrantz and Guildenstern are Dead* is a notable, but by no means unique example, of theatrical foregrounding to open up a discourse on political oppression. In *Not to Disturb* the power vested in the master/servant relationship is an issue, ironically inverted to give the servants the appearance of controlling events which are merely running their course. Theirs is the power of knowledge, the dramatic irony perceived by the audience as the characters in the play stumble along to the tragic outcome. The cleverness of *Not to Disturb* is to transpose privileged information, which in the theatre has no practical use, into economic terms, as the servants prepare to benefit from the denouement. The sense of their own destiny, a product of that privileged information, allows them to reify their employers in a way that reverses the power structure of the relationship: '" – they were good for a purpose so long as they lasted,"' Lister says. '"As paper cups are useful for occasions, you use them and throw them away"' (p 31). In deciding not to cook dinner, they quote Marie Antoinette: '"Let them eat cake"' (p. 29).

Nabokov's *Pale Fire* has given us the phrase 'lexical playfields' (p. 291) which in itself is an apt description of the kind of text it is – one that, to quote Tony Tanner, 'is nearly all foreground'[12]. Indeed, the overt theme is words: both what they signify for the user and the ways in which they may be interpreted by others. Published in 1962, it has been a central influence on the development of American postmodernist writing, as Tony Tanner argues in *City of Words*.

It takes the form of a poem, 'Pale Fire', which is one line short of 1000, and the critical apparatus – a Foreword, a long editorial commentary and an index – with which it is brought to press following the poet's untimely death. The form of the novel – immediately apparent at a typographical level – at once suggests either fraud or parody and invites an element of suspicion in the reader's response to the text. The very fact that it is rare to find critical comment on *Pale Fire* which takes the poem seriously as a poem suggests that readerly expectation works against the presence of a 'real' poem within a 'real' novel. One of the key principles in the writing of *Pale Fire* – form, word play, the kinds of transactions taking place with the reader – is to demonstrate that the construction of a 'reality' through words excludes and devalues other possible realities that may be constructed.

The Foreword to the poem introduces us to its editor, Charles Kinbote who, having gained control of the text of the poem, uses his editorial position to impose on the reader his own preferred version of himself. An exile from the central European country of Zembla, which has recently undergone a revolution, he is treated as an outsider by the East Coast academic establishment, envious both of his access to a larger world and of his 'close friendship' (p. 29) with the poem's author, John Shade. This friendship, and the fact that as Shade's next door neighbour he enjoyed some degree of physical proximity to the poet during the time of the poem's composition, are offered as qualifications for his role as editor, along with a general trustworthiness which is expressed in terms unusual in a 'document' of the kind that this purports to be: 'My free and simple demeanour set everybody at ease' (p. 22).

The naivety of the Foreword puts the reader on guard as belonging to quite a different kind of discourse from that of the professional critic. Moreover, his statement of editorial principles shows Kinbote to be at odds both with the formalist criticism which dominated American critical practice at the time of *Pale Fire*'s publication – a practice which insisted on the self-contained autonomy of the text – and with Nabokov's own expressed view, that the 'reality' of a work of literature was not to be confused with the 'reality' of the writer's life:

> Let me state that without my notes Shade's text simply has no human reality at all since the human reality of such a poem as his (being too skittish and reticent for an autobiographical work), with the omission of many pithy lines carelessly rejected by him, has to depend entirely on the reality of its author and his surroundings, attachments and so forth, a reality that only my notes can provide. To this statement my dear poet would probably not have subscribed, but, for better or worse, it is the commentator who has the last word. (p. 31)

Since the irony in Nabokov never works in one direction, however, it seems likely that academic criticism is also being targeted, in particular that feature which it shares with Kinbote's approach, of claiming for the critic a status comparable with that of the creative writer.

Kinbote's description of the creative process, as he perceived it at work in John Shade, is celebratory:

> perceiving and transforming the world, taking it in and taking it apart, re-combining its elements in the very process of storing them up so as to produce at some unspecified date an organic miracle . . . (p. 30)

He fails to recognize, however, that any verbal construct – including his own and others which call themselves 'criticism' – re-orders and re-combines a world, though 'an organic miracle' may not necessarily result. Shade's poem, by contrast, opens with an image which, in the context already established by Kinbote's 'Foreword', asserts the impossibility of an unmediated window on the world:

> I was the shadow of the waxwing slain
> By the false azure in the windowpane. (p. 35)

This is immediately followed by a description of the interior of the poet's house at night as reflected on the window, where that reflection is superimposed on the garden beyond. The opening image takes on a particular resonance in the Commentary following the poem, with its many references to the poet glimpsed through the window of his house by his neighbour, Kinbote, ironizing the latter's attributions of meaning in the poem.

The poem itself is described by G.M. Hyde as: 'a deceptively limpid all-American poem by a notably self-effacing poet (appropriately named Shade).'[13] Critics have found in it a pastiche of the work of Robert Frost, with which it shares a respect for Augustan and Wordsworthian poetic values, transposed to a New England setting. Andrew Field[14] has noted its resemblance to Wordsworth's 'Prelude', both in its autobiographical themes and in the fact of posthumous publication. Like Wordsworth's poem, 'Pale Fire' stresses the primacy of experience and the role it plays in poetic composition; celebrates common human values and family bonds – in Shade's case, his love for his wife Sybil and continuing grief for the suicide of his daughter, Hazel. The poem closes with Shade's stated expectation of living to complete the poem and of the established pattern of his life continuing.

What follows the poem is, to quote G.M. Hyde again, 'a deranged and pedantic commentary appended by a mad Central European. . . .'[15]

To this the reader's first reaction is likely to be one of humorous outrage. Every rule of critical practice is flouted. Kinbote, whose

Commentary was written in a log cabin retreat remote from libraries, anyway sees himself to be above the drudgery of tracing references:

> Anybody having access to a good library could, no doubt, easily trace the story to its source and find the name of the lady; but such humdrum potterings are beneath true scholarship. (p. 286)

He subverts the values of the poem – those of 'decent' middle-class America – in favour of his own. A homosexual himself, he is particularly dismissive of the poem's celebration of married love, having the further motive of blaming Sybil Shade for thwarting his friendship with her husband. It soon becomes clear that the editorial role is a pretext for telling his own 'story', as he manipulates the Commentary into a narrative form.

He claims to have provided Shade with reminiscences of pre-revolutionary Zembla – a baroque, romantic world, far removed from the middle-class America of the poem – as material for 'Pale Fire'. The exclusion of that material on, he affirms, the insistence of Sybil Shade, justifies its inclusion in the Commentary. His Zembla is a richly detailed compensatory fantasy world, where homosexuality is a mark of superior taste and refinement, and with himself – the hints become more explicit as the Commentary proceeds – at the centre as King. As his story develops, the reader comes to realize that his project is to appropriate, not just Shade's poem, but his death, which provides the Commentary's narrative with its climax. The official version of Shade's death is that he was murdered by an escaped psychopath (Jack Grey) who mistook Shade for the man responsible for sending him to an asylum. Kinbote's version is that 'Grey' was an alias for 'Gradus', a Zemblan revolutionary who mistook Shade for his neighbour. Assassination – or proof of intended assassination – would of course validate Kinbote's claim to be king. Grey is now dead, and so beyond affirmation or denial. Kinbote is now completely estranged from Sybil, who gave him her husband's poem to edit immediately after the murder, when she was under the impression that Kinbote had intervened to save her husband's life.

The common-sense reading of *Pale Fire* is to give the poem priority over the commentary, to allow meaning to Shade and deny it to Kinbote; but the movement of irony in a Nabokov text is, as we have noticed, never so easy to chart. Ontological uncertainty is built into the text, at the most readily accessible level, in Nabokov's inviting the reader to identify Kinbote with himself – an identification which would, in a realist text, give him a special status. Kinbote, a European exile now teaching in a New England college, reflects some of the circumstances of Nabokov's own life, as well as a number of his opinions, in particular his well known contempt for Marx and Freud. The teasing of the reader with just such an identification becomes explicit at the end of the novel:

> I may turn up yet, on another campus, an an old, happy, healthy, heterosexual Russian, a writer in exile, sans fame, sans future, sans audience, sans anything but his art. (p. 337)

Of course Nabokov's work is full of such ploys, designed both to tempt into, and warn against, 'locating' him in his work. Nonetheless, the one quality which he undeniably shares with his character Kinbote, the condition of exile, gives both a particular perspective on America, allowing them to see, not only what America believes itself to be, but what has been excluded in the creation of that entity. This feature of *Pale Fire* parallels, and is indeed dependent on, the textual foregrounding. The juxtaposition of the two discrete elements in the text – the poem and the commentary – draws attention to an aspect of the creative process which is concealed in unselfconscious modes of writing (like Shade's poem) – its selectivity. A poem like 'Pale Fire' is implicitly an expression of eternal and universal human values. Kinbote's attempts to intrude himself into Shade's poem, during the composition and by using his editorial position to tell his own story, are absurd, but they draw attention to the truth of his own exclusion both from Shade's world and from the world of the poem. The complete text, if not the poem, is conscious of that exclusion in a way that is comparable to Shakespeare's use of homosexual characters who cannot be included in the heterosexual paradise that the plays otherwise seem to be celebrating at the end of *The Merchant of Venice* and *Twelfth Night*.

Shade's world, characterized by its tranquillity, decency and humanism, is further ironized by the eruption of violence into it – his own senseless death and, more suggestively, his daughter's suicide because she lacked the looks and charm to prosper in the American dating system. Kinbote's claim to identify with Hazel Shade – easily dismissed as yet another of his many appropriations – at the same time extends the reader's awareness of what is excluded from the cosy New England world celebrated in the poem to include Shade's own daughter. Kinbote's fantasy life takes more account of violence and disruption than Shade does, yet Shade is himself afflicted by them.

Pale Fire shows two quite different versions of reality competing in the text in a way that suggests there can be no common reality which accommodates the complexity and diversity of human experience. Moreover, such reality as the text possesses is itself textual. The name 'Shade' suggests an uncertain ontological status. Mary McCarthy, in her review of the novel when it was first published,[16] traced Zembla to

Nova Zembla in Swift's 'The Battle of the Books', where it is the home of criticism. The real audacity of *Pale Fire*, of course, is to give Zembla – which is not confined to the commentary but mentioned in the poem – a comparable status to America, with the results described by Tony Tanner:

> when Nabokov says America and Zembla and puts them together in the same frame as though belonging to the same dimensions – cohabiting on one plane – then our reading of the signs is necessarily more confused, the old associations are unsettled, the normal confidences as to the location of the 'real' are shaken.[17]

To quote Tanner again: 'On lexical playfields a man can be a king. . . .'[18] This applies, not just to Kinbote, who through his commentary has given a textual reality to the kingdom of his fantasy life, but to Nabokov himself, whose evident enjoyment of the creative faculty sets him apart from other writerly novelists, whose sense of the power of the text often expresses itself as anxiety.

The New York Trilogy, the first full-length work of Paul Auster (born in New Jersey in 1947), shares with *Pale Fire* a foregrounding of the text, and its power to create its own reality, which in turn confuses the reader's certainty about everyday reality. Each of the three parts of the *Trilogy* ('City of Glass', 'Ghosts' and 'The Locked Room') includes some discourse on the nature of language, as the expectations of the characters that language will render meaning are confounded by its stubbornly self-generating qualities. Auster both uses and subverts the conventions of American detective fiction, taking account of the consolations peculiar to the genre only to withhold them from the reader; thus creating, as each part succeeds the other, a sense of infinite regression. He plays with the boundaries of the text, teasingly suggesting autobiographical sources for the work, only to leave the reader still guessing at the end. The *Trilogy* is further enriched by a literary frame of reference which includes early Puritan theology, the writings of the nineteenth-century New England Transcendentalists and the fiction of Samuel Beckett, particularly his 'Trilogy', which is never mentioned by name but is nonetheless 'present' throughout.

   The New York Trilogy is, as its title suggests, set in New York, with excursions in the final part to Paris and New England; but like the 'America' of *Pale Fire* it is a New York self-consciously mediated through the text, in this case the detective novel and film. The central character of the first part, 'City of Glass', is Quinn, a writer of detective stories who is himself aware of the priority given by genre fiction to the genre itself over the world: 'What interested him about the stories he wrote was not their relation to the world but their relation to other stories' (p. 7). Quinn, who turned from other forms of writing to detective fiction after the death of his wife and son, finds in it not just the consolations of narrative – the addictive and sedative qualities of the genre are brought into play throughout the *Trilogy* – but the opportunities it offers the writer for concealment through regression. He uses the pseudonym of William Wilson and has as his private eye narrator Max Work, who:

> Over the years . . . had become very close to Quinn. . . . In the triad of selves that Quinn had become, Wilson served as a kind of ventriloquist. Quinn himself was the dummy, and Work was the animated voice that gave purpose to the enterprise. (p. 6)

Since Quinn no longer has any friends, his fiction has become his world.

'City of Glass' opens, in the time-honoured manner of detective fiction, with a telephone call, the caller asking for Paul Auster (who is of course unknown to Quinn). Quinn decides to impersonate Auster, who is being sought as private eye to protect a potential murder victim, Peter Stillman. When Quinn meets Stillman and his wife Virginia he finds them curiously lacking in spontaneity. Virginia Stillman is 'searching for an attitude of unshakeable honesty' (p. 25); while Stillman's mechanical responses are explained by his having been locked in a room as a child for nine years by his father, for experimental purposes. Stillman Senior is about to be released from prison after serving a long sentence for his treatment of his son, and the Stillmans want protection from Auster/Quinn from what they see as a likely murder attempt by the father on the son. Quinn's agreement is influenced by the fact that his own son was called Peter, and to protect another vulnerable son will serve some need of his own.

Naming, the organization of meaning through language and the relation of words to what they signify – all assume great importance in the central section of the narrative. Quinn, who has assumed the identity of Auster, finds that by:

> a deft little twist of naming, he felt incomparably lighter and freer. (p. 50)

Released from the burden of memory and feeling:

> He . . . had to remain solely on his own surface, looking outward for sustenance. (p. 61)

He buys a red notebook to record his impressions of the Stillman case:

> In that way, perhaps, things might not get out of control. (p. 38)

Through the library, he acquaints himself with Stillman Senior's theoretical justification for the incarceration of his son.

Stillman, the scion of an old Boston family and a Harvard scholar, was testing the theories of a Boston divine called Henry Dark. (Auster, like Pynchon in *Gravity's Rainbow*, finds in a reconstructed seventeenth-century Puritanism a vehicle for expressing late twentieth-century postmodernist concerns.) Dark's, and Stillman's, central precept is that before the Fall language carried the essence of meaning, so that the arbitrary relationship between language and what it signifies is a feature of man's fallen state. In locking up his son, Stillman hoped to reproduce the conditions in which 'pure' language might be generated. Quinn follows Stillman in his perambulations round the city after the latter's release from prison and can find no pattern in his movements until they are mapped out on paper and are seen to form the letters of TOWER OF BABEL. Quinn gets into conversation with Stillman, who confesses that Henry Dark and his paper were his own invention. In the course of following Stillman – trying to read him, penetrate his meaning – Quinn had lost an illusion which is crucial to a writer of detective fiction:

> that human behaviour could be understood, that beneath the infinite façade of gestures, tics, and silences, there was finally a coherence, an order, a source of motivation. (p. 67)

These are all deeply writerly concerns, and it is at this point that Auster – or an Auster mediated through the text – enters the narrative. Drawing a blank with his own investigations, Quinn locates Auster through the telephone book and goes to see him, hoping for help. Auster has a wife and small son whose presence revives the pain of Quinn's own losses; while the son, like Quinn, is called Daniel, reminding us that in another dimension, outside the frame of the novel, Quinn is Auster's 'son', in the sense of owing his existence to him. Auster is working on an essay on *Don Quixote* which raises the issues of how fact relates to fiction, fantasy to reality, and the place of the writer in his own work. Auster's evident pleasure in his own theories on the pleasure of the text is described as:

> a kind of soundless laughter, a joke that stopped short of its punchline, a generalized mirth that had no object. (p. 100)

Auster's behaviour, baffling to Quinn, enacts his view of the ultimate 'pointlessness' of the text, which is an end in itself rather than a way of penetrating meaning. This view is there to be tested against the events of the narrative of 'City of Glass'. Stillman Senior went mad in his search for pure meaning and deprived his son of human identity in the process. Quinn, now embarked on his quest, becomes possessed by it. In order, as he sees it, to pursue the Stillmans' case more effectively, he stations himself among the garbage outside their apartment and denies himself food and sleep to the point where he becomes unrecognizable even to himself. When he runs out of money to supply his now minimal needs and is forced to re-emerge into the world, he finds that Stillman senior has committed suicide, the younger Stillmans have fled without trace and the cheque they gave him as payment has bounced. He returns to his apartment to find somebody else in possession and all sign of his earlier occupation obliterated: 'He had come to the end of himself' (p. 125).

He returns to the Stillmans' empty apartment, where he slowly disintegrates. A first-person narrator – a friend, we are told, of Auster's – takes over at the end to explain that the events have been reconstructed from Quinn's red notebook.

It is this final sequence of 'City of Glass' which most powerfully evokes Beckett's work, particularly the 'Moran' section of *Molloy*. Like Moran (who is also some kind of investigator) Quinn has only to move a short distance from home and his familiar routine to lose his physical identity and his orientation in time and space. What happens to Moran and to Quinn suggests the clear dependence of what we take to be ultimate certainties on what we have ourselves constructed, life's necessary fictions. Moreover, like Moran, Quinn becomes the thing he pursues – for the Stillman whom he trailed around New York had assumed a tramp's life on leaving prison: the end of all searching, it seems, is the self, and finally loss of self, for the search exposes the self's frailty.

The fate of both Stillman senior and Quinn – both in search of an end which does not exist – would appear to validate the priority that 'Auster' gives, in his discussion of *Don Quixote*, to means over end, in life as in the text. 'The City of Glass', which begins like a detective novel, and indeed plays with the conventions of the genre throughout, not only withholds meaning and resolution, but exposes the flaws in a genre which holds out the promise of them. Nonetheless, the use made of 'Paul Auster' in the text implicates him in the quest for meaning, despite the god-like serenity with which he claims to be above it. The Stillmans' first telephone call to 'Paul Auster' establishes a link between the private eye and the writer. Moreover, the parallel sets of fathers and sons also open up teasing possibilities. Again, the point of serenity is 'Auster' 's happy relationship with his son. So why has he chosen to write about the vulnerability of sons and emotionally devastated and mad fathers?

Towards the end of 'The Locked Room', the third part of the *Trilogy*, the unnamed first-person narrator suddenly takes up a position outside the frame in order to comment, as author, on the three parts of the *Trilogy*, which he describes as: 'the same story, but each

one represents a different stage in my awareness of what it is about'
(p. 294).

The three parts share common components of plot, but in 'Ghosts',
the second part, the form is at its most diagrammatic. Blue, a private
detective, is employed by White to follow Black. White has rented an
apartment across from Black's for Blue to occupy; Blue is to prepare a
weekly report and be paid by cheque, with no immediate prospect of a
further meeting with White, whom Blue anyway suspects of having
worn a disguise. In his new solitude, Blue begins to lose his bearings:

> For the first time in his life, he finds that he has been thrown back on
> himself, with nothing to grab hold of, nothing to distinguish one mo-
> ment from the next. (p. 143)

Aware for the first time of 'the world inside him', he begins to make up
stories about Black and:

> he discovers that making up stories can be a pleasure in itself. (p. 144)

Among his other discoveries are a curious reluctance to telephone his
fiancée, and a new unease with language when he comes to write his
reports. Words, which he had assumed to be 'transparent . . . great
windows which stand between him and the world' (p. 146) have taken
on an inconvenient life of their own:

> It's as though his words, instead of drawing out the facts and making
> them sit palpably in the world, have induced them to disappear.
> (p. 147)

His reports reveal nothing about Black, whereas the stories he makes
up say a good deal about himself.

As time goes on and nothing happens, Blue begins to feel like a
character in a book, one that:

> will go on being written for as long as he stays in the room. . . .
> (p. 170)

It is a book with

> no story, no plot, no action – nothing but a man sitting alone in a room
> and writing a book. (p. 169)

The sense of being condemned like a character in a book (as of course
he is) with no control over his own destiny, is reinforced by the reflection of himself that he finds in Black. Black's life appears to be as
empty as Blue's, and he too spends most of his time writing. Looking
at Black, and knowing everything and nothing about him, Blue
reflects that: 'It is not possible for such a man as Black to exist'
(p. 170). Blue begins to wonder whether Black is not another of

White's hirelings, paid to watch him. This suspicion seems to be confirmed when he meets Black in a bar and the latter describes himself as a private detective engaged on a boring case of watching somebody who appears to do nothing. He fails to recognize Blue, however, so bringing into question not just the 'point' of Blue's life but how far he is in fact there. When Blue breaks into Black's apartment and finds it bare of clues, he is confronted by the same kind of extremity reached by Quinn in watching the Stillmans' apartment:

> It's a no man's land, the place you come to at the end of the world.
> (p. 185)

The writerly concerns of 'Ghosts' and of 'The City of Glass' – of a plot and a language which are outside the individual's control – raise the broader issues of personal freedom and destiny. Both Blue and Quinn, once forced back on their inner lives, become incapable of breaking out of the plot, however unrewarding, as though in the expectation of a final answer. Discourse on these questions is broadened by the use Auster makes of two crucial periods of American cultural history. I have already mentioned the Puritan background to Stillman's theories, which admits into the frame of reference that historical moment when the power of the individual to will his own destiny becomes crucial to American thinking. In 'Ghosts' Black (and then Blue, in search of clues) is reading Thoreau's *Walden*. Black talks to Blue, at this point disguised as a tramp, about Walt Whitman, whose 'Leaves of Grass' was printed in Brooklyn, where 'Ghosts' is set. These references bring into play the ideas of the New England Transcendentalists of the mid-nineteenth century and their central belief in the power of the individual, in communion with himself, in however confined and solitary circumstances, to find the world illuminated with meaning.

The Transcendentalists are ironic and ghostly presences in the background as, at the end of 'Ghosts', Blue batters Black to death with a gun that Black had drawn on him. He reads Black's notebook, whose contents are withheld from the reader, which confirms his suspicion that he knew all that there was to know at the beginning. There is no White, only Blue and Black. Blue leaves the room at the end and disappears.

The final part of *The New York Trilogy*, 'The Locked Room', again combines writerly concerns with an investigative plot, but here the conventions of detective fiction are suggested as possible parallels rather than used to dictate the terms of the plot. This is accompanied by a feature of more conventional fiction which is minimized in the two earlier parts of the *Trilogy* – some psychological exploration of character in relation to circumstances and background. The effect of this, however, is not to provide a final human explanation for the unsolved mysteries of the two earlier books, but to expose some of the human needs which, by a process of displacement, detective fiction is used by the consumer to fill.

The theme of knowing another person – or rather, the urge that drives human beings to seek such knowledge – is important in 'The Locked Room' as it is in 'The City of Glass' and 'Ghosts', but is more firmly rooted in biographical circumstances. The unnamed first-person narrator – who, as a web of detail is formed throughout the novel, is ambiguously identified with Paul Auster himself – is unexpectedly confronted with his own past. He receives a telephone call from Sophie Fanshawe, the wife of a friend of his from childhood and adolescence who has since dropped out of his life. Sophie tells him that her husband has disappeared, and having drawn a blank in trying to find him – she employed Quinn the private detective for this purpose – has decided to act on the instructions Fanshawe gave her in the event of his death. These are that she should ask the narrator (whom I shall henceforward refer to as N) to act as his literary executor. N, who is a writer himself, agrees, and finds himself in possession of a suitcase of unpublished manuscripts.

This revives for N memories of Fanshawe, from whom as a child he was virtually inseparable.

> It would be impossible, I think, for me to know anyone as well as I knew Fanshawe then. (p. 213)

The first-person narrative through which Fanshawe is filtered allows him to acquire a mythic status similar to that conferred on Jay Gatsby and Sebastian Flyte by similar means in *The Great Gatsby* and *Brideshead Revisited*. He is described as being:

> more in harmony with himself, more ideally a normal child than any of the rest of us. (p. 214)

That harmony, however, was combined with outstanding achievement in every field of activity. The death of Fanshawe's father is recalled, and Fanshawe's devoted care of him – this is the most poignant rendering of the father/son configuration in the *Trilogy* – both being seen as significant in terms of Fanshawe's subsequent development. No longer able to confine himself to a conventional pattern of existence, he took to a wandering life which came to an end when he married Sophie.

The collection of manuscripts confirms N's judgement of Fanshawe as a man of extraordinary talent, and when the novels are published and the plays performed that judgement is confirmed by widespread critical acclaim. N becomes emotionally and sexually involved with

Sophie. The relationship brings its own special kind of knowledge and gives N his 'true place in the world'. He is widely assumed to be the 'real' author of Fanshawe's work, and although he denies this, he begins to wonder 'whether or not a writer has a real life anyway' (p. 236). At this point the reader might well begin to ask similar questions about Auster. In 'City of Glass' he is shown with a beautiful wife, Siri, who is Norwegian, 'By way of Northfield, Minnesota' (p. 102), and a son, Daniel. Sophie too is a Norwegian from Minnesota, has a son, Ben, by Fanshawe, and when she marries N they go to live on Riverside Drive, like the Austers of 'City of Glass'. Knowing nothing of the circumstances of the Auster who is outside the frame of the novel, the reader is inevitably drawn to speculate. Since, given the self-consciousness of the work as a whole, we can probably acquit the author of a naive reliance for material on the detail of his own life, is he exposing the process by which biographical fact is turned into fiction, or the ways in which fiction may be used to express those latent anxieties which are a kind of alternative biography?[19]

The conventionally happy family picture that is drawn in 'The Locked Room', containing and harmonizing as it does elements from the past with prospects for the future, and recalling the picture of the 'Austers' of 'City of Glass', suggests a possible closure which relies on the reader's experience of other stories and other endings. It is at this point, however, that the novel begins to darken. N has had a letter from Fanshawe partly explaining his motives; and the knowledge that he is still alive (which he concealed from Sophie, though he insisted that she obtain a divorce before their own marriage), together with his agreement with a publisher that he write a biography of Fanshawe, begin to corrode his life. His relationship with Sophie sours; he visits Fanshawe's mother in search of material and brutally makes love to her. His feelings for Fanshawe become violent and his work on the biography becomes a disguised search for Fanshawe himself, whom he wants to kill.

Or has Fanshawe scripted even this, and chosen N to be his exterminator? The more N discovers about Fanshawe, the more enigmatic he becomes, no longer irradiated by the clear light of childhood memory, but, as his mother remembers him, '"cold inside"' (p. 261). A resemblance between N and Fanshawe is increasingly noticed, to the point where N is mistaken for his missing friend.

His search takes him to France where, paralleling Blue in 'Ghosts', he loses the urge to telephone Sophie – who links him to the world, the past and the future – and is finally confronted by himself:

> After all these months of trying to find him, I felt as though I was the one who had been found. Instead of looking for Fanshawe, I had

actually been running away from him. The work I had contrived for myself – the false book, the endless detours – had been no more than an attempt to ward him off, a ruse to keep him as far away from me as possible. (p. 292)

Like hell in Marlowe's *Doctor Faustus*:

Fanshawe was exactly where I was, and he had been there since the beginning. (p. 292)

The locked room where he eventually finds Fanshawe has both a physical location – in Boston – and is his own mind, where Fanshawe has always been.

By the time the meeting takes place, N has been reconciled to Sophie, who has borne him a son of his own; the biography has been abandoned and they are no longer living off the proceeds of Fanshawe's work. Fanshawe summons him to Boston, where he is using the name of 'Henry Dark', Stillman's invented New England Puritan. There are further echoes of the earlier parts of the *Trilogy*, as Fanshawe reveals that he camped outside N's and Sophie's apartment in order to watch them. He gives N a red notebook – Quinn uses a red notebook for his investigations – which is intended to offer an explanation, but:

Each sentence erased the sentence before it, each paragraph made the next paragraph impossible. It is odd, then, that the feeling that survives from this notebook is one of great lucidity. It is as if Fanshawe knew his final work had to subvert every expectation I had for it. (p. 314)

All three novels of the *New York Trilogy* turn on the quest for knowledge of another person which is finally either withheld, or granted in a form which is meaningless. All three quests are ultimately internalized and expose within the self, not an answer, but a frightening void. Their inter-textuality, creating an effect of endless doubling back, subverts the linear plot of the quest, with which they all play. The relationship of the narrator with Fanshawe in 'The Locked Room' is particularly interesting, as being the most psychologically realized. On the one hand it suggests that knowledge of another person can never be pure, but is always coloured by what we want to find: the mythic and heroic Fanshawe of the narrator's youth, is replaced by a Fanshawe who is beyond the human in a more disturbing, even diabolical way, as he takes on the burden of the narrator's fears and resentment. On the other hand it is never clear whether Fanshawe is not, for the narrator, an alter ego who is destroyed (Fanshawe's intentions at the end are suicidal) once he has outlived his usefulness. There is an echo here of the merging of Moran and Molloy in the first part of the Beckett Trilogy.

Needs which life cannot fulfil are served by fantasy and fiction, the detective novel in particular offering the prospect that all will finally be known, all mysteries solved. That is the nature of the consolation which the genre offers us, the source of its addictive and sedative powers. Both Quinn and the narrator in one episode in 'The Locked Room' use detective fiction to ease pain. Auster, while always teasing us with the possibility of such consolation in *The New York Trilogy*, finally withholds it. But it is a withholding that provokes no anger, since his own intrusions into the narrative are designed to suggest that the writer, too, is driven by need. What is left, for both writer and reader, is an ever recurring cycle of further narratives.

Afterword: *The Satanic Verses*, 'Alternative Realities' and Absolute Truth

Postmodernist writing resists closure. It also belongs to an historical and cultural cycle which cannot yet be viewed as complete. Unfinished, it cannot be discussed with the same air of finality as, say, the Elizabethan Drama or the Victorian Novel. It seems appropriate, therefore, to end this book 'in the midst', or by entering what Salman Rushdie in his essay 'Outside the Whale', called 'the unceasing storm, the continuing quarrel, the dialectic of history.'[1]

He was referring, in a general way, to the responsibility the writer owes to his own political and historical moment. Now Rushdie himself has made history with his most recent novel, *The Satanic Verses*; and as I write this (September 1989), the situation created, and the issues raised, by *The Satanic Verses*, are still tragically unresolved and threatening.

Those Western readers who read *The Satanic Verses* between its publication in September 1988 and the beginning of 1989 when, for the Western world, it first became a news item, might be able to claim a naive or 'pure' reading of the novel (assuming that that is ever possible). But for those who read it after the storm broke, the sequence of events provoked by the novel's publication now inevitably colours their reading of it.[2] Its own engagement with history has become part of the phenomenology we take to the reading of it. This in itself would be enough to make *The Satanic Verses* an exemplary text in any examination of the postmodernist project. Beyond that, however, the events which have followed its publication are difficult to interpret, and generate more irreconcilable patterns of irony the more closely one looks at them – and that is so even if one confines oneself, as I must, given my own limitations, to a Western, secular viewpoint. When the commentary on the novel, and on the situation to which it had given rise, was at its fiercest, in the early months of 1989, there appeared to be a babble of voices, clamouring to be heard, impossible to harmonize, each ironizing the others. By a supreme irony this in itself, apart from the considerable literary merits of *The Satanic Verses*, would seem to justify the kind of novel that it is. It acknowledges the world's complexity, through irony, through a wide variety of destabilizing techniques and by offering alternative readings of reality.

The secular attack on *The Satanic Verses* on aesthetic grounds has been almost as fierce as the Muslim outrage at its religious transgressiveness. Widely and popularly held to be 'obscure' and 'unreadable' – criticisms that were also levelled against *Ulysses*, a novel that it much resembles in its knowing play with another text (the *Quran*), in its inclusiveness and in the tight structure underpinning the surface chaos – its reception by the general public demonstrates that postmodernist fiction still needs defending. Yet the sequence of events following the publication of Rushdie's novel, and the issues raised by them, are themselves the stuff of postmodernist fiction; and indeed, were it 'fictionalized', could hardly be rendered in realist form. What is immediately apparent is the impossibility of constructing a frame to hold everything that is part of this particular picture, in that the West and Islam are in themselves two discrete systems of reality. The Muslim response – book-burnings, large public demonstrations, and, in February 1989, the death threat issued against Rushdie by the Ayatolla Khomeini, then spiritual leader of Iran – has confirmed the West's sense of the 'otherness' of Islam, and of its primitive handling of crisis. Western explanations of Islamic behaviour, however, have been marked by a different kind of primitivism, in the simplistic use of historical argument.

One popular and widely canvassed 'theory' is that, since Islam was founded 600 years or so later than Christianity, it is that much 'behind' Christianity in civilized development; as though the Western pattern of development should be taken as a 'universal' norm, and therefore a model by which other civilizations might be usefully measured. More seriously, the Muslim response has created difficulties in precisely those liberal circles in Britain which have traditionally championed the rights of immigrants. The British Labour Party in particular has found it impossible to reconcile the conflicting principles of the writer's right to publish with its commitment to the aspirations of minority groups.

What we have been seeing are two irreconcilable systems of value in collision. On one side, the right to freedom of speech, observed by Western societies, has been upheld to the point where the British government is giving police protection to a writer who in this same book lampoons both the British Prime Minister (thinly disguised as Mrs Torture) and the British police force. On the other side, behind Khomeini's death threat there is an absolute reverence for revealed religious truth which supersedes personal freedoms, albeit that the 'offensive' episodes – a transgressive, 'alternative' life of Muhammed which shows him in doubt on the issue of assimilating pagan goddesses – might appear to liberal Western perceptions to be balanced by a passionate defence of the rights of Muslims in the Western societies of their colonial overlords.

There are ironies enough in this bald account, and as one looks further they multiply, not always in ways that favour the West. *The Satanic Verses* is a deeply subversive work, subverting a range of received realities with a variety of postmodernist techniques. The fact that it was perceived as subversive by Islam might be felt to argue, not a lack of sophistication, but a respect for the word which is no longer held in the West. It was clear from the reports of the PEN conference in New York in March 1989, and in particular from the embattled tone adopted by Norman Mailer, one of the principal speakers, that the issue had generated a certain excitement among writers that they were at last in the front line. When, in the weeks following the death threat, Britain's Foreign Secretary, Sir Geoffrey Howe, described *The Satanic Verses* as:

> deeply critical and rude about us. It compares Britain with Hitler's Germany. We don't like that any more than the people of the Muslim faith like the attack on their faith contained in the book.[3]

it seemed clear that only then had somebody in government circles taken the trouble to read the book.

Postmodernist writing is a deeply subversive mode, but it is difficult to be subversive in a society that refuses to listen. It might be argued – and the Rushdie affair has brought this into particularly sharp focus – that the growth of this kind of writing in Western societies over the last forty years or so is itself a response to a widespread loss of principle and passion. One of the less edifying by-products of the controversy has been the opportunity it has offered to denigrate a work – and beyond that, a whole mode of writing – which few people have taken the trouble to understand. 'The underlying tragedy' concluded a leader in the *Independent* entitled 'Viking Must Stand Firm', 'is that the book has acquired a significance beyond its due'.

In the light of this, the accusations of collusion between the British government and Rushdie, made by Muslims states, are absurd, proof of a misunderstanding by Muslims of the West as profound as the West's misunderstanding of Islam. Political rhetoric, however, is itself a form of fiction which is effective to the degree that it is received as reality. This is an aspect of the world which postmodernist novelists, Rushdie among them, are uniquely able to address, in their relentless exposure of the processes of fiction. The novelist Magie Gee, at an ICA conference on the issues raised by *The Satanic Verses*, described it as:

the final irony . . . that it isn't actually Rushdie's novel which has caused this furore, but cruder, smaller fictions about his novel, propagated by powerful elites. Thus has his novel fallen back into the hands of the very same public fictions that the novel has from its origins challenged.[4]

Rushdie, who among contemporary novelists has shown perhaps the greatest awareness of the complex historical forces and cultural exploitation which determine the fate of the immigrant, has now become a scapegoat, the focus for long-standing injustices experienced by immigrants. And while the fictions generated about his novel have for him been personally tragic, viewed from another perspective, they may be said to justify the underlying theory of postmodernism.

In *Midnight's Children* he wrote of 'the alternative realities . . . beloved of poets' (p. 217). One reading of *The Satanic Verses* is as a discourse on the power of imagined reality, within the context of exile and immigration, and of religious experience. The two central characters, Gibreel Faroushta and Saladin Chamcha, are actors and therefore professionally involved in creating alternative realities – Gibreel in the Bombay film industry, where his speciality is 'theological movies', Saladin more modestly in London doing voice-overs for television commercials. Towards the end of a flight from Bombay to London – Saladin returning from a visit to his father, Gibreel in pursuit of Alleluia Cone, whom he met when she was in India on an Everest expedition – the plane is blown up by terrorists and the two men fall from the skies to begin a series of metamorphic adventures.

Chamcha, the fully anglicized Indian and apologist for Western cultural values, is partly transformed into a goat; after violent handling by the British police, who are indifferent to his claims to be a British citizen, he finds himself in a hospital with other deformed creatures, where his condition is explained to him by another inmate:

> 'They describe us. . . . That's all. They have the power of description, and we succumb to the pictures they construct.' (p. 168)

(As in *Midnight's Children*, language is seen, not as an inert medium, but as a dynamic force in its own right; and metaphor, rather than illuminating reality, creates its own.) Escaped from the hospital, and rejected by his English wife Pamela, he goes into hiding with the Sufyans, proprietors of the Shandaar Cafe, who further exhibit the confusions inherent in the immigrant's position. The socialist Muhammed Sufyan left Pakistan on political principle; his wife, unknown to him, is growing rich by letting rooms to families left homeless by government housing policy. Their two teenage daughters are complete cultural hybrids. During his time in hiding with them,

Chamcha, who has taken pride in his 'English' self-control, learns to hate – a development which restores him to his original appearance.

Gibreel initially fares better. His love affair with the blonde Everest queen Alleluia Cone – who, as the daughter of Polish Jews exiled in London, contributes to the novel's discourse on immigration – prospers; and his metamorphosis is invisible. He believes himself to be the Angel Gibreel, and in that capacity, in a sequence of dreams, he intervenes in the development of the religion in the desert established by the Prophet Mahound (Muhammad); in his waking life he appoints himself the saviour of the once great city of London, whose inner corruption he is enabled to see. His belief in his own powers, however, is not matched by his still human physical capacities, and he nearly dies in an act of outrageous daring. While he is recovering, Chamcha reappears in his life and sets out to wreck Gibreel's relationship with Allie Cone. A series of anonymous telephone calls, in which Chamcha exploits to the full his skill with voices, convinces Gibreel, an Othello to Chamcha's Iago, that Alleluia is unfaithful to him. At the end of the novel, when the action has switched to Bombay, Gibreel kills Alleluia and then himself.

Chamcha's telephone calls, of which he repents too late, are the 'satanic verses' of the title, paralleling the verses in the *Quran*, later removed, which tell of the Prophet's brief assimilation of pagan deities into the new religion in the desert. *The Satanic Verses* opens with a quotation from Defoe's 'The History of the Devil' describing the omnipresence of Satan; and one way of describing *The Satanic Verses* would be as a discourse on the nature of evil, which is seen as a kind of impurity or adulteration of the 'whole'. Since impurity is lurking everywhere in the world, then nothing which includes human agency – even the world's great religions – can avoid a brush with it. This is further explored in the 'Mahound' narrative when the girls in a brothel in Jahilia (Mecca) assume the names and to a degree the characteristics of the Prophet's wives, for the delectation of their clients. Here the appearance of holiness sharpens the appetite for what is shameful. At the same time, since the narrative is persistently ambiguous, the whole episode exposes the futility of trying to fix and regulate human life, which in the novel is subject to a constant process of metamorphosis, – a project on which Mahound embarks with a proliferation of new laws on his triumphant return to Jahilia.

The source of the evil in the central narrative is Chamcha, the uprooted, self-invented man. Upright, righteous, the complete English gentleman, he becomes embittered when he realizes that he can never finally be accepted on those terms by the society in which he thought himself to be assimilated; while Gibreel, flamboyantly and unashamedly Indian, wins the desirable Alleluia Cone. Gibreel himself, a one-time philanderer, is surprised by the depth of his feeling for Alleluia, and this leaves him vulnerable. Anything of value invites, and carries the seeds of its own, destruction.

The dichotomy present in the novel's depiction of the honourable Chamcha, who is shocked into dishonour, and of Gibreel's 'pure' love for Alleluia, which becomes violent, also characterizes the moving account of a pilgrimage to the Arabian Sea led by a young mystic, Ayesha, who claims that the sea will part and the pilgrims – an entire village – will be able to walk to Mecca. The dichotomy here is one of interpretation, of how absolute religious faith is viewed by the secularized sceptic – a position assigned in the novel to the wealthy Mirza Saeed, whose wife Mishall, Ayesha's principal pilgrim, is dying of cancer. What happens when the pilgrims reach the sea is left in doubt, but it is worth noting, in view of the outrage that *The Satanic Verses* has provoked in religious circles, that the sceptics who watch the pilgrimage have their scepticism shaken:

> these visitors were amazed, and retreated with confounded expecta-
> tions, that is to say with a hole in their pictures of the world that they
> could not paper over. (p. 488)

At the end of the novel, while Gibreel dies, Chamcha is given a second chance. He returns to India for the death of his father, from whom he has been estranged, and finds him purified by the approach of death. The illness which had stripped him of flesh:

> had also stripped him of his faults, of all that had been domineering,
> tyrannical and cruel in him, so that the mischievous, loving and
> brilliant man underneath lay exposed, once again, for all to see.
> (p. 524)

Once home, Chamcha is reconciled to the first Indian woman he had ever made love to, Zeeny Vakil, a doctor who works with the homeless in Bombay.

The ending of the novel recalls Dickens's work, in its closing sequence of homecoming, reconciliation, moving death-bed scene and reformed hero rewarded with a woman whose virtue is re-defined in twentieth-century terms. Perhaps the final irony of the *Satanic Verses* story – an irony generated by the play between the story within the novel and the 'story' it has provoked – is that it has attracted almost as much opprobrium from non-Muslims for its moral offensiveness and textual obscurity as it has from Muslims for its blasphemy. Yet it displays many of those features of nineteenth-century fiction – rich and detailed characterization, the ability to move to laughter and to tears, a plot which reaches a 'satisfactory' conclusion and a continuous spirit of moral inquiry – whose passing is most lamented in Britain by what used to be known as the common reader. That these qualities are combined with an extraordinary linguistic resourcefulness, a playfulness and a breadth of reference more characteristic of its own times, makes the reader's experience of *The Satanic Verses* all the richer.

Notes to Chapters

CHAPTER ONE

1 George Eliot, *Middlemarch*, Penguin English Library, 1965, p. 30.

2 See in particular *Modernism*, edited by Malcolm Bradbury and James McFarlane, Penguin, 1976.

3 Quoted by David Minter in *William Faulkner: His Life and Work*, Johns Hopkins University Press, 1980, p. 99.

4 James Joyce, *A Portrait of the Artist as a Young Man*, Triad/Panther, 1977, p. 195.

5 See in particular Eagleton's *Criticism and Ideology*, Verso, 1976, and Said's *The World, the Text, and the Critic*, Harvard University Press, 1983, Faber & Faber, 1984.

6 Frank Kermode, *The Sense of an Ending*, OUP, 1966, p. 112 paperback edition.

7 Roland Barthes, *Writing Degree Zero*, translated by Annette Lavers and Colin Smith, New York: Hill & Wang, 1977, p. 46; *Barthes: Selected Writings*, introduced by Susan Sontag, Fontana, 1983.

8 David Lodge, *Working with Structuralism*, Routledge & Kegan Paul, 1981, pp. 3–16.

9 The relevant passage from *Das Kapital* may be found in *Twentieth Century Interpretations of Robinson Crusoe*, edited by Frank Ellis, Prentice Hall, 1969, pp. 91–2.

10 Alexander Selkirk's account of his experiences was published by Sterne in the *Englishman* on 3 December 1713.

11 Patricia Waugh, *Metafiction*, Methuen, 1984, p. 99.

12 Deirdre Bair, *Samuel Beckett*, Jonathan Cape, 1978, Pan 1980, p. 389.

13 Roland Barthes, 'Authors and Writers', written in 1960, included in *Critical Essays*, Northwestern University Press, 1972; *Barthes: Selected Writings*, p. 187.

14 Kermode, *The Sense of an Ending*. These ideas are discussed, from different perspectives, throughout the book.

15 Among recent novels exploring apocalyptic ideas in environmental terms are Ben Elton's *Stark*, published in 1988, and Martin Amis's *London Fields*, published in 1989.

16 Terry Eagleton's 'Capitalism, Modernism and Postmodernism' is included in *Against the Grain*, Verso, 1986. This quotation, p. 146.

17 Kermode, *The Sense of an Ending*, p. 101.

18 Philip Roth, 'Writing American Fiction', included in *The Novel Today*, edited by Malcolm Bradbury, Fontana, 1977. This quotation, p. 34.

edited by Malcolm Bradbury, Fontana, 1977. This quotation, p. 34.
19 Brian McHale, *Postmodernist Fiction*, Methuen, 1987, p. xii.

CHAPTER TWO

1 See Chapter 1, p. 11.
2 James Joyce, *Ulysses*, published in 1922 in Paris; this quotation, p. 23
Bodley Head 1960 edition.
3 Salman Rushdie in 'Desert Island Discs', broadcast BBC Radio 4, 18
September 1988.
4 Joyce, *Ulysses*, p. 255.
5 Samuel Beckett, *Proust*, Chatto & Windus, 1931.
6 Deirdre Bair, *Samuel Beckett*, Jonathan Cape, 1978; Pan 1980, p. 243.
7 See Note 13 to Chapter I.

CHAPTER THREE

1 For a brief introduction to this group of writers, see Marcus Cunliffe,
The Literature of the United States, Penguin, 1986, 'Southland' chapter,
p. 343; and for further study of the subject, his Bibliography to that chapter.
2 As quoted by David Minter in *William Faulkner: His Life and Work*,
Johns Hopkins University Press, 1980, p. 96.
3 *ibid.*, p. 99.
4 See Chapter 2 for a discussion of Joyce's aesthetic.
5 Minter, *William Faulkner*, pp. 96–7.
6 For a discussion of this feature of Russian Formalist critical practice, see
Peter Brooks, *Reading for the Plot*, Vintage Books, 1985, Chapter 1,
'Reading for the Plot'.
7 See Roland Binns, *Malcolm Lowry*, Methuen, 1984, for a more comprehensive discussion of Lowry's literary frame of reference.
8 Binns, *Malcolm Lowry*, p. 56.
9 See Chapter 1.
10 Mark Kinead-Weekes and Ian Gregor, *William Golding: A Critical
Study*, Faber & Faber, 1984, pp. 121–64.
11 Richard Ellmann, *Four Dubliners*, Hamish Hamilton, 1987; Sphere
Books, 1988, p. 82.
12 *ibid.*, p. 85.
13 *ibid.*, p. 88.
14 John Fletcher, *Novels of Samuel Beckett*, Chatto & Windus, 1964.
15 Jean-Jacques Mayoux, 'Samuel Beckett and Universal Parody', from
Vivants Piliers. Le roman anglo-saxon et les symboles, Paris: Editions René
Juillard, 1960. Translated by Barbara Bray in *Samuel Beckett: A Collection
of Critical Essays*, edited by Martin Esslin, Prentice Hall, 1965; this quotation, pp. 88–9.

CHAPTER FOUR

1 Andrew Field, *VN: The Life and Art of Vladimir Nabokov*, Crown Publishers Inc, 1986, New York; Futura, 1988, p. 310.
2 *ibid.*, p. 310.
3 George Steiner, 'Book-keeping of torture', *The Sunday Times*, 10 April 1988.

CHAPTER FIVE

1 See in particular Middleton and Rowley's *The Changeling*.
2 See Chapter 3, p. 46.
3 Frank Kermode, *The Sense of an Ending*, OUP, 1966; 1981 paperback, p. 112.
4 Malcolm Brabury, *Saul Bellow*, Methuen, 1982, p. 73.
5 Bradbury, *Saul Bellow*, p. 73.
6 Malcolm Bradbury, *The Novel Today*, Fontana, 1977.
7 Philip Roth, 'Writing American Fiction', from *Reading Myself and Others*, Farrar, Straus & Giroux, 1975; reprinted in Bradbury, *The Novel Today*, pp. 32–47.
8 Saul Bellow, 'Some Notes on Recent American Fiction', *Encounter*, 1963; reprinted in Bradbury, *The Novel Today*, pp. 54–69.
9 *The Novel Today*, p. 62.
10 *ibid.*, p. 69.
11 *ibid.*, p. 69.
12 *ibid.*, p. 66.
13 *ibid.*, p. 66.
14 George Steiner, 'Book-keeping of Torture', *The Sunday Times*, 10 April 1988.

CHAPTER SIX

1 As reported by, for example, *The Sunday Times* on 10 July 1988.
2 See Tony Tanner, *Thomas Pynchon*, Methuen, 1982, in particular the first chapter, 'Thomas Pynchon and the death of the author', pp. 11–19.
3 *ibid.*, p. 11.
4 Roland Barthes, 'Death of the Author', 1968, in *Image-Music-Text*, Fontana, 1977.
5 Roland Barthes, *Mythologies*, 1957; Jonathan Cape, 1972.
6 Tanner, *Thomas Pynchon*, p. 60.
7 David Lodge, 'Modernism, Antimodernism and Postmodernism', in *Working with Structuralism*, Routledge & Kegan Paul, 1981; this quotation p. 16.

CHAPTER SEVEN

1 Georg Lukacs, *The Historical Novel*, Pelican, 1981, p. 20.
2 *ibid.*, p. 20.
3 *ibid.*, p. 224.
4 *ibid.*, p. 279.
5 *ibid.*, p. 278.
6 *ibid.*, p. 276.
7 See the Foreword to *The Magus*, Triad/Panther, 1977, p. 6.
8 Heinrich von Kleist, 'Michael Kohlhaas', in *Erzählungen* (1810–11); English translation, 1960.
9 See, 'The marked man: a writer driven by life to dissent', *The Sunday Times*, 19 February 1989; reprinted in *The Rushdie File*, edited by Lisa Appignanesi and Sara Maitland, Fourth Estate Ltd, 1989, p. 3.
10 In BBC Radio 4, 'Desert Island Discs', 18 September 1988.
11 For example, the date given for the death of Mahatma Gandhi, *Midnight's Children*, p. 161.
12 As reported in the *Observer*, 22 January 1989; reprinted in Appignanesi and Maitland, *The Rushdie File*, p. 75.
13 'Bandung File', 14 February 1989, Channel 4; reproduced in Appignanesi and Maitland, *The Rushdie File*, p. 29.

CHAPTER EIGHT

1 Tony Tanner, *City of Words*, Jonathan Cape, 1971; 1979 Cape paperback, p. 27.
2 Tanner, *City of Words*, p. 83.
3 'Ripeness is all', *King Lear*, V, ii.
4 Brian McHale, *Postmodernist Fiction*, Methuen, 1987, p. 16.
5 Tony Tanner, *Thomas Pynchon*, Methuen, 1982, p. 74.

CHAPTER NINE

1 Iris Murdoch, 'Against Dryness', *Encounter*, January 1961.
2 Anne Righter, *Shakespeare and the Idea of the Play*, Chatto & Windus, 1962; Penguin Shakespeare Library, 1967.
3 Peter Conradi, *John Fowles*, Methuen, 1983, p. 54.
4 David Lodge, *The Modes of Modern Writing*, Edward Arnold, 1977; 1979 paperback edition, p. 226.
5 Peter Conradi, *Iris Murdoch: the Saint and the Artist*, Macmillan 1986, p. 15.
6 *ibid.*, p. 230.
7 See 'Against Dryness', *Encounter*, January 1961.
8 See Iris Murdoch, *The Sovereignty of Good*, Routledge & Kegan Paul, 1970.
9 'Against Dryness'.
10 Conradi, *Iris Murdoch*, p. 248.

11 *ibid.*, p. 262.
12 Tony Tanner, *City of Words*, Cape, 1971; 1976 Cape paperback, p. 33.
13 G. M. Hyde, *Vladimir Nabokov, America's Russian Novelist*, Calder & Boyars Ltd, 1977, p. 171.
14 Andrew Field, *VN: The Life and Art of Vladimir Nabokov*, Crown Publishers Inc, 1986; Futura, 1988, p. 339.
15 Hyde, *Vladimir Nabokov*, p. 171.
16 See Tanner, *City of Words*, p. 33 for a summary and discussion of McCarthy's review.
17 *ibid.*, p. 34.
18 *ibid.*, p. 38.
19 Auster's autobiographical essay, *The Invention of Solitude*, Sun Press, 1982, Faber 1988, suggests interesting autobiographical sources for these anxieties.

AFTERWORD
1 'Outside the Whale', Granta, 1984.
2 For a full chronology of events, see *The Rushdie File*, edited by Lisa Appignanesi and Sara Maitland, Fourth Estate, 1989.
3 *Sunday Times*, 5 March 1989.
4 *The Rushdie File*, p. 200.

Index